D0267984
EGYPT
UGANDA
EXIT
REPUBLIC OF FIJI
PERMITTED TO ENTER AS A VISITOR
FOR 4 MONTH
FROM 21 OCT 1995
NOT AUTHORISED TO ENGAGE
IN ANY BUSINESS OR EMPLOYMENT
KENYA
JKIA-NAIROBI
20. 12. 2004
IMMIGRATION OFFICER
EXIT
KENYA
20. 12. 2004
IMMIGRATION
ARRIVED
21 NOV 1995
CAIRNS AIRPORT
IMMIGRATION DEPARTMENT
06 NOV 1995
JALISCO
10 ABR 08 E
REPUBLIQUE RWANDAISE
KANOMBE
DATE
NATIONAL SECURITY SERVICE
15.08.07
15.08.07

POLICIA DE INVESTIGACIONES
CONTROL MIGRATORIO
CHILE
AEROPUERTO
07 JUN 02
SRI LANKA
LEAVE TO ENTER FOR SIX MONTHS:
EMPLOYMENT AND RECOURSE TO
PUBLIC FUNDS PROHIBITED
28 MR 2001
P.I.A./A.I.P.
IMMIGRATION OFFICER
-3 JUN 1999
CHANNEL TUNNEL
UGANDA
22 FEB
ENTEBBE
REP. DEM. DU CONGO
IMMIGRATION
AERO - BUNIA
ENTREE - SORTIE
21.08.2004
AUG 15
CT2007
入境后可停留030
DURATION OF EACH STAY
DAYS
PR2007
签发地点
ISSUED AT
芝加哥
2007-04-27
WESTBY
VIETNAM IMMIGRATION
210396
MOC BAI
U.S. IMMIGRATION
ADMITTED
AUG 21 20
CLASS
Děčín
15 08 7 08

Advance Praise for *Fortune Favors The Brave*

"Kiri Westby is a walking miracle of a person, and her brave and beautiful book gives a thrilling ride through a life dedicated to freedom and love, hurtling straight in the face of some of the most horrendous situations people have recklessly created for each other on our endangered planet. I couldn't stop reading it, enjoyed every vividly written page, and relished the whole blessed secret world she reveals of totemic action women heroes who never give up. The special delight of it comes from the sense I get that they are certain to prevail, no matter how stubborn seem the pseudo-powerful, blue meany bad guys everywhere! You all should read this book!"

—Robert A. F. Tenzin Thurman,
Professor Emeritus, Columbia University,
Author, Grandpa, Activist

"In this fierce, heartbreaking, beautiful book, Kiri Westby describes her near-fatal descent into the heart of darkness, and how she came back with compassion and fury. As a boots-on-the-ground activist and born Buddhist, barely out of her teens, she set out to save the world and came to meet a group of extraordinary women who taught her what it means to be brave in the terrible face of violence and fear. I am deeply moved by her bravery and grateful for her wisdom."

—Mark Matousek, Author, *When You're Falling, Dive: Lessons in the Art of Living*

"In *Fortune Favors The Brave,* Kiri Westby transforms from a naïve, adventurous ingénue into a mature and deeply committed human rights defender. What I loved most about this book was the real, and sometimes raw and unromantic, truth of her journey. I was fortunate to have witnessed some of Kiri's growth firsthand and am impressed by her ability to recall and capture poignant lessons behind our work establishing UAF. Absorbing, brave, and often humorous, it is worth a slow and thoughtful read. Thank you, Kiri!"

—Julia Shaw, AKA "The Mountain Goat."
Co-Founder, Urgent Action Fund for
Women's Human Rights (UAF)

An Extraordinary Memoir

FORTUNE FAVORS THE BRAVE

An Extraordinary Memoir

FORTUNE FAVORS THE BRAVE

BY *Kiri Westby*

A POST HILL PRESS BOOK
ISBN: 978-1-64293-343-7
ISBN (eBook): 978-1-64293-344-4

Fortune Favors The Brave:
An Extraordinary Memoir

Cover Concept by Phill Bartell
Cover Design by Cody Corcoran
Author Photo by Andrea Chavez, Luz y Tiempo Photography

All people, locations, events, and situations are portrayed to the best of the author's memory. While all of the events described are true, many names and identifying details have been changed to protect the privacy of the people involved.

Post Hill Press
New York • Nashville
posthillpress.com

Published in the United States of America

Dedication

May All Beings Be Free.

Author's Statement

All of the events described in this book actually happened, and I've written about them as I witnessed and experienced them directly, though others present may recall them differently. Many names have been changed or invented to protect privacy and security, while some events have been compressed, and some dialogue recreated. Capturing the past with words is a fickle business, and we must acknowledge that human memory is imperfect and partial. Our memories, however, inform our understanding of how life has uniquely shaped us and, for me, it is less important to recall exact details and more illuminating to examine how big events—and their lingering footprints—play into the choices I've made. Within these pages, I have attempted to paint an accurate picture of what took place in my past, while focusing my recollections on the transformations that occurred within me along the way.

Contents

Chapter One

CHINESE PRISON

"*Who made the sig*?" Scary Fat Man spits as he yells in my direction, tiny droplets dotting the space between my drooping body and his rotund mass, shaking with anger. He hardly fits into his military uniform and, since he's removed his jacket, his dress shirt is coming untucked at the waist, revealing the soft flesh of his belly. It's the most animated I've seen him or any of my Chinese captors since I was arrested with four other American protesters at Mount Everest Base Camp two days ago. Most of the characters in this charade tread quietly, letting their leaders lead. Others, like Angry Dark Man in the corner, practically turned to stone the moment he sat down. He stares silently, unceasingly, exposing me under all this goose down and Neoprene. I'm still wearing layers of donated mountain gear, sponsored through Students for a Free Tibet, the Tibetan independence organization that recruited me for this mission. I put home out of my mind and try to pretend Angry Dark Man is stone and, therefore, can't hurt me.

"*Who carried the fire alarm*?" He pounds his fat fist on the bedside table emphasizing frustration, making sure I understand that he's not fucking kidding. The big problem is I keep bursting into laughter. I bite my tongue hard to prevent more giggles, until I taste blood, but it's a lost cause; I can't stifle them. *What the fuck is he talking about?* Scary Fat Man looks like he might snap if I don't stop insulting him in front of his colleagues and, while I know this could bring his interrogation to a far more painful point, I honestly don't know what he's asking. His insistence that I do is making the whole charade absurd, like *Laurel-and-Hardy* hysterical, and I wish my dad were here to see it. I wish anyone else were here to see this but, most likely, at this point, no one will ever hear my story about "that one time my Chinese interrogator used an old electronic translator and came out sounding like a broken robot." That thought is strong enough to finally freeze my relentless chuckles.

My throat is sore and crusty—dust and vomit compounded with forty hours of through-the-teeth lying. I don't want to talk anymore. Even if I wanted to tell the truth now, at this point, we've gone so far off track that the path back to the truth seems impossible. They think my name is Westin and that I'm from Laramie, Wyoming, so that is who I must become. There's nothing funny about my situation and, for the majority of the time since our arrest, I've been openly bawling, like snot-on-the-sleeves, grief-bawling, not laughing. Just last night, The Worst held my head over a cliff as I retched, and shook, and prepared for my death. Fear-vomiting—a raw, emotional, physical response to terror that caught me entirely off guard. There's probably some training manual for how to deal with this much fear all at once, without spontaneous vomiting or uncontrollable laughter, but these are highly-trained soldiers, working for the most oppressive political regime on earth, and they broke me like a stick of butter.

My response now—laughing right in my interrogator's face—is not bravado, nor obstinacy. It comes, instead, from a place of resignation; a detaching from my physical body; a total divestment in my future; a letting go of everything that was "my life" before the protest…and it's all coming out as more of a bizarre cackle than a real laugh; a subtle soundtrack to a good horror film. If this were any other cross-cultural experience, we might all be cracking up at the inaccurate auto-translator, but it's the second day of this dance, somewhere deep in central Tibet, and it's clear they're getting pissed off by my antics. Scary Fat Man is so angry and frustrated that, again, he tells Scrawny Translator Woman to remind me that I may never go home, never see my family again, that I must answer his questions truthfully if I don't want to go to prison. I am beginning to believe his poorly-translated lies and to accept the fact that I may never leave this place. My adopted Tibetan brother, Romeo, warned me about the disappearances, accidental deaths, poisoning that many Tibetans faced after being arrested. He begged me to never let them get me alone and not to eat one bite of food they provide. I've already broken both those promises.

I've told so many half-truths and sideways lies that, at this point, I've entered my own fairytale and I'm clinging to it like Alice to the White Rabbit. Buttery puddle that I am, I am still alive, which feels miraculous after witnessing my death on that windy cliffside roughly sixteen hours ago. I know that we are in some type of police station or detention center or prison complex, from what I could determine coming in, though I only had moments to look around. I saw my colleagues Tendor, then Laurel, and then Shannon hauled into the building before me, wondering if they'd ever come out or if I'd ever see their faces again.

And now I'm sweating profusely in a too-hot, oddly-furnished room that feels more like a cheap motel room than the torture chamber I was expecting. I'm panicking about how badly my throat hurts, every swallow sandpapery, wishing I had refused their offered cigarettes in the jailhouse at Everest, instead of breaking my two-year nicotine hiatus. *I'm just getting a cold. Or maybe I've contracted a bug and need antibiotics? Did they put something in the food that's making me sick, like Romeo feared they would? Why did I eat the food? Shit! Everyone else was eating. If I were poisoned, wouldn't we all be dead by now? How long would it take? How long have I been in this room? How many times has he asked the same questions? Maybe sustained terror has flu-like symptoms? Do I have a fever? It's a million degrees in here. If I could just take off my clothes, I could think straight!* My mind spins upside down, stuck on a stifling merry-go-round; I've completely lost track of time, and I'm trying to solve an unsolvable puzzle. My aching muscles scream out that they are beyond tired, my entire body thirsts for sleep, for an escape from this fiery, surreal production, with its cast of eccentric stone men and leading torturers.

The louder and more animated Scary Fat Man gets—and he's practically splitting his pants with rage at this point—the quieter and more anxious Scrawny Translator Woman becomes. She keeps imploring me with intense whispers and piercing glares, to "just answer his questions," her wild eyes contrasting her perfectly pressed, navy skirt suit. She is acting like she's on my side and, for that, I love her and hold her innocent. I give her my best *I seriously would if I could* look back, but I doubt it's getting across.

I try to use the moment to take off my down coat, but Scary Fat Man insists that I keep it on, as well as all the layers one needs to survive at the foot of Mount Everest where we first met. Judging how half the room of officers has stripped down to short-sleeves, I'm guessing they've upped the temperature on purpose—they're trying to sweat me out. Their earlier threats to let us freeze to death in a cement cell with a clear view of Everest—my mind calculating the number of hours before hypothermia would set in—still echo on my skin, helping me mentally welcome this intense heat. I try to imagine that I'm just in a sauna back home, at a fancy sports club, and that the heat is healing my lungs and helping my throat. A steady drip of sweat between my shoulder blades burns a swath across my chaffed lower back, the consequence of constant rubbing against worn police car upholstery for many hours, now helping to keep me awake in this tense sauna standoff. Almost unwillingly, I drop into meditation.

I am eighteen again, alone and scared, going through my final stage of Warriorship training, what is called the "Rites of Warriorship" program. I am frozen in fear but know I must act to save myself. Drawing on the young warrior woman that was born that day, the deep source of bravery I discovered facing the dark woods alone, I begin to chant, mouthing words silently, hoping my captors think I've gone mad. "This is what heat feels like. I welcome it. This is what heat feels like. I welcome it." And then the story of Palden Gyatso comes to mind, which I also heard at age eighteen, just after he escaped from Tibet and testified in front of the United Nations. Palden Gyatso spent thirty-three years being heinously tortured in Chinese prisons for non-violently resisting the Chinese occupation in 1959. While his testimony revealed the abject horrors occurring inside Tibet—he even snuck some of their torture devices out as proof—his kind words for his torturers were what shocked humanity most. I'll never forget being dumbfounded as he explained what he had feared most during his three decades in prison was "losing his compassion for the Chinese." He forgave them for their horrific crimes against him because he knew they were acting out of ignorance and still deserved compassion. *How could someone withstand so much pain and anger and still come out urging kindness for his torturers?* I'd pondered that question for many years, holding myself up to the "Palden Gyatso standard" and failing time and again to muster real forgiveness for those who murder, occupy, and oppress. My work in war zones had taught me that most of the foot soldiers were also often victims of the war. Many were conscripted to fight against their will, orphaned as young children, left with no option but to fight or die. But behind those frontline soldiers are the leaders in charge, those making the ultimate decisions to destroy and maim. I struggled to find compassion in my heart for them. I still do. Now, amazingly, I find myself in a slightly similar situation to Palden

Gyatso, and all I feel is rage, especially for The Worst, who recently pretended to kill me for laughs.

I have no idea where I am on a map, but we arrived at this police compound roughly eight hours after we left Base Camp, just as the rising sun bathed the barren landscape a bold, premonitory red. And now the fading light, tiny slivers streaming under the door to the hallway, plus the occasional yawn offered up by Scrawny Translator Woman, tell me that I'm about to enter a second night in this hell realm—not that I expect to get any sleep. I need to prepare myself for another twelve rounds with Scary Fat Man. The sweat and ever-present cigarette smoke is burning my eyes, which I can hardly keep open, drifting off repeatedly mid-sentence.

One young officer, whose only apparent job is to shine a bright laser into my pupils, squeezes my cheeks hard to pop my lids back open. I am only half awake, my mind getting used to his interruptions. "Westin! Westin! Wake up! We are not finished!" He speaks like he knows me, though my name is not Westin. He must know that by now, with copies of my passport on Scary Fat Man's makeshift office/TV stand to prove it. Controlling my head by the jaw, he pulls all my attention back into my body and I am wide awake again. Over my years of working in war zones, I've learned to sleep through almost anything—gunshots, bombs, crying children—but not Laser Boy. If he serves only one purpose in this inferno, he does it exceptionally well. After his visits, I'm ready for more questioning. Fear and lasers, it turns out, are tantalizing uppers.

Laser Boy has forcibly awakened me twice now, giving no indication of how long I'd slept. Each time I come back, there is a fraction of time when I don't know where I am. When reality hits and my situation re-dawns on me, I want to crawl out of my crawling, burning skin. I want to be anywhere on the planet but back in this nightmare smokebox. I fantasize sipping warm, honeyed tea in my soft living room and, in the most cliché way, I imagine my mom coming in to save me and I want to just apologize and start over; like I did the time my brother and I drove through our neighbor's fence while testing his driver's permit. I am folding, calling "uncle," but there's no visible way out of this one, no apology big enough to save face for this evil regime. We've embarrassed China on the international stage, in front of all their well-bought Olympic cameras, and they're not going to let us off easy. *How crazy to think that five individuals could take on China and win*? I've finally gone too far.

I imagine my mom's anger and then disappointment upon hearing I've been locked up for life; my father's profound sadness; my brother's loss of his ever-faithful baby sister; my husband's eternal loneliness, forever wondering what could have been. I think of my mentors in the human rights field, The Mountain Goat, The Eagle, The Tortoise, the debates they'll have about the idiocy of offering my life up like this. The Bear will not be impressed. The remorse is devastating. A part of me starts to wish they had thrown me over the cliff, that I could be a forever casualty of this nearly-erased conflict, that I won't have to face the impending consequences of our actions.

When Scary Fat Man began the interrogation, I was ready for him. I had memorized my well-crafted backstory and I almost had fun with the banter. There are not many times in life when we're given full rein to lie with reckless abandon and stand behind it. In my short training before the protest, I learned that Chinese law requires official interrogations to be meticulously transcribed and translated. I was told to talk as much as possible, in one continuous stream, to buy myself time through oversharing. So I told them about my cousin going to rehab, and my aunt the librarian in California. I shared a lot of information about the jobs my parents held and the fear we had around my brother's childhood cancer. Scary Fat Man squinted in irritation each time Scrawny Translator Woman repeated detail after inane detail about real (and imaginary) relatives and their imaginary (but sometimes real) life choices. He was clearly not amused.

For some reason, I insisted at the beginning that I am from Laramie, Wyoming, a place where the real me once played a basketball tournament in high school, and I never once waivered from that invented detail. Most of what I recounted was pure fiction, but I had to memorize my responses as quickly as I came up with them. If a detail made its way into a storyline, I'd hold onto it for life, program it into my other false memories and begin to believe it myself.

Now that we've gone around and around, covering every detail surrounding us getting into Tibet and pulling off the most visible Tibetan independence protest in decades, I'm not having any fun. The strange part is, if we succeeded in getting video of the protest out through the "Great Firewall of China," they must know I'm lying. They should know exactly who I am and precisely where I come from. If Jeff made it out with the videotapes, the whole world would be demanding to know where we are by now. Students for a Free Tibet, Lhadon Tethong at the helm, my family and friends, hundreds of people I've never met, should be pushing for the United States government to find us and insist we get home. I'm counting on all of them. I picture strangers clicking through the night to the glow of laptops, issuing press releases, pressuring senators to intervene. I focus on Laurel's "golden ripples," and their light buoys me as I sit in my smoky sauna and spin my fairytale fantastic.

Finally, exasperated, Scary Fat Man breaks into Mandarin, ordering the others to take a break, or at least their movements imply as much. Angry Dark Man stays frozen in the corner, staring at the same newspaper but never turning the page, monitoring me hour after hour. I imagine he's a human lie detector, measuring my pulse, calculating my levels of guilt, noting the places where my story has shifted slightly. We are the only ones in the room who know exactly how full of shit I am. As the room empties, all humor exits with the guards, my sadness reinforced by near-constant reminders from The Worst that

I am never getting out of here and how happy that makes her. All my remaining hope slips away with the tiny slips of dusk under the door.

Scary Fat Man's sweat-beaded brow and the accumulation of spittle on his chin turn his image monstrous, repulsive. I drop my head, close my eyes, and attempt sleep during the break. He finally walks out, but not before turning to me and adding, conclusively, "I think we both know who carried the fire alarm, little sister." I purse my lips to suffocate another snickering response, squeeze my eyes tight and pray for a long reprieve before Laser Boy hits repeat.

I did not end up in this room by accident and, though isolated, I never feel completely alone. Alongside my rapid heartbeats are the imprints, etchings left by hundreds of activists from my path here—women who left me skinned brave by their impossible acts of courage. Their spirits bolster me now, keeping away the despair, providing a temporary place to rest my tortured mind. As I try not to drown in a sea of fear and anger, each of their stories arises underfoot, like dependable stepping stones. Some new and shiny, some mossy and worn, they position a path for me to rehinge my damaged psyche. "Don't be scared," they encourage, "Let our bravery guide you." My body releases time and space, dipping into a dream where lasers and lashings cannot reach. I fall sideways, out of my chair, face-first onto the bed in the center of the room, no longer asking permission, nor heeding instructions. I am held tightly along a sacred thread of courage that my captors cannot see, accompanied even now as I tumble into a dreamless, futureless abyss....

Chapter Two

GROWING BRAVE

I am shivering and can't see my hands, even when held close. How am I supposed to light a fire with invisible, shaking hands? Night flipped black like a switch and completely enveloped me before I could prepare for it. I had a good flame burning earlier, but I ran out of wood as my mind started running away. It's hard to stay focused when there is nothing to do. Lighting a fire now feels more a necessity than the novelty it was during daylight; now it's a crucial lifeline and I've lost it. More than needing warmth, I desperately need to see my hands, and I know wild animals fear fire. I need fire to stay alive. Any number of hungry beasts—from bears to mountain lions to badgers—could be circling, waiting for me to fall asleep, seeing clearly in this blackness while I sit blind.

My eighteen-year-old body is lean and strong, molded by thousands of "suicide" drills on the basketball court, hundreds of hours running across lacrosse fields. Though I'm sore from days of romping about these mountains with other camp kids, the need to find firewood overrides all my aches. There's also the small problem of the rules. When the elders placed me here, I was forbidden from leaving a fifteen-foot radius, but I've already harvested all the kindling and burnable wood from my particular rocky circle. The rules are contrasting with my basic survival needs and, at the end of the day (literally), it is up to me to take care of myself in this world, which feels like the entire point of this program.

I was originally placed in a wooded glen full of soft grasses and swaying aspen trees. I was stoked about the spot, settling right into building a home for the foreseeable future. They gave no indication of when they'd be back for me. After half a day—and a ton of hard work constructing a comfy shelter—a staff member arrived and silently moved me to this inhospitable, craggy hilltop. There are no trees, only a plethora of rattlesnake-sized holes that dusk transformed into a pile of skulls and dangerous crevasses. I spent my first few hours brooding over the change of address, convinced I was being singled out and punished by the elders. I was two years older than the others in the program and think maybe they are making it extra hard for me. I wasted precious time wondering about the spots they'd given my friends, sure I was getting shafted and, somehow, missing out on the importance of the entire program by having to navigate my shitty location. I wailed against the injustice of it all while the sagebrush and moss mocked my futility. In the meantime, I wasted precious sunlight.

When anger has no other living creature to take itself out on, no place outside of you where it can stick, it quickly dissipates. I am used to my mom being the target of most of my anger—my dad a close second—my big brother in a pinch but I'd never before been so thoroughly upset, while also so utterly alone. I could feel the anger burning inside of me, like a living, growing thing, and I searched for a direction to throw it, someone to blame, anything to ease the discomfort. All the tears I've shed gave me this headache and dehydrated me further; all the screaming to no one, trying to solve an unsolvable problem, amounted to nothing but more suffering. I had no idea where the staff was, having arrived blindfolded, and I had no choice but to let my anger go. With no food, barely any water, and just enough clothes on my back to keep me from freezing to death, I had to move beyond my personal storyline, stop playing the victim, and get busy saving myself.

Judging by the excessively happy stars and the icy chill, it's well into night now. I am shivering, and I have to make a fire. The moon rising over the nearby ridge helps me decide to leave my limiting little circle and, like a ninja, creep down from the mountaintop to find something I can burn. It's still too dark to see much, but the moonlight lends a cinematic quality. Staying low to the ground, I gather pine needles and shove them in my pockets, the smell of freshly dug up earth and aromatic sage keeping me calm. I don't know if someone is watching. Finally, I make out a dead branch, illuminated against the moon glow, and belly-crawl over to it. What was once just a rotting tree, an object hardly noticeable when warm and full, becomes my midnight savior. "Hello," I say out loud.

I have always made friends with trees, often felt my most comfortable in their presence. When I was eight years old, I had a grand mal seizure, and the hospital doctors diagnosed me with epilepsy. My mother, never one to accept the word of others, especially not hospital doctors, refused their diagnosis and their prescribed medications for it. Instead, my parents took me to see a medium, what some people might call a psychic but what my family called a Channeler. It would be decades before I was allowed to hear the recorded tapes from those few, poignant sessions with the Channeler, my parents choosing to keep most of what he revealed secret to my third-grade ears; but his prescriptions were applied immediately. His diagnosis was unresolved trauma from a past life; his recommended remedy was to spend more time in nature.

"Time to take your walk, Chani[1]," my dad would gently remind me after school, "Go be with your trees. Take Jezebel." I would leave my house with my basset hound and we would make the rounds, vis-

---

1 "Chani" is my family nickname and will occasionally show up in reference to me when quoting a close family member.

iting each tree-friend in sequence, discussing the day's ups and downs. I kept a journal with their stories, just as they'd recount them to me, so that, someday, someone could read what I'd meticulously translated. The trees were so happy for the company and the attention, but mainly they were thrilled to tell their stories.

I learned then, in an eight-year-old way, that listening was a gift. The simple act of asking someone (or something) to tell their story, especially the hard parts, could make them feel better. It was a medicine. A powerful prescription, as effective as any I'd tried. It was then that I also began to feel healed by telling someone (or something) my hard parts. That same year, 1985, my mom had a late-stage miscarriage, taking with it all the excitement and plans I'd made for a younger sibling. I spent that evening by an old maple tree, weeping for the loss of a dream, for the ending of such a short story. The maple understood, having lost many saplings over the years, and still it grew, surviving on the promise of rebirth, the cycle of dying and becoming reincarnate, the way nature renews.

Thus began my love affair with trees, as well as an unrealistic collection of notebooks filled with the tall tales they wove, the lessons they imparted. My walks became a part of my inner life, a chance to inhale all the pain and sadness I felt from the day, to exhale those big emotions back into the earth via its sapling soldiers, my branchy friends, whom I learned to trust most of all.

Before my seizure, the bulk of our family's worry revolved around my older brother, Noah. Colicky as a child and prone to constant ear infections, my brother struggled to be in his body from the moment he was born. My mom would one day tell me that she believes Noah, conceived near Nagasaki, Japan, entered his life as a shattered soul from the A-bomb, a remnant of the unimaginable shock of nuclear destruction; that it was incredible he chose to reincarnate at all. The hospital doctors, however, confirmed that Noah's illnesses were the result of a rare kidney tumor called "Wilms," which was slowly taking his life.

Memories of my brother's childhood battle with cancer are as much fiction as fact, as I was only two at the time, but there is one event from the years our family spent in the Children's Hospital in Denver that has been told and retold so many times, it has morphed into a family mythology:

> *Noah was dying. He'd been given a 50 percent chance to live, before the surgery and chemotherapy began, but, that day, the nurses' tones shifted from optimistic to accepting, and my parents' energy went from solid to crumbly. Even two-year-old eyes can tell the difference between a real and a fake smile, between happiness and a "good face." The adults were preparing for something terrible, but I refused to accept such surrender. I marched my little frame into Noah's hospital room, the adults watching in amazement, determined to save him. He hadn't eaten for days and he would no longer smile or respond, though my parents offered him everything from ice cream to Disneyland. They said he was "losing his will to live." I was barely tall enough to reach the bed, but I was strong, and my entire universe revolved around Noah. I grabbed him by the legs and pulled him out of the bed. I then forced him across the room, prodding him down the hall and into the children's playroom. The way my mom tells it, "Noah laughed for the first time a few minutes later and he ate his first meal that afternoon." The doctors couldn't believe the sudden change, and everyone noted the power of a sister's love and the miracle of baby Noah surviving.*

As the story of his survival folded itself into my growing memories, combined with the irrationality of youth, I convinced myself that I had magical powers and that, with enough determination and special wishes, no obstacle was insurmountable.

When I was just a few months old, I was presented by my parents to their guru, a Tibetan meditation master named Chögyam Trungpa Rinpoche. At that meeting, he officially gave me my middle name "Norbu," which translates loosely from Tibetan into "wish-fulfilling jewel," and represents the perfect combination of compassion and wisdom. It has always felt like a lot of name to live up to. I've heard there are roughly four hundred of us spread around the globe, each named separately, the children whose Western parents took Buddhist "Refuge Vows" with "Trungpa" (as he was affectionately known). He was the first Tibetan meditation master to offer esoteric Buddhist teachings to Westerners, in English. In our community, us named children are referred to lovingly as the Dharma Brats, though more by the older generation than amongst ourselves—not that the moniker doesn't fit.

I say "our community" because that's exactly how it felt. We called ourselves a "Sangha" (the Sanskrit word for community), and, by all recollection, I grew up in a country within a country. We sang our own anthem, raised our own flag, founded our own schools, and adhered to our Buddhist way of living. Our Sangha was modeled after a Monarchy, with Trungpa Rinpoche as the King, his young British wife, Diana, as the Queen, and their close attendants referred to as the "Royal Court." They lived together in a giant house in central Boulder, Colorado. The rest of us children in the Sangha were raised to be princes and princesses and taught to regard ourselves as exceptional, our human birth as extremely fortunate. Most of us attended private Buddhist schools and began training in esoteric meditation techniques at as young as four years old, depending on the household. My mom and two other mothers started the first Buddhist Preschool in Boulder when I was just three weeks old, named "Alaya" by Trungpa himself. While I don't remember any lengthy meditation instruction in preschool, I can recall sitting through long group silences—during which I would carefully inspect the features of the many eclectic adults our Sangha attracted—and I recall falling asleep on mountains of meditation cushions during unending community gatherings, which consisted mostly of waiting, meditating, and feasting.

If I close my eyes and conjure my earliest felt experience of meditation, I am tiny and sitting snuggled for an eternity in my father's lap. His gentle swaying as I daydream, moving slightly forward, then slightly backward, keeping me perfectly contained within a rhythmic, upright posture; his mumbled mantras and clacking prayer beads eventually lulling me into real sleep. By the time I entered our Sangha's private elementary school at age five, it was perfectly normal to start each class with a meditation session or to spend the entire thirty-minute lunch break contemplating the origins and taste of my food. Once children in our Sangha turned eight, we entered formal training in the five Dharmic arts of Ikebana (flower arranging), Kyūdō (archery), Drutsa (calligraphy), Oryoki (food ceremony), and Haiku (spontaneous poetry containing precisely seventeen syllables). These practices were taken mostly from the Japanese Zen Buddhist tradition and were the result of a lifelong friendship between Chögyam Trungpa and Onyumishi Kanjuro Shibata Sensei, who served as the Imperial Bowmaker to the Emperor of Japan for thirty-five years before coming to teach in our Sangha.

Me and my big brother Noah, heading off to "Vidya," our Sangha's private elementary school where we wore uniforms and trained in Meditation, Oryoki, Ikebana, Kūydō, Elocution, Calligraphy, Haiku, Maitrī, and more.

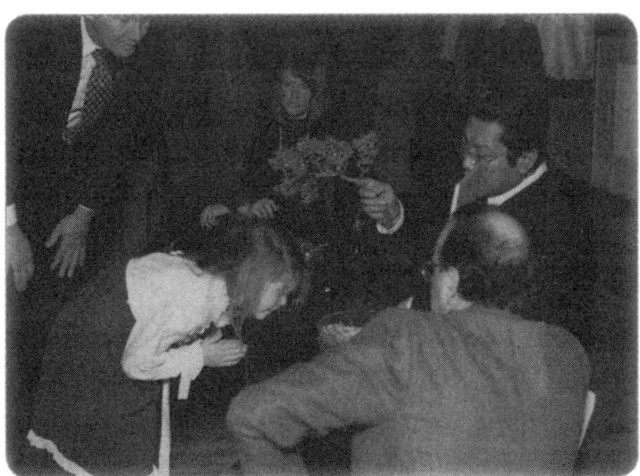

Receiving a children's blessing from Chögyam Trungpa Rinpoche at six years old in 1983.

At the end of this initial training, around age eight or nine, we made our first vows in a program called "Rites of Passage," taking our initial, communally-acknowledged step away from the care of our parents and into our lives as individuals, now expected to begin the difficult task of taking responsibility for ourselves and our actions in the world.

Rites of Passage were the first of several vows offered to young practitioners in our Sangha. When I turned eleven, with my closest friend, Eve, by my side, under the guidance of Khenchen Thrangu Rinpoche, I took my official Refuge Vows into Buddhism. Vowing to seek spiritual refuge in "the Buddha, the Dharma, and the Sangha," I formally became a Buddhist in my own right. Thrangu Rinpoche gave me the refuge name Tamcho Lhamo, which translates roughly to "holy Dharma divine feminine"—yet another big name to try and embody.

The summer I turned eight, I started attending Shambhala Sun Summer Camp. "Sun Camp" was a child's dream, at least to me. One week in the woods with no schedules and no parents. Eve and I were both lucky that we had older brothers at camp to show us the ropes, and we could hardly wait to turn fourteen, when we'd be invited up three days early for the Cadet Command Workshop (CCW). CCW meant taking on the responsibility of caring for the younger campers and running specific aspects of the camp. Plus, CCW had its own, highly-secretive vow ceremony that I'd heard snippets about from Noah. The Sun Camp adult staff stayed up on a nearby hill, wordlessly watching, occasionally intervening in the chaos of a hundred, unbound children, redirecting us to do camp chores, march in military-style drills, or meditate. But, for the most part, the staff stayed out of the way and let the Cadets and the Warriors run the camp. The Warriors—or "ROWS," as we called them—were in their final year as campers and preparing for the "Rights of Warriorship" program that took place directly after camp. None of us knew anything about that program; it was top secret, and the sixteen-to-twenty-year-olds that went in rarely came out the same…I couldn't wait to be a ROW.

Shambhala Sun Summer Camp, 1987, where I trained in Kasungship and nonviolent conflict transformation from the age of ten to eighteen.

Trungpa introduced us early on to a meditation-in-action practice he called Kasungship. "Kasung" loosely translates as "invincible" in English, though I've also read it written as "command control," meaning to hold control over a situation. Kasungship adopted many of the Western military forms—uniforms, ranks, drill—but applied them to a nonviolent context, to building an army for goodness. During long, hot, Colorado summer days, we marched on "parade grounds" until our feet blistered, our minds spinning with complex drill maneuvers. Our slogan was "Victory Over War!" and we shouted it until our lungs ached.

We also spent hours making up fun call-and-response songs about ending violence and slaying ignorance by waking up humanity. Camp was divided into three gangs, each with an invented name and assigned flag. At the end of the week, we held a massive, daylong game of Capture the Flag that we called "The Skirmish." Inevitably, close friends and family members were pitted against each other and the raw emotions of conflict emerged. We felt the awful sensation of friends turning into enemies, the gut-wrenching anger at being outmaneuvered on the battlefield, or betrayed by close friends. Invariably, one gang would fall and be absorbed into another, and the final battle would come down to two limping armies, facing off over an open field. With nowhere left to hide and nothing left to lose, we would march out into the center, flour-bag weapons cocked, hatred and desire pouring out of us until—boom!—we would stop a few feet away, lock eyes with our rivals, and recognize that the others are actually us, defending their territory with the same passion and intensity, two sides of the very same coin. We were then taught to model true bravery by making a different choice at that crucial moment; to drop our weapons first, recognize our shared humanity, see our similarities over our differences, and bow to one another instead of fighting further.

It was an exercise in holding one's mind steady in the midst of extreme chaos and confusion; of overriding the instinct to destroy or be destroyed; of outsmarting the pitfalls that had plagued humanity for millennia. We had simulated nationalism and now we were replicating war and how to overcome it—though I wouldn't understand that for another decade. To my young mind, we were just playing an awesome, adult-free, all-day game in the woods and I loved every minute of it. At the end of that exhausting day, enemies would become friends again, we would drop our illusory gripes, and we'd collectively declare victory over the three poisons of passion, aggression, and ignorance.

Kasungship was more than just simulated war games, though; it was also about learning to hold a space—to "create a container," we would say—for everyone to feel safe, accepted, heard, and loved. My early experiences with older Cadets rushing to my cries in the lonely night, bandaging my skinned knees and soothing my sunburnt shoulders, had me longing to be a Cadet myself, to have the confidence and trust to take care of another person in need. Similar to what a nurse or doctors might feel when they have healed someone or taken away their suffering, helping others was addictive, and Sun Camp got me hooked.

Each step along the path of growing up in our Sangha had its allure and careful planning, with ceremonies and pins, special gifts and community responsibilities. Each new stage was designed by Trungpa to instill the tenets of nonviolent Warriorship deeply within us. From the time I was eight until the summer I turned eighteen, I walked that invisible spiritual road, graduating from trainings, just as I did grades in school, making lifelong vows along the way to love myself, to help humanity, and to combat the futility of war.

It wasn't until I entered public school in third grade that I realized not everyone makes such principled promises, and not everyone had been taught to take less so there would be enough to go around. I was both shocked and embarrassed by mainstream American culture. Shocked at the obvious—even celebrated—inequalities and embarrassed that humanity still hadn't figured out how to stop stepping on one another to get ahead. From the playground, to the classroom, to my home, all of my early life lessons were about sharing and conserving, about lifting others up when they faltered. Now that morphed into messages of winning at any cost and taking advantage of weakness in others. Sun Camp became my summer salvation from this cruel new world, my fellow Dharma Brats life rafts in the storms of change. If not for them and my daily cavorting with the trees, the transition into America might have destroyed me.

I was ten years old when Trungpa died. In his wake, he left a community in distress, several fatherless children, and public scandal in an AIDS-ravaged, post-Hippie dystopia called "the nineties." Replacing the sexual revolution with profound sexual revelations, shortly after Trungpa passed away, so did his successor Thomas Rich, who had contracted HIV, denied its effect on him, and, in the process, infected some of his loyal students, who also died. Stories about Trungpa's unorthodox and often outrageous teaching techniques with adults began to emerge posthumously, as well as the fact that he had officially taken on seven female "consorts." The public scandals rocked our secluded world like an earthquake, exposing us to the harsh judgment of Judeo-Christian society. Just as I was awakening to the fact that the world wasn't as safe or inherently good as I'd imagined, my home country disappeared and I became as a refugee in a foreign country I didn't relate to nor fully understand.

And then my mom was diagnosed with breast cancer and my universe collapsed.

▪ ▪ ▪

"Remember you are magic…remember you are magic…remember you are magic…." I repeat the words like a chant, half believing them, half hoping that, if I say them enough, my mom will survive, the way Noah did. The world spun, my primordial ground shook, as I imagined, for the first time in my short life, my mom's death. I've seen death a few times now, our Sangha gathering for traditional "Sukhāvatī" funeral rites, even for strangers, bodies on display and untouched, no matter how gruesome the end. One body, badly damaged in a car accident, its severed limbs tied together with cloth. One corpse felled by cancer, shrunken and turned inward, the blue-gray shade of newborn eyes, only half the size of when a soul had inhabited it just days earlier. I was terrified to see my mom that way.

It made sense now, why everyone around me was acting strange, their smiles too wide, and their tones too loud, as if they could drown out the truth with volume. I saw the motivation behind the extra bedtime cuddles from Daddy, the gentle way Grandma let me lick her batter-thick spoons from Sunday's meringue. Come to think of it, even Noah has been unusually generous with the remote control and the bigger ice cream scoops. It seems I am the last to know that Mom is sick, and that alone is infuriating. No one remembers I have magical powers. No one thinks I'm even old enough to include in their Cancer Plans.

The morning Mom finally told me about it, she was being extra strange, wringing her hands, and pacing the house. Dad took Noah to school, which was unusual because she was one of the school's Head Directors and we usually all rode together. It was just the two of us, sitting on the scratchy living room couch. Her patting invitation almost untrustworthy after she said, seriously, "Chani, we need to talk." We sat too close for the size of the sectional, the claustrophobic proximity of our bodies mirroring the tightening at the back of my throat. *Something was wrong.* I imagined the worst thing I could, based on the Richter scale of my mom's pained expressions, bracing for news that Grandma had died. A girl in my class lost her grandma last year, and I'd thought of it a lot over the summer; the concept of losing a family member sitting heavy on my naïve heart, the wound of nearly losing Noah freshly opened.

But the words from my mom's lips were not what I'd imagined and, at first, they landed foreign on my ears, untranslatable by my young mind. *So Grandma's alive? What did she mean SHE was sick? Like Noah had been sick? Like surgery, hospitals, and losing-one's-will-to-live sick?* All attempts to spin a silver lining—to remind me how Noah was still with us and healthy; to promise she would get better too—

passed right over me. Instead, I took in the light pink paint peeling in the corner of the room; the floral pattern on the navy, quilted curtains that employed a modern magnet system to seal out the cold; the smell of her "Tea Rose" perfume; and the staggering number of travel tchotchkes crowding the rattan shelving on the far side of the TV.

I began memorizing every detail of our world, as if it was crumbling as fast as my ground; as if I had to chronicle the way things were before this conversation, if I stood a chance of surviving things after. It was my first experience of how the world slows to a crawl in the face of trauma. The full knowing that we have zero control over how or when our lives will end; one day, healthy; the next day, sick; the next day, dead, an empty corpse on the community pyre, returning back to dirt. I couldn't allow my mom to become soil yet; I still needed her to hold me at night and teach me about all the things I didn't know. And I didn't know how Noah would survive the loss of her, his ever-present walking stick, helping him navigate a fragile post-cancer adolescence. And so, I hatched my own Cancer Plan.

I didn't go to school that day, or maybe it was a Saturday and my dad had taken Noah to the movies, but I remember staying in and plotting. I got out all of my best pens and fancy notebooks. I'd stopped Noah from dying when no one else could, and I was going to save my mom too. I had to conjure enough magic by cashing in all my birthday wishes and favors with the Tooth Fairy, leaving troll notes under every bridge, and writing to Santa personally. I could, and I would, do whatever it took for her to pull through and there was no time to waste. With zero understanding of how it was going to work, but complete faith in myself as a magical being, I began to write for her life.

For the next six months, my mom fought like hell to save herself from the consuming depths of cancer. Though I wouldn't know it for many years, her battle began with local doctors insisting on a mastectomy, driving her to insist on an experimental lumpectomy surgery instead, and raging into a super ability to withstand dangerously high levels of chemo in exchange for keeping her breasts. She weathered it all with an impenetrable resolve to shield Noah and me from the effects of her treatment. Within weeks of the morning she slowed time on our scratchy living room couch, all her hair fell out. Grandma took her shopping for a high-quality wig at The Crossroads mall and I secretly hoped no one I knew would recognize her. I wanted her to look normal again and for it all to end.

In many ways, because she chose to have the experimental treatment in Illinois—the only place in the United States performing lumpectomies in 1988—her cancer *was* something that happened outside of my life. Every couple of weeks or so, she would leave for a week of treatment, Grandma moving in to try and fill her place. Mom would return with chocolates from a famous factory near the hospital, filling the awkward air with obligatory smiles and promises to take me one day. I would tell her about the sixth-grade drama she'd missed as she crawled into bed and "didn't feel well" for the next few days. The following Monday, she'd resume her role in the carpool, back at her desk in the head office.

Cancer must not be too bad, I reasoned, never knowing that I was witnessing a giant's strength, never exposed to the night-sweats and endless vomiting, nor the terrifying hair loss and aching bones. Just as she had done with Noah's cancer, mom put on a suit of armor and went into battle alone.

It wasn't until much later, on a blind date in high school, while watching Julia Roberts star in *Dying Young*, a film depicting a man's death through chemotherapy, that I truly understood what cancer was. I ran from the theater retching, regurgitated Dr. Pepper and popcorn filling the lobby trashcan, providing the perfect excuse to go home early. It terrified me more than any horror film I'd ever seen. The understanding of what she'd gone through, my dad home alone to put food on our table and privately worry, the bravery she'd mustered to get on that plane for poison-treatments, month after month. It made me sad that she'd hidden it all from me, that she'd put on a happy mask for us all, that she'd carried that burden for me and Noah, never letting us see her crack. And that's how I saw life, even at eleven—like a series of painful burdens to bear with nothing guaranteed; like facing death at age two or forty-two was perfectly normal; like I was already running out of time to be of benefit to the world during my short, unpredictable life.

Chapter Three

STAYING BRAVE

The same year Mom leaves home for cancer treatments I go on my first humanitarian mission abroad. Our elementary school adopted a "sister school" in a small Costa Rican village and a few teachers are bringing a select group of sixth graders down to visit them over spring break. Maybe it's my annoying persistence that I be amongst the delegates, or maybe the chaperones felt bad for the girl whose mom is dying, or perhaps it was Mom's influence as Director that seals the deal, but it's not long before I'm packing my bags for my first international trip without my parents.

I had been to small pueblos in Mexico, where the poverty levels are high and people live off the land and the sea more than grocery stores. When I was six, walking the cobblestone streets of a large Mexican city, I saw a mother in rags, begging with her infant child. The child was malnourished and wearing a tiny cast on its arm. The entire scene shattered my heart. I pleaded with my parents to help them, to share our food and money. I could think of nothing else. They explained that it was a common scam, and the mother had most likely broken the child's arm to solicit charity or, more likely, the cast was a fake. *How can poverty be a scam?* I raged. Thinking of the Bodhi School tales of the Buddha with his begging bowl, of cautionary morals against greed and hoarding, of the fundamental teachings around karma.

I felt powerless to help the beggar, while simultaneously determined to do so. A conflict ignited in my belly, the ancient rub between generosity and self-preservation. *How do you know when you have enough and when you've shared too much?* While my external world emphasized competition and survival of the fittest, my internal world obsessed over building merit by helping those in need. I calculated, in my frightened young mind, that my daily actions and decisions were being computed in some giant universal machine, that the Karma Gods were weighing the consequences of each choice I made, choosing to either keep my mom alive or let her die.

This universal bargaining played out daily in little ways, like avoiding sidewalk cracks or offering the larger slice of Sunday's pie. But I also adopted whales, wrote to the U.S. Attorney General about the "perils of cigarettes," and led a successful petition to increase the timing of the walk signal at our elementary school's main traffic light (making sure the elderly and disabled had enough time to cross). I won an award for being the "Boulder County Student of the Month," writing all my good deeds in a locked journal, where I also took stock of my moments of selfishness or meanness, vowing to improve.

I tell no one but the trees about my bartering system, my clandestine plan to keep my mom healthy. I fixate my efforts on the impending trip to Costa Rica, a chance to aid an entire village of children, which coincides on the calendar with the end of her treatment trips to Illinois. Costa Rica is my last major opportunity to accrue enough merit to put me over the top. My mom's life hangs in the balance, and I'm not going to let her down, no matter how scared I am to leave home alone.

▪ ▪ ▪

"*Su nombre es Maria*," I practice writing in Spanish on a postcard bound for Boulder. Maria is my first Costa Rican friend. Even though she doesn't speak English, and my Spanish is terrible, I *know* we are friends. She's curious about my hair, my skin, and all my fancy clothes and jewelry. I've never considered myself enviable and, through her eyes, I'm like a movie star. I'm amazed that she's allowed to drink coffee at just ten years old, which her mom makes for her in an old tube-sock strainer, and that she can climb high into the trees without permission or ropes. She is wild and free, and we instantly recognize the other's spirit.

I haven't missed home, not the way I thought I would. Every day is fresh and full compared to life in Boulder, to weathering Mom's illness with its perpetual sadness and stress. In Costa Rica, I've eaten mangoes picked fresh on the side of the road, showered outside in a torrential rainstorm, and watched a sloth give birth in a cloud forest. I never knew that the world was this colorful and delicious. I want to eat it whole.

Living in Maria's house, in a forested village two days' drive from anywhere, is fantastically liberating. I imagine this is my real life and that her people are my people. My host family embraces me as one of their own, welcoming me into their warm, buzzing nest. The village children don't have to wear shoes and, since I hate wearing shoes, it's like a magical place tailored just for me. Maria and I run barefoot through the jungle in the same clothes as yesterday, drinking soda out of plastic bags, and laughing at jokes neither of us fully understand. I get to know her smile more than her story and, in that sense, our connection is true and present in the moment, free from judgment or context.

The soccer games at recess go on forever and, even when it's time to go inside to study, the school's missing windows infuse our classroom with exotic floral scents and random laughter. It's nothing like going to school in Boulder. Learning Spanish has never been more important, mainly so I can share my secrets with Maria. I'm speaking more and more of this foreign tongue every day. The words, once so alien, become a melody I can memorize, like lyrics to a song I can't stop singing. I'd never thought of language as its own unique expression before, more like Haiku than a direct translation from English. Before long, I drop English all together and start using Spanish to learn more Spanish.

The supplies we brought down—bought at Target with profits from our "World Peace Calendar" sales—appear shiny on the shelf next to dusty, torn textbooks. I've never seen anyone so excited about new pencils, "with erasers!" the kids marvel. In fact, my new classmates appreciate a lot of things I've never thought about. Pens, books, and backpacks always appear to me before school starts in the fall and I hardly question where they come from or what learning would feel like without them. Sometimes I get mad at my mom for choosing the wrong color or shape of my supplies, rolling my eyes at her social ignorance. It's staggering to realize that I've had so much at my disposal and barely noticed, taken all of it for granted.

Seeing myself in Maria's eyes, my relative wealth compared to this tiny village, I drop the masks I've been wearing at home. I can be anyone I want here, and what I want is to stop worrying about cancer and having cool things, the attention of boys, or being popular. Suddenly, the world is full of real things to worry about, like making sure every child has food and shelter, and basic school supplies to learn! I want to be a part of solving that problem. My life up until now appears trivial, even the bouts with cancer, when compared to the life-and-death struggles of the people around me. Their poverty illuminates my immense privilege, dwarfing all of my problems.

Maria's House, Costa Rica, 1988.

In Boulder, I complain about being poor, about our old house smelling like incense, even when there isn't any burning, and my handed-down, outdated clothes. I rarely invite friends over, unless they're already in our Sangha. I spend a lot of time comparing myself to the rich, Christian girls and coming up short. But, here in Costa Rica, I'm the rich girl and I begin to understand that wealth is a state of mind and, therefore, so is poverty. This realization forces me to reevaluate how I feel about my life at home. In the middle of the Costa Rican jungle, dirty-footed and feral, I am the freest I have ever felt. I am a little girl again, unbound and fearless. *Does Maria know how lucky she is? What a treasure her village life is?* It's easy to calculate what she doesn't have, to feel sorry for her lack of material abundance, but, when I add up the freedoms she enjoys and compare them to life in Boulder, I only feel sorry for myself. I want the life she has just as much as she wants the life I have.

We are leaving tonight and, after two life-changing weeks as a Costa Rican villager, I am dreading the trip back home. I don't want to lose all the magic I've discovered here. It is most independent I've felt, and I never want that liberated sensation to end. I'm going to miss my new friends deeply, especially Maria, and, though we promise to write letters, the thought of never seeing her again brings rivers of tears.

We've been sent to our host homes to pack our things for the evening bus ride back to San José. I desperately want to hold on to all they've given me, to somehow take Costa Rica with me. Collecting my stuff, I notice my favorite silver bracelet is missing. After searching the whole room, emptying my bags and scouring the house, I know it's gone. My heightened emotions around leaving cause my tears to morph into wails. Finding my bracelet becomes the most important thing in the world and I won't leave without it. I tear a path through the village like a lunatic, searching with raw eyes, making a huge scene. My host mother alerts the neighborhood and, before long, the entire village is looking for my bracelet. And then the worst happens. Maria's brother finds the bracelet hidden under her mattress, where's she stashed it. It's clear from the ashamed look on her face that she's been caught.

How could my new friend steal from me? I'm outraged and want her to be punished for this betrayal. I'm inconsolable, crouched on the ground in the town center, while Maria is standing on the other side, head bowed, weeping softly. There is a lot of discussion in Spanish amongst the adults and it is clear, despite my teacher's attempts to intervene, that the village will handle this their way. Everyone is there. All of my fellow exchange students and most of the school, even a few old grandmas who didn't seem mobile until now. I'm playing the victim perfectly, my sadness and pain melding into a grand performance. I enjoy the way it makes me the center of attention, the wronged one, and the one deserving everyone's sympathy. Which makes Maria the bad one, the one to be punished, and there is much tongue-clicking and finger-wagging in her direction.

The man in charge steps up and declares, "*Es un problema muy serio. Maria tiene que ser castigada*!" "This is a big problem. Maria must be punished," our teacher translates. Maria's tear-filled reaction cracks my resolve. Suddenly, I just want to run to my friend and embrace her. He continues, "*Hemos decidido dejar que Kristina va a determinar la sanción, porque ella es la herida.*" We have decided to let Kristina decide her punishment, because she is the one Maria hurt. My mouth goes dry hearing the translation, my surprised eyes blinking away wetness, replaced with confusion. *I'm the one who has to punish Maria?* It feels horrible. *How can I possibly punish her without punishing myself?* Images of the rich girls back home flash into view, how I covet their expensive clothes and trendy makeup. I see myself stealing a pair of earrings at the mall last year, my desire for them outweighing my better judgment, lucky I didn't get busted. And I can still feel the desperation I had only this morning, looking around the village for one last time, wanting to hold on to it, to take a piece of Costa Rice with me. She is me.

Maria's eyes meet mine apologetically. I admire her courage and her strength, and I want to be just like her, stolen bracelet and all. I run over to throw my arms around her and we fall to the ground embracing. We are both weeping now, for the friendship we are losing, and for the confusing end to our beautiful time together. Everyone claps and cheers, a few mothers crying along with us, a few adults laughing at the ridiculousness of it all. There doesn't have to be any punishment, only forgiveness and understanding, which need no translation.

Shortly after, as our bus begins the long climb out of the village, dozens of schoolmates run alongside, waving final farewells. I look down at the bracelet, shiny and heavy against my wrist, and know exactly what I to do. "Stop the bus!" I scream, "I forgot something!" The teachers can't believe I'm causing yet another dramatic delay, but I run past their protests, uncaring. Maria is there, near the door, when I jump down. I wrap the bracelet around her thin brown wrist, saying

"*Un regalo! Sí! Sí! Es un regalo*! A present for you!" She is shaking her head no, but smiling, and laughing along with me. I should have just given her the bracelet last week when she said she liked it so much, avoided all this unnecessary pain. She's given me everything I needed in just two weeks, and I know I'm leaving here wealthier than when I arrived. Meeting Maria and her entire village taught me that we all feel rich and then poor; happy and then sad; scared and then brave, from one moment to the next, and that's what makes us the same. No language or skin color or customs can alter that universal truth. Our fundamental similarities are more powerful than all the superficial differences that divide us.

In this muddy moment, laughing by the side of the road, marveling at the absurdity of the entire afternoon, I understand that what I got out of my friendship with Maria is a gift I can't repay. What I don't understand, at only eleven years old, is that the poignant lesson I learned from my short, intense friendship with Maria will stay with me for life, emerging like a long-lost friend in my most conflicted moments, reminding me that generosity is the key to sowing peace.

▪ ▪ ▪

Mom's ongoing battle with cancer, combined with the gauntlet that is junior high school, turned me inward, a shadow of the barefooted tree climber I was with Maria by my side. Mom was still sick when the seventh-grade bullying got so bad I started skipping school, choosing to be with my trees in the hills above Boulder instead. I switched to a different school for eighth grade, but the main qualities that transferred with me were a shitty attitude and half-decent basketball skills. I became a bully, taking my pain and confusion out on those I cared about most.

Now, in my junior year of high school, I tell my parents casually over the dinner table that I will "throw myself off the Second Flatiron in the mountains above Boulder if I have to keep going to high school." The shock on their faces stems from the belief that I am "doing much better," even thriving. My grades are up, I am dating boys, and my social status as a jock is firmly cemented by joining the basketball, lacrosse, and volleyball teams. Inside, however, I feel I am dying a slow, meaningless death. The sensation that Costa Rica unlocked in me is so juicy, so addictive, that dreams of a different life, one of adventure and global impact, consume me; I want to be a real-life wanderer, like the aesthetics I'd read about in Bodhi school, not just another teenager in Boulder. I ache to get far away from my predictable, anti-bacterialized existence and into a life that matters.

My parent's eventual solution to my grumbling is, like any good hippies, to send me to Bali. They had lived there in the early 1970s designing jewelry and studying Hinduism. Naropa University, a contemplative university founded by Trungpa Rinpoche, was beginning a study abroad program there, and my oldest friend Eve's mom was tapped to direct it. Dad showed me a photo of him and Mom posing at a lonely dirt crossroads with a small sign that read "Kuta Beach," telling me that Bali was paradise on earth. So, at the mature age of sixteen, I left high school, bailed on the varsity basketball team a few weeks before the state championship playoffs, and re-packed my bags for parts unknown.

▪ ▪ ▪

Wayan combs coconut oil through her long black hair, which hangs almost to her waist. A few drops fall onto her white kebaya, sending frangipani fumes around the room. She doesn't seem to notice or mind. We are preparing for temple down in Ubud, the town below the village of Campuhan where I've been living for weeks. Wayan has been giggling all afternoon at the sight of me in traditional Balinese dress, attempting to balance large baskets of fruit on my awkward, round head. She is two years older but often acts younger. We became fast friends in the short time I've been here; she invited me into her private world like a sister. As I did with Spanish, I opened my mind to learning Indonesian, and it flooded in quickly. Our long conversations helped, Wayan working shifts in her family's store, discussing everything from boys, to sex, to marriage and babies, the topics that fascinate teenage minds. I feel it again, the wonder of discovering another person from a completely alien world who, in many ways, is just like me. The mesmerizing sensation of unlocking the way another culture works, the intricacies of Balinese customs holding a stark mirror to my life in Colorado. Here, they make offerings each morning to the lower realms before leaving the house. Before beginning to work, they make offerings to the gods of abundance. Before each meal, they throw a bite of food on the ground for less-fortunate beings (the street dogs and bugs living well off the generosity). Daily life is so infused with spirituality, in fact, that it's hard to differentiate when people are praying and when they are working.

In the West, our spirituality is sequestered behind church, temple, and synagogue doors. Even our Buddhist center in Boulder operates outside of the mundane world, our spirituality neatly scheduled. But what happens to that spirituality when you walk back out the temple doors? The sensation of living with daily, even hourly, rituals of one's faith feels warm and alluring, reminding me of my early childhood in our Sangha. The aspects of my life that stand out queerly at home—from our eclectic incense-filled household to my obsession with talking trees—are fascinating in Wayan's eyes, making me freshly interesting to myself. My friendship with Wayan reintroduces me to my own nature, painting my self-confidence a brilliant gold again, just the way Maria had.

With Wayan, Campuhan, Bali, 1994.

Me in Bali practicing my head-balancing skills before temple, 1995.

Plus, I have fallen in love with Wayan's good friend Ida Bagus. He's strikingly handsome, tall for a Balinese, and we began making eyes at each other the day I arrived. He says he loves me too and that we will find a way to be together forever. I believe him the way a sixteen-year-old believes she is in control of her future, the way I still believed in fairytales and shiny-armored knights and happily ever after.

"I want to stay in Bali forever," I share with Wayan once we are alone. "I'm making secret plans to stay and be with Ida Bagus. My parents will be angry, but they will understand eventually." Her reaction is far from what I expect, more confused than agreeing. "What is it?" I pry. She confesses that, while she's happy at the thought of my staying, I must know by now that Ida Bagus is betrothed to someone else, just as she is already promised to marry a boy from her village. Whereas we were indistinguishable "sisters" a moment before, I immediately see myself as the foreigner I am, threatening to upend generations of tradition, asking someone I care about to risk everything they know and love me instead. She explains that Ida Bagus' family is looking the other way at our obvious affair, because I'm going home soon, but that I could never stay in Bali and expect to be with him. It would ruin his whole life and shame his family. Then she says something that rings even more painful. "You must go home, Kiri. Study and go to university. Do something great with your wild American life. Girls like me don't have that chance." As rejecting as it is, I know that she's right. Bali is not the end of the line for me. I have the opportunity to accomplish great things, to study whatever I want, to be in control of my destiny...plus I still owe the Karma Gods for all my childhood bargaining. My mom is alive and well, now five years cancer-free, but I feel I still have a cosmic debt to pay.

I vow then and there to use the good fortune of my birth, and the unrestricted access that my citizenship grants me, to transform some of the suffering in this cruel world. It's both a profound realization and a heavy weight to carry. If I'm going to let the dream of a simple life in Bali die, I will do my part to try to make this world better for all girls, for all the Wayans and their children. I leave Bali drowning in sorrow, sobbing the entire thirty-six-hour trip back to Colorado, depressed for weeks afterwards. The love letters and phone calls from Ida Bagus become fewer and fewer. I harden my heart to the pitfalls of love, especially for girls, and buckle down to fulfill promises to my faraway friend and to the fierce warrior she's reawakened inside of me.

▪ ▪ ▪

I'd reached my limit. I wasn't aware that I had one but, the moment I hit it, I was certain. It turns out I draw the line at eating cockroaches. It's taken me eighteen years, with at least a dozen countries visited now, to refuse offered food. I'd eaten cow brains in Mexico, snake flesh in Vietnam, dog meat in Bali, and all sorts of slimy, raw sea creatures in between, but I could not—would not—eat a cockroach. Visions of them scurrying around my grandma's apartment in Queens, her sweeping and crushing and trapping them, have forever turned cockroaches into filth in my mind, unaware that it's the only source of protein for many in this part of the world.

The young Cambodian girl outside our taxi looks at me with suspecting eyes, unsure of how I can possibly refuse her scaraby gift. Pulling her arm back out the car window, she flips off the bug's outer shell and pops the roasted insect in her mouth with a disturbing crunch. The old woman selling the steaming mound of cooked roaches from which she has been lifting, notices her standing too close and shoos her away with disgust, waving a greasy red cloth in her direction. She yells something in Khmer at the girl, the tone of her voice and the motion of her hands translating to, "Scram, you street urchin, and don't let me catch you stealing my product again!" With a wink and a smile, the girl grabs an even younger boy by the hand and ducks behind a painted cargo truck, which is sandwiched in an endless procession of cars, trucks, and motorcycles waiting to pass through the security checkpoint that guards Cambodia's capital city of Phnom Penh.

I quickly roll the window up to prevent the entire platter of nauseating snacks from entering the car as well, simultaneously waving my other hand in the universal "No!" motion to the old woman who thinks I've taken an interest in her roaches. The traffic jam is swarming with people on foot, hawking wares between bumpers, advertising special deals and delicacies. A plate of boiled turtles walks by and I grow queasier. It's not helping that it's well over a hundred degrees and, now that the windows are all closed, stifling.

A Cambodian boy sells boiled turtles to the packed trucks of travelers waiting to enter Phnom Penh, 1996.

We've been backpacking through the South Pacific and Southeast Asia for six months now. My best friend from high school, Katie, and I saved our graduation money and worked all summer to afford the trip. My parents, sensing my reluctance to go to college, knowing my time in Bali had only piqued my wanderlust, made me a deal no teenager could refuse. If I got accepted to a college and landed a year-long deferment, then they would help pay for me to travel the world during that gap year. They knew, more than me, that it can be hard to apply for college once you're out of high school and that the first year of college anywhere would pale in comparison to the lessons I would learn after a year on the road. Katie's mom followed my parents' lead and she was offered a similar deal. We both landed college deferments, bought plane tickets, and left home in the weeks following our eighteenth birthdays.

We spent the first months away making our way from Hawaii to Fiji to New Zealand to Australia, and then across Indonesia, where I reconnected with Wayan and Ida Bagus. It had been two years since I was a student in Bali and Wayan was already married with her first baby, while Ida Bagus was engaged to an arranged wife. All of Wayan's predictions had rung true and I felt like a tourist visiting, more foreign to their island and community than before, still friends but resigned to following our divergent life paths.

Katie and I continued traveling up through Thailand, expanding our minds at the "Full Moon Party" on the island of Ko Pha-Ngan, and marveling at the depth and history of Thai culture, their form of Buddhism familiar yet distinct. From Bangkok, we had flown to Vietnam, a place that loomed ominous in the psyches of my parents and their entire generation, where my uncle had fought and survived the Viet Cong. Once we had made it that far, as if pulled by an invisible call, I began to work out the dangerous details of entering Cambodia.

Now we've been on the road to Phnom Penh for several hours and, at the rate we're crawling, we won't reach the capital before nightfall. Maybe this wasn't such a good idea? Katie reluctantly agreed to join me on this insane part of our journey, into an active war zone, and we somehow sweet-talked our way into a "limited-travel, six-day visa" into Cambodia at the barely-operating U.S. Consulate in Ho Chi Minh City. The young man at the consulate had made us promise not to leave Phnom Penh. "Not allowed!" he'd emphasized with a stiff finger-metronome, but I'm hoping to sneak up country to the lost ruins of Angkor, one of the remaining Seven Wonders of the World.

Travel permit in hand, the trip from Ho Chi Minh City to the Cambodian border was a harrowing ride on the back of a motorcycle. My backpack wedged upright between the driver and me, like a third person, our collective weight threatening to topple us at every turn. I kept a sharp eye on Katie's back far ahead, bumping along on her own twin-stroke engine. The surrounding countryside revealed endless hues of green rice paddies, hundreds of makeshift homes and farms, and the occasional overgrown metal skeleton of an abandoned tank or downed plane from the decades-old war. My driver was fond of pointing them out, screaming, "America!" each time he saw a new wreckage site. Parts of helicopters and broken military vehicles, nearly covered now in creeping vegetation, evidence of a violent conflict that cost the lives of 57,939 American sons; to say nothing of the 250,000 South Vietnamese soldiers who fought and died alongside them.

Now we are well into Cambodian territory and far from the relative safety of Vietnam. I suppose that I had imagined a war zone to look like a cross between *Apocalypse Now* and *M.A.S.H.*, with people fearing for their lives and bullets flying. On the contrary, a thriving scene of survival meets us on the outskirts of the capital, as millions of Cambodians go about their daily business, civil war or not. Making do with scraped-together housing and old clothing, selling anything that can be salvaged and reused, squeezing a life out of virtually nothing. By the time we finally cross security and enter Phnom Penh, the sun is beginning to set, while the war with the Khmer Rouge and their ruthless leader, Pol Pot, actively rages in the Western provinces.

My heart is beating double time as our taxi navigates the madness of a large, crowded metropolis with hardly any central governance. I get the giddy, fearful sensation of being out past curfew or breaking into a public pool at night, like we're definitely not supposed to be here. We'd made quick collect calls to our parents when we were back in Vietnam, and we'd checked in with Katie's family friends at the Dutch Embassy, like we promised. They warned us not to go to Cambodia but, despite Katie's anxiety that we heed that warning, I was going to Cambodia with or without her.

We'd heard about a backpacker's guesthouse in Phnom Penh called "Cloud 9," and instructed the taxi driver to bring us there. He looked at us as if to say, "Of course, that's where you're going," our packs and clothing giving us away. We'd gotten in this taxi at the border, along with a tightly-held Israeli woman, traveling alone with a small bag and a permanent scowl. She didn't even ask if she could share our ride, plopping in the back seat and daring us to make her leave. I could smell the sweaty shirt stuck to her neckline, which looked as if it'd been there long enough to leave an imprint. Like many young Israelis, she'd recently been discharged from her mandatory military service and was taking a holiday to decompress—by herself—in the war zones of Cambodia. She seemed agitated with the inefficiency of the border crossing and downright appalled at the naiveté that Katie and I offered everyone we met. At some point along the long drive, she caught me examining her. Before I could look away, our eyes locked in a gaze that was more hostile than friendly. I was fascinated with this woman, who had known the foul taste of war and remained drawn to it, even when far from home. I didn't yet understand the addictive quality of war, nor how it can seduce you into carrying its weight around long after the bullets stop flying.

We almost didn't make it across the border at all. Ignorant of border-crossing customs, Katie and I were awed by the scene between Vietnam and Cambodia, two distinct borders with a mile-long, dirt road "buffer zone" between. Hundreds of migrants, bicycles and motorbikes stacked to the brim with goods, flooded the no-man's land, the cacophony of commerce in two foreign languages amplified by the heat and the crowds. I immediately started taking photos of the outlandish scene. Moments later, a gun-waving soldier began screaming "No photo! No photo!" pointing in our direction. We were taken into a small room on the Cambodian side, where a man behind the desk explained in broken English that we had broken the law. We hadn't even crossed into Cambodia and we were already at risk of being kicked out.

Eventually, the border guards let us pass but only after confiscating the film rolls from our camera and scolding us repeatedly in front of other travelers. The Israeli woman watched the entire charade amused, staring at us like zoo animals surviving in the wild against the odds. She continued to regard us that way as we drove across Phnom Penh to the guesthouse. As soon as we reached our destination, she put as much distance between herself and us as possible, as if our innocence itself was a liability and she wanted nothing to do with the trouble it would eventually stir up.

The sign at the guesthouse entrance, scrawled in drippy spray paint along a crudely-constructed wall, read, "Welcome to Cloud 9. You can check out anytime you like, but you can never leave." Katie and I exchanged a mutual look that said both, "Sounds dangerous" and "I'm up for it." Rounding the ominous wall, I was struck to see that the entire guesthouse was on stilts, perched precariously and expansively over an enormous lake. The sounds of the city fell away as a tranquil scene of lily pads, birds, and frogs beckoned us in. I didn't even know that there was a lake in Phnom Penh and felt like an idiot for not knowing where we'd ended up on a map. The sun was setting in vivid reds and oranges, reflecting bright fractal light beams that bathed the entire scene in a rosy glow. Just like that, the movie set changed from a sweltering, chaotic border crossing to a relaxed, waterfront sunset lounge. It was disorienting and fantastic, both enticing and completely surreal.

The second thing that struck me was the overwhelming smell of marijuana in the air, plumes of smoke billowed from the low-lying tables and hammocks that filled the lounge. On the coffee table near the reception desk sat an open pack of rolled joints that were apparently being offered free with check-in. My body relaxed for the first time since leaving Vietnam. Growing up the way I did, pot was no stranger, and the smell brought an odd sense of calm. We snagged two beds in a basic dorm room with a shared toilet, freshened up, and headed back to the lounge to gather info.

Most of the travellers aren't much interested in making small talk. But a cute French boy in Thai fisherman pants makes eyes at me, so I strike up a conversation about the beauty of our shared surroundings. His English is poor and my French is nonexistent but I learn that he's been at Cloud 9 for more than a week and has yet to even leave the guesthouse. As opposed to us, he seems in no hurry to get anywhere. He says he's heard about the ancient ruins of Angkor, but he's not planning to leave Phnom Penh. He offers me a joint from his own pack and sits back to light another for himself, explaining how dangerous—not to mention illegal—the trip across Cambodia has become. A large boat traveling up the Mekong River to the ruins had caught on fire the week before and sank. People he knew were injured and stranded on the banks of the river, in the middle of Cambodia. He was high but also genuinely scared. He explained that weed was prolific, and practically free in the city, with huge marketplaces selling marijuana by the kilo for practically nothing. Looking around the lounge, everyone seemed suspended in a state of non-action. *Stoned and stuck on Cloud 9.*

I knew we were going to have to find a better source of information and make plans to get out of there quickly, lest we end up incapacitated in a cloud of smoke, missing the extraordinary wonders we'd come all this way to see. War or no war—Pol Pot or not—I was getting to those ruins. I can't quite explain the urgency, except to say that I was compelled to discover something other than prepackaged tourist traps, determined that this journey lead somewhere significant, illuminate a future path before we head home. Later that night, as Katie slept, I snuck back out to the lounge and made out with the French boy until sunrise, which was equally stunning along the lakeside. He may have been a frightened stoner, but he was also super cute.

Cloud 9's front receptionist, a shifty-eyed man who always seemed in the middle of a shady deal, arranged a dirt-cheap way for us to get north to the ruins once we admitted that we were living on a rough budget of seven US dollars a day. The fast boat to Angkor cost twenty dollars per person and may have been worth it, but the recent fire had stalled its operations for the foreseeable future, making us both wary. Plus, my instincts told me that traveling with large groups of wealthy tourists through a war zone was a bad idea; that the boat fire may not have been an accident. The safest option, according to Shifty, was to take the local route by truck and then canoe, which would only cost a few dollars each. The catch was that tourists were not technically supposed to travel this way, and we were going to have to trust him to connect us with good people who would help keep us safe en route. Being guideless and ignorant, we chose the cheapest way and crossed our fingers.

Loading into the back of a pickup truck, the sun was just waking to the rhythms of the central marketplace. At first, our ride felt rather spacious—not too bad for a six-hour trip to the river, where we were instructed to continue the trip by boat. Two wooden benches hugged the truck bed's long sides, and the top was covered in a thick canvas tarp that could be rolled up or tied down. I was optimistic and nervous, ready for adventure. Before long, passenger after passenger arrived with more and more luggage, squishing us closer and closer together. By the time we pulled out of the bustling market, the truck held fifteen Cambodians, two large sacks of rice, three live chickens, Katie, and me.

In the beginning, our travel companions are skeptical of our presence but, as we drive on, we share honest smiles and warm hand gestures. An elderly woman with a toothless grin offers us some of her breakfast, cooked cactus that she's kept warm in a wrapped cloth. I try it politely. *What must she think of us?* I contemplate, feeling self-conscious of my hippie beach clothes, my too-bare midriff, clueless of local customs or culture. It takes less time to leave the checkpoints of Phnom Penh than it had taken to enter, and, before long, we are speeding down a potholed, paved road, out of the city, towards the unknown.

Twenty minutes later, the pavement ends abruptly, and even the dirt road seems to deteriorate the further on we drive. Several times, the driver veers off the road altogether, avoiding enormous craters and bombed-out bridges, navigating the truck through withered riverbeds and dry, flat land. "No wonder they don't want tourists to travel this way," I say to Katie, as the visible signs of war appear. I wonder how long it's been since those bridges were bombed and when, if ever, they will be rebuilt. When there's no government in place, no one fixes roads or bridges.

The countryside flies by, lifeless and unkempt, barren as if abandoned for years, and so it has been. Farming: another invisible victim of war. The truck occasionally stops on the side of the road to drop a few travelers—everyone grateful for the additional butt room—and I watch them head off, on foot, into open fields, a few mud huts in the far distance their obvious destination. *What if that was my home? Who would I be today?* I ponder the bigger picture of my life, where I come from, all the invisible rights I was born into—like roads and working bridges. My manicured hometown of Boulder, Colorado, is so clean and resourced in comparison. I think of our annual Tulip Festival, with its thousands of temporary flowers, displayed in hundreds of colors. How would my fellow travelers react to seeing such opulence in the face of their ongoing misery? I have a hard time reconciling how one part of humanity can be so rich, while another side starves to death.

Arriving at the first military checkpoint, I'm surprised when our traveling companions urge Katie and I to get down into the middle of the truck bed, with the rice and chickens, and cover our faces with bandanas. One woman imitates the position we should assume, her head tucked between her knees, facing downward.

We comply with their demands, not understanding why, but trusting their intentions to shelter us. The young man who sold us these seats in Phnom Penh has been riding upright on the back bumper, hanging onto the top of the canopy, like a sanitation worker back home. He jumps down and offers the soldiers money for our passage. I see the offered bribe out of the corner of my eye as I further lodge myself against the truck's floor bed. I hear them laugh mockingly at the meager amount, making gestures for our vehicle to turn around and head back, heads shaking, refusing entry. Apparently, no civilian vehicles are allowed to travel this road, carrying tourists or locals. *Had Shifty betrayed us, stolen our money? Was this the end of our attempt to see Angkor? Or the end of our lives?* Our fate is clearly not in our hands. Katie is sweating and breathing heavy; like me, she has no idea what's happening. The bumper boy continues to implore the soldiers to let us pass, as one man raises an angry voice. Peering through the legs of the cactus-offerer, my head level with her calves, I see the soldier strike our boy hard in the head, hear him drop to the ground. I squeeze my eyes and tuck my head harder into my knees, trying to un-see it.

If I can't see them, maybe they can't see me. It's a child's game of hide-and-seek, only, this time, for keeps. A soldier moves around to the back of the truck, looking over the passengers, pointing his gun at random faces. I can't tell if he can see us down in the middle, or recognizes that we're foreigners, but he finally speaks in a more relaxed tone and the truck begins to move forward. Taking the boy's money, the soldier kicks him in the butt as he tries to jump back onto the bumper, eventually making it back up to join us. I am not entirely sure what just happened. What is clear are the stoic, sad expressions worn by our travelmates after we pull away. Their morning smiles fade into despair. This is the reality they must endure, what they've been forced to withstand for decades, the ever-present fear of traveling these dangerous roads, littered with landmines and AK-47s, their daily fate at the whim of war-weary men. Katie and I have placed our fate in those same hands and, again, I question what we are doing here and feel deeply in over our heads. The French boy was right to be scared.

Over the next six hours, we pass through a dozen similar checkpoints, the abusive tango with the soldiers becoming routine as the boy on the back bumper takes the brunt of their aggression in exchange for our ambitions. Each time we stop, I am sure we will be discovered, pulled from the truck, and disappeared. Each time, we must trust strangers with our lives. Each time, they keep us well-covered with bags of rice. The gravity of the situation I've gotten us into becomes crystal clear. Katie didn't want to come here in the first place, but I insisted. For weeks, I've been pushing us further and further from her comfort zone, searching for something, desperate to find a spark or a sign that will tell me what I am meant to do in this crazy, crowded world. In my drive to find it, I may have driven us too far.

The truck stops for lunch in a dusty town that serves as a sort of weigh station for vehicles traveling these unprotected roads. Even in war, commerce and life find a way of carrying on. We dismount, butts numb, and are led into a small teahouse where our driver and travel mates begin unpacking snacks from their bags and ordering food. Nothing on the menu is recognizable, and no one speaks much English. Instead of getting dysentery from some suspicious-looking stew, I opt for a bag of potato chips and an orange soda. I notice a fenced-in camp across the road and move to get a closer look. The Red Cross on the front gate, guarded by heavily-armed soldiers, tells me it's an official camp—a refugee camp. Though I only glimpse inside, it's the first sign of the international response to this war that we've seen, and now it makes sense why this is a safe rest stop. Until now, I thought the world had forgotten about Cambodia, that these poor people were left alone to pick up the mess of a brutal, ongoing civil war. When Pol Pot and the Khmer Rouge held Phnom Penh, they murdered two million people, or roughly 25 percent of the entire population of Cambodia. Those wounds will take generations to heal, and Pol Pot is still actively killing in the West. I see men and women working inside the camp, doing something useful to help the displaced, responding to the needs of innocent victims, and I long to be inside. This is no childish war game in the woods. This is real-life war, suffering on a massive scale, and I desperately want in.

In hindsight, I know this brief moment was my spark—a tiny window into my future. A few minutes spent staring into that camp, through a chain-link fence, becomes the inception of my life's pursuits. Though I didn't know it then, the impression Cambodia leaves on me serves as the driving force behind my work for the next ten years. What I do know, in that very instant, is that there is a role for me to play in this suffering world, the camp is clear evidence of that, and I finally know—without a doubt—what I want to be when I grow up.

Katie, however, is starting to feel sick. She is clammy and too sweaty, even for this heat. We'll need to find food and shelter for her soon and we still have many hours of hard travel ahead of us. Roughly five hours after leaving Phnom Penh, the road melts straight into the banks of the Tonlé Sap River. It is, literally, the end of the road. From a distance, it appears like any other river we've seen in Asia: muddy, ochre shades of water, drifting along slowly but steadily, banked with dense, green vegetation. But, as we draw closer, something extraordinary emerges: the river has thousands of people living on top of it. An entire city built on stilts stretching far into the water, emerges before us. The ground gives way to narrow, muddy paths lined with enormous mounds of garbage. Trash piles as high as I can see, boasting a stench that grabs hold of my nose and makes me gag. I can't imagine staying here another five minutes, much less existing here permanently. But the place is crawling with humans, most of them small.

The mounds of waste come alive with hundreds of children picking through the refuse, searching for something to eat or sell or repurpose. A little girl in an oversized, tattered sun hat, which might have once belonged to a Hollywood starlet, raises her head at the sound of our approaching engine. She smiles and waves, as if to adoring fans. The sounds of play and laughter stand in glaring contrast to her backdrop. *What could they possibly have to be so happy about?* I compare the scene with my neighborhood growing up, the exquisite maple tree-lined streets, to these kids running around in tatters of the same Western civilizations that have caused their people so much strife. A deep pang of injustice washes over me. *Why are these children born into rags, while others into riches? Why did these innocent lives deserve such misery? How do they not seem to know they're miserable? Who will help them, if not me?* The emotions the scene on the riverbanks elicit will stay with me for life, returning each time I witness the destruction of war firsthand, the abject poverty it produces, affecting, above all else, the blameless children.

We offload from the truck and onto a narrow, covered canoe, having lost and gained several companions along the way. More trucks arrive, and even more people pile into the waiting boat, three of whom are not Cambodian, making them the first foreigners we've encountered since leaving the capital. They're all men, dressed like they're on safari, and say they're part of a documentary film team. They seem genuinely shocked to find us there, either impressed or marveling at our incredible stupidity. For the second time today, I am embarrassed by my brightly-colored, tummy-baring Thai beach clothes. For the hundredth time today, I feel completely out of my element. Even the other foreigners don't think we belong here. Katie looks like she's gonna pass out and I help her lay down, urging her to drink some water.

The boat captain tells us that we have another six hours before we'll reach Siem Reap, the closest city to the Angkor ruins. I lay claim to some personal territory, stretching out on my backpack to make myself comfortable for the long trip. At this point, Katie is miserable, and I'm worried she'll throw up or have diarrhea along the way. This is not the time to need a toilet. I know we'll need to find a decent hotel in Siem Reap and hunker down until she gets better. I calculate that we can afford one day to convalesce if we're gonna see the ruins before our visas run out and we end up in Cambodia illegally. We can't afford for anything to go wrong.

Stilted dwellings stretch far into the water, with residents navigating the passageways in open canoes. We motor through a floating city of homes and shops, witnessing everyday life on the river. Canoe-based businesses, loaded with food and household goods, sell their bounty to villagers leaning over moldy front porch railings. People bathe and wash their clothes in eddies by the banks, while babies pee out open windows and gasoline spews from our old outboard motor. We putter along murky brown waters towards a mystical destination: the Lost City of Angkor. I feel like Indiana Jane and look to share my excitement with Katie, but she's finally fallen asleep. Cambodia is undoubtedly unlike any place I've ever imagined and, instead of sleeping too, I stare at the moving banks numbly, trying to process everything I've seen today. I'm dumbfounded by the recent discovery that humans can survive—even thrive—on garbage and sewage.

As the outboard motor thumps our passage up the Mekong River, images from the refugee camp return. I see my future self, working in such a place, recognize the charged chaos from Sun Camp games, the teachings to react calmly and with confidence. I've been training for environments like this since that day in Noah's hospital room, preparing my mind to work with suffering on this scale. Only now do I see how my upbringing has uniquely prepared me to navigate such a conflicted and painful world. *Why were we recreating war scenarios in the woods at such a young age? What was Trungpa preparing us for, if not this?* I try to join Katie in getting some rest, but my insides are jumping around, motivated by this newfound inspiration for my life and I don't want to miss an instant of it.

▪ ▪ ▪

"Hiiiiyaaaa!" I jump around the corner, stick-sword brandished and ready for battle, but Katie's not there. *Where's she hiding?* I hear her approach from behind, turning quickly. Stick-meets-stick in a mock battle for the captured princess…or something like that. I began the make-believe sword fight in an effort to keep our minds off the fact that we had just snuck into the Angkor ruins illegally, but also to disregard the 4:00 a.m. darkness, the chilling cold, and the creepy sounds emanating from the surrounding forest. Katie is playing along, so I continue the charade, for both our sakes.

We'd found a room in the only clean-looking guesthouse in Siem Reap, and spent the first twenty-four hours sleeping, reading, and nursing Katie back to health. Once her fever broke, I knew she was in the clear, just another case of undiagnosed traveler's illness. During the downtime, I met a Cambodian boy who said he could sneak us into the ruins for "free," which meant that, for a small fee, he could get us past the guard station at the entrance. They charge a whopping twenty US dollars to enter the ruins, which is equal to three whole days of our budget. Not only are we broke but the only bank in Siem Reap is completely out of money and there is no way to get more. Plus, our visa days are dwindling as fast as our wallets and, once Katie is on her feet, we have to either finish the journey or start back toward Vietnam. There was no time to waste on trivial things, like entrance fees.

Quietly motoring past the sleeping guard station, which would start charging visitors at 6:00 a.m., our accomplices silently left us by a stone path, in the pitch dark, and drove off without headlights. Neither of us have a clue where we are, nor any idea what we were supposed to be seeing, but we've made it inside. I've started to enjoy the giddy feeling that accompanies breaking the rules, the lawlessness reminding me of an old western movie. Holding hands, we inched up the path to a tall building, barely visible against a barely starry sky. I can tell that Katie is genuinely scared and I'm shaking too. I draw on the courage I found that cold night alone during Rights of Warriorship, forced to move past fear into action. Our efforts to save money suddenly feel silly in the face of dealing with thieves or soldiers, out here in the middle of the thick jungle, in the middle of the night. This was probably another bad idea. For comic relief, I began a mock duel, using laughter to overcome the fear, and it's doing the trick, as we're both starting to have fun.

Slowly, the sun rises on our imitation battlefield, my eyes adjusting to the growing light and, above us, I see the face of Buddha. A giant, beautiful, serene visage staring down, knowingly, watching our play. Jumping back, as if our silly shenanigans were suddenly sacrilegious, looking around to see if anyone else has been watching, I notice Katie staring up at yet another face, and then another. Spinning 360, taking in the entirety of the temple, we are surrounded by giant Buddha faces, a silent, stoney audience that neither applauds nor jeers at our imaginary battle. One moment, we are stranded travelers in the Cambodian jungle, terrified of getting caught, and the next, we are among dozens of monolithic allies, sharing a momentary secret that will remain hidden among these ruins forever. I get the feeling these old, wise rocks hold many secrets.

In the full daylight, the Bayon temple is breathtaking. Intricate and complex, hundreds of massive heads overlook a series of hallways and small rooms full of incense and flowers. I can now read that this temple marks Cambodia's transition from Hinduism to Mahayana Buddhism, the same tradition of my youth; the enormous stone faces, each an expression of Avalokiteshvara, the embodiment of compassion. It's as if they're here for me, confirming all of my recent life realizations. Buddhist mythology, delicately carved in bas-relief, decorates every inch of the temple's foundation. It's unlike anything in the Western world and stands proof of a time when art and spirituality were inextricably linked. Being in this one temple, clandestinely performing for its stone guardians throughout a magnificent sunrise, makes the perilous journey to get here well worth it.

We spend the rest of the day exploring other ruins, realizing that we could spend a whole week within the ancient city of Angkor, from dawn to dusk, and still not see it all. It is an immense, antique metropolis that once held a massive civilization but, without a guide, we have very little idea what we're seeing, other than what's written on sparse, poorly-translated signs. I vow to return one day, when I'm older, maybe even while working for the Red Cross, when I can spend a week studying these temples; when I can easily cover a twenty-dollar entrance fee. For now, we will just have to let its mysteries soak into us, and listen to what the ruins have to say instead of the history books.

Here I am in front of Angkor Wat, buying crafts from local kids, 1996.

Midday, we bump into an out-of-place group of American men, speaking English loudly while exploring the main temple, Angkor

Wat. They are the second set of Westerners we've seen since leaving Phnom Penh. Katie strikes up a conversation and they invite us to lunch, their treat. Broke and hungry, we accept. Over the course of the meal, we learn that we are dining with high-level U.S. military personnel, stationed in Cambodia to help train local forces to defeat the final contingent of the Khmer Rouge. *What the fuck are U.S. soldiers doing deep in the jungles of Cambodia?* I think. *How do I not know about this? Who does know about this?* They admit that their mission is top secret, part of an effort to "support and guide" recently-appointed Cambodian leadership, transitioning into power after decades of armed conflict. I realize that I know little about the war surrounding us, who's involved, how it began, or what is being done to stop it.

The more I think about it, the more I see how ignorant I am to all the world's wars, clueless about most of the conflicts plaguing our planet. For the first time since leaving high school, I feel an urgency to know more, to get involved, to play a part in ending this insanity, in helping those children get off the trash piles. I have traversed the ravaged roads of a country destroyed by war and grown enormously as a result. I don't understand how, but Cambodia feels like an initiation, a dress rehearsal for putting my Warriorship training to work. My feet have never felt so firmly planted in any direction. It is the trailhead I've been searching for. I set my intention to see it through to the end, even if it kills me, and I have a sneaking suspicion that it just might. I am strangely at peace with that kind of end.

In just a few days, among the ruins of what was once one of the world's greatest empires, I have located my life's purpose, the thing I've been seeking all these months away. I set my sights on building a future that will help those innocently entangled in the evil clutches of war. With a deep sigh, I exhale all the longing and searching that has consumed me since I left home. Turning my head toward the sky, I inhale a new sense of knowing and comfort, finally here and fully dedicated. I have found the beginning of my path.

Chapter Four

LOVE AND TRAUMA

In deconstructing the roots of my feminism and global activism, I seek to untwine the many ways my identity and my sexuality were enmeshed with my sense of self worth and personal power in the world. Taking stock of all of it, I see myself growing into my strengths through my history of intimate relationships with others…

The Destroyer

He was the coolest kid on the block. Older than my big brother, Noah, who, along with the rest of the neighborhood, admired him and let him lead…which is how it happened…everyone did what he said. I wish I could remember back to a time when my sexuality was free, when it wasn't woven into my shame and guilt and trauma. But I was only six when it happened, and I hardly remember anything beforehand.

"Why don't you leave the tent, Noah?" or something like that, was all that it took for us to be alone together. He said he had a new game and that I was lucky he chose me to play first. I felt honored. He instructed me to take off my clothes, like it was the most natural thing in the world, and the next image I recall, I was naked and lying on a wooden bench, in the bright, yellow-tinted, ten-person tent, which stayed permanently pitched in the neighbor's backyard. "Ready?" he asked, as if I knew what was about to happen and could've somehow prepared myself. He inserted his fingers into my vagina and spread them to make room. Then he began placing something pokey inside. "What is that?" I can imagine myself asking. "We're just gonna see how many sticks I can fit inside," he replied as if he was doing an experiment, one he'd performed before. It felt foreign and scratchy and uncomfortable. I wanted to say something, but I also wanted him to like me, to win the invisible contest he was holding.

I remember the sound of Noah's voice shouting, more than the look on his face, and then the shouting was growing distant, heading in the direction of home. Before I could get dressed and reach my front door, my father grabbed me and threw me inside, ordering me upstairs to my room. I never knew what happened to the boy, only that the game we were playing was obviously upsetting to the adults, and I was in big trouble for having played it.

I was grounded for a week, which, at age six, might as well have been a year. Noah was still allowed to play around the neighborhood until the streetlights came on, which was the universal sign to head home where we lived. I sat alone in my room, crying and confused about why I was being punished, unconsciously comingling my sexuality with shame. Even at six, I began to understand that, if boys hurt girls, it was because they were provoked to do so, that our victimhood was somehow always our own doing, while "boys would be boys" with social impunity.

In a matter of minutes, on a warm summer afternoon in the neighborhood play-tent, I went from feeling lucky and honored to bearing the full weight of sexism and shame that our society bestows to girls. With a few abusively-placed branches of a tree—of all things—he destroyed any chance I had of escaping the clutches of patriarchy and the virgin/whore trap with which it ensnares all women.

The First

His name, Ida Bagus, literally means "good idea" in English. If I was looking for a sign that this was the right time or that he was the right person, his name was surely it. At sixteen, I am the last virgin amongst my close girlfriends and they all tease me for it. Sex came onto our scene like lightning and, suddenly, all the girls were doing it, mostly with older boys. Ida Bagus is older than me too, by a couple of years, but Boulder High School is exactly 9,123 miles away and none of the home rules apply here in Bali.

He says he loves me, and I think I love him, though I've never said those words to anyone unrelated. We've been frolicking all over this island for months now, me holding tight to his waist from the back of his motorbike like a lifeline, burying my head in his leather jacket while passing too-large trucks on too-tight curves, our youth duping us into a state of complete immortality. We've been making out in waterfalls and staying awake until dawn on pristine deserted beaches, sharing our dreams and planning a future together. He's it, I'm sure. I just need to figure out the right moment to "offer him my flower," as my mom embarrassingly calls it.

She's been telling me to "guard it with my life" since the day I ran out of seventh-grade math class, the red stains on the desk chair matching the ones on the back of my jeans. I got to leave school early that day but had to endure a mortifying conversation about "cycles," and "tampons," and "blood flow" on the drive home. My dad came home from work early, a wrapped present in his outstretched hands. "Congratulations on becoming a woman!" He pronounced too loudly, turning my face red to purple. "How do you feel?" he pried, turning the uncomfortable to awkward.

"Fine," I most likely replied shortly, unsure how I *should* feel, and pretty sure that none of my girlfriends had talks with their dads about getting their period.

"I'm here if you need me," he assured, like he always did with the big friend fights, and the big game losses.

Now that I am considering having sex for the first time, I kind of wish I'd asked him and Mom for a few pointers. My best friends, Katie and Eve, had detailed their first times to me, neither of which had been particularly pleasant, and I have years of Sex-Ed under my belt, but I still feel terrified. It's such a huge, trusting thing: to let another person's body enter into yours…and I'm afraid it will hurt.

I haven't felt this open since I was in Costa Rica, and a huge part of that freedom is the liberty to explore being a woman, and no longer a girl. Untethered from the heaviness of The Destroyer's shadow, I yearn to reclaim something stolen from me, to step into my womanhood proudly and on my terms. So I chose the time and the place and offered my virginity to "The First." It was raining and misty and we found a secret place, far from prying eyes; surrounded by emerald rice patties and dragonflies and the tiny white birds they attract. We fell into each other completely, creating a moment of intimacy that felt right, and mutual, and empowering rather than manipulative or confusing.

In a matter of minutes, fractals of golden-green light bathed our bodies in rivers of acceptance and love, restoring a sense of strength and connection to my body. My sexuality became mine again, was made whole again. I arrived in Bali a girl and I left a few months later a young woman, more sure of myself and the type of loving partnership I deserved.

The Dreamer

I've never believed in love at first sight, nor the concept of "the one," nor that I needed anyone outside of myself to "complete me." So I can't explain how I fell so hard and so fast for "The Dreamer." Maybe it's because he was the kind of man whose smile preceded him, like it walked into a room first, a split second early, catching you off guard. Before you knew it, you were smiling too.

His smile greeted me at the freshman dorm registration table on my first official day at Occidental College in Eagle Rock, California. My mom insisted she make the long, hot August drive from Boulder, Colorado to Los Angeles to help me settle in, even if it was embarrassingly unnecessary in my mind. I had traveled the world without her and, after Cambodia, there was little innocence or helplessness left in me. But it was nice that she paid for my huge haul of dorm-sized goods and, once we got on campus, she obviously wasn't the only parent tagging—and nagging—along. Though not the case with my assigned roommate, at least not by the time I got there and found her completely moved in and chatting familiarly on her bed with another brown-skinned girl with long, black hair. They both looked me up and down skeptically, their smiles conveying distrust and curiosity. It didn't help my case that my mom was right behind me.

My roommate put on her best professional voice, what we would later refer to as her "white girl voice," and made some excuse to leave and let us move into what was clearly my empty side of the small, cement dorm room. I would soon learn that she was Filipino-American and the first member of her family to attend college in the U.S. She would soon learn that I was the strangest white girl she had ever met, though she admitted early on that she had never actually spoken to many white people. Occidental was one of the "most diverse" liberal arts colleges in the country, and we had both been accepted to live in the "Multicultural Hall," an experimental dorm that assigned incoming freshmen roommates from a culture distinct to their own. The idea was that cohabitating, coupled with lots of group discussion, training, and team-building, would force us out of our racial and cultural comfort zones and, in turn, break down some of the ignorance and fear that divided us. In reality, the M.C. Hall became a beautiful family: one that fought and grew and protected one another within the broader campus ecosystem.

I came into Oxy so confident and cocky, convinced that I wasn't like other white Americans. I had lived with, traveled with, and loved people from many different races and cultures. I had been raised to be proudly "colorblind." My years at Oxy slowly and painfully helped me realize that that only meant I had spent my entire life blind to the experiences of people of color in the US…and it all began with "The Dreamer" and his radiant, infectious smile.

"What?! You really walked across the border of Vietnam and Cambodia and then illegally drove across an active war zone?" I nodded.

"Girl, I've met some interesting white people during my time at Oxy, but you might just be the craziest white girl I've ever met. Hell, you might be the craziest person I've ever met."

I was showing off. Not just because of his luminous smile, but because he was smart and interesting and full of life. He was also a senior and, I'd since learned, a star basketball player. And much of our love blossomed on a basketball court, over game upon game of "horse," talking about everything from politics to polar bears; talking trash while shooting hoops and opening up about the vastly different worlds we came from. He helped me realize that I had traveled the entire world to expose myself and learn from cultures different from my own, and I knew almost nothing about Black Culture in America. I was woefully ignorant about much of my own country, having been spoon-fed a Cosby Family, Michael and Whitney-loving, post-racial, white man's version of Black America.

I was mainly confused, and sad, when his family rejected our union and we started receiving hate from other black students on campus. Black women approached me in the cafeteria wondering "why I couldn't find a nice white boy to date." He began to receive notes and public snickering about "betraying his people."

For me, it was unfamiliar and unfair criticism that I brushed off, saying, "What is this, the 1950s?" As if their facts and their fears were completely misplaced there in 1996. For him, it was just another weight added to the burdens he bore. He was the first in his family to attend such a prestigious college, his parent's youngest son, and his community's great hope, as well as the poster boy for Oxy's winning basketball program. But, alone with me, he was goofy and creative, queer and peculiar, inquisitive and wicked-smart. He could recite the name of every country in the world, even though he had never left his own, and had memorized the Latin names for all 206 bones in the human body.

"I've never met anyone like you."The Dreamer said one day, out of the blue. We were talking about love and possession and how, for me, the two are oxymorons (a term we loved to call ourselves, as two Oxy students from opposite worlds). I had just declared that I was never getting married and wanted him to understand that not only did I believe in the separation of church and state—making tax breaks for married couples illegal by definition—but that anyone who is a feminist and an advocate of gay rights can't, in good conscience, support the misogynistic and homophobic institution of marriage as it stands.

"I wish you wouldn't use those words," he replied.

"What words?" I questioned honestly.

"'Feminist' and 'gay.'"

"What's wrong 'with those words'?" I practically shouted.

"Where I'm from, those are fighting words. Whispered words."

"Well, that's just ignorant and wrong. Equality for all or equality for none." I ended the discussion there, never realizing that my own ignorance was blatant, that I had no idea what it was like to walk through the world as a black man, nor that all of his fears, and his mother's fears, were perfectly founded. He looked at me that day in total disbelief and perhaps I never fully looked back.

As our love grew, so did The Dreamer's confidence. He admitted that he found no joy in playing basketball anymore and was considering quitting the team midseason. "Do it!" I urged, saying "Life is too short and too precious to spend one moment in misery." When I went home for holiday break that first year, he did it. He wrote a letter to his coaches and his team explaining his decision to follow his happiness and explore other life goals. He skipped a big game and took himself to the movies instead. The fallout was severe. I failed to understand how the same community that supported his athletic career wouldn't support his decision to focus on his academic and spiritual growth. To me, he was evolving, finally dreaming out loud. To his community, he had lost his mind and, clearly, our relationship was the root of the problem.

We weathered the storm together, attacked on all sides by those who felt abandoned and betrayed by his choosing not to play basketball. As if this talented, beautiful student lost all his value to the school and their pride when he chose to step off the court. Never mind that he had a plausible dream to revolutionize sports medicine, his currency was his contribution to the school's athletic department and not his brilliance in the classroom. That spring, he fell into a deep depression and attempted to take his own life. I found him in a state of overdose, unresponsive, and my roommate, who had become one of my closest friends, helped me drive him to the emergency room. They pumped his stomach and revived him. He made me promise not to tell a soul saying, "The only thing worse than a suicide is a failed suicide." I knew it was a cry for help, but I had no idea how to heed it.

By the time The Dreamer graduated in the full-blown Los Angeles summer heat, he was different, and I was different. We were still in love but there was a filmy layer to our relationship that was hard to name. I started to feel suffocated around him, like his life was balancing precariously in my hands, like I held the keys to his freedom as well as my own. I desperately wanted to see him fly free but worried that he'd never make it far from the nest. We planned a cross-country road trip after his graduation, back to my home in Colorado, noting that it would be the furthest he would've ever travelled from LA.

His mom called the night before our trip, hysterical, begging him not to drive out of California alone in the car with a "white woman." But we were undeterred. For me, her fears were delusional, stating "It is 1997, after all," without a thought of the near-fatal beating of Rodney King by the L.A.P.D. five years earlier. For him, he had already begun to risk everything with our relationship, to live differently than his parents' dreams, and there was no going back. The Dreamer and I were born on the same day of the year, at roughly the same hour, and, that summer, we celebrated my twentieth and his twenty-second birthday. He would never celebrate a twenty-third.

The post-graduation road trip to Colorado was fun and full of firsts and, thankfully, rather uneventful. We managed to rope in two of his close friends and fellow graduates to caravan our way there, making everyone feel safer. The largest obstacle we encountered was a broken water pump in my old Volvo, which had us stopping every fifty miles of the last leg to refill, lest we overheated. The Dreamer's experience of Boulder was fascinating to witness, and, through his eyes, I saw how truly homogenous my hometown is. He had never been around so many well-meaning white folks in his life, some of whom, embarrassingly, waved to him on the street for no apparent reason. I tried to explain such strange behavior, chalk it up to a welcoming community spirit, but I struggled to understand it myself. In the end, we laughed over it, deciding they must assume that he's famous or a star athlete, as those are the only black folks that make it into the fabled "People's Republic of Boulder." In fact, I did grow up with some black students, a few of whom were close friends but, in reality, there were so few black kids in my high school that we had only fifteen black students in our graduating class of 459.

The Dreamer said that being in Boulder, surrounded by only white people, made him feel "like someone had turned on the lights and shown him that the boogeyman wasn't so scary, after all." We joked about the absurdity of it all, both young and delusional to the evidence and efficacy of institutionalized racism all around us. At the same time, we needed a break from one another. Racial tensions aside, we had weathered a difficult semester, and we both had some serious soul-searching to do. I felt far from the badass girl who had trekked across Cambodia in the midst of civil war, and I was emotionally drained. It was my first experience with the trap of codependency, at least on that level, and, in some ways, our year together at Oxy had sent me to a place more unfamiliar to myself than any of the traveling I'd done.

I made plans to spend the summer in Paris, with the excuse that I needed to work on my French, having done poorly in French 101 my second semester; The Dreamer's depression and attempted suicide filling my mind and heart more than the desire to tackle a foreign language from a foreign land. He made plans to work on his Spanish at a school in Costa Rica and bought a one-way ticket there. His parents were freaking out at the thought of his leaving the country but I was his biggest supporter. I knew what traveling had done to force me out of my shell to see life differently. We spoke on our birthday, me from Paris and he from Costa Rica, and he promised to pick me up at LAX in a month's time. We said, "I love you," and, "I'll see you soon."

The morning his mom called my mom, the old landline on the kitchen wall rang like a warning alarm, notifying me that my world was about to be forever altered. The details were few and confusing. The Dreamer had last been on a Costa Rican beach with friends, other students from the language program, celebrating the end of their classes. He was days away from flying home to L.A. The other students, one of whom I spoke to for a moment, reported that they had left the beach and that he had chosen to stay alone, saying he'd be back up to their lodging soon.

His body washed onto shore in the morning, having been lifeless for many hours. He was alone at the end and only he knows the truth of what happened. Maybe that was his parting gift to all of us who loved him, to not know exactly how it ended. Because in the not knowing lies the freedom to write whatever end serves us best, whatever storyline we need to continue on living. I know that he died having bravely completed his first solo mission out into the world and, to me, that is better than a lifetime of living in fear.

My entire childhood was steeped in death, my mom's favorite reminder to me, "Death comes without warning; this body will be a corpse. At that time, the Dharma will be my only help; I must practice it with exertion." And, while I had those words posted on the wall near my teenage bed, it wasn't until The Dreamer died that I fully understood and felt them. Life ends in a moment, and that moment is awaiting all of us. His final gift to me would be that understanding. I vowed to carry it with me, evidenced by the scar across my heart, and to live the rest of my days as if they were truly my last.

The Lover

Before The Dreamer died, during my carefree summer in Paris, I met The Lover. I call him that because, thanks to his patient teachings, sex went from confusing and shameful to filled with sensuality and pleasure. The Lover was slow and communicative and knowledgeable about a woman's body in all the ways that American Puritanism despises. The Lover was never satisfied until I was. I had given myself orgasms but never had I felt relaxed enough to go there with another person…The Destroyer had made sure of that. Never before had my pleasure been so central to my partner's mind and focus, as if his desire was entirely dependent on mine being fulfilled. The Lover took my tiny, rose-bud of a flower and turned it into a full-blooming beauty; sex was transformed from an act that someone else did *to me,* to an act I was fully participating in. It was intoxicating and addictive, and we spent the end of the summer at his family's home in the south of France, drinking too much wine, visiting nude beaches, and making love every moment we could. And it was there that I met his grandparents, whose own love affair spanned decades, and there that his grandfather and I developed an uncanny and unexpected friendship that would also last for decades.

I bade farewell to The Lover in a scene out of a movie, on a small plane heading for Paris, him waving from the runway. I wrote in my journal that I was sure I'd never see him again. I had just gotten my first email address, and we promised to keep in touch, but, when I left him, it was The Dreamer I was heading towards, our impending reunion at LAX, and I could hardly wait to hear all about his time in Costa Rica. But that reunion never happened, and I returned to L.A. a week early, instead, to attend his funeral.

Because so much of my love life with The Dreamer had taken place on our own private island—away from the judgment and fear that our dissonant skin tones elicited—I grieved the loss of him alone. Few people knew of his attempted suicide earlier in the year and his death was ruled an "unfortunate accident," though I maintained my doubts. There were several memorials during which his family, his basketball coaches, and members of the Black Student Alliance spoke about a man I never knew. While a few of his close friends knew how much he meant to me, I struggled to make sense of how a person's memory can become fractured and skewed to fit individual narratives, how an entire lifetime of secrets can die along with us. I was angry that no one else was grieving the same version of The Dreamer that I was, too young to know how common that is, how death allows each of us to rewrite history, to sweep the ugly stuff under the rug and choose the most palatable ending to hold on to. I didn't blame his family nor his friends for memorializing versions of him that they knew and loved best, but I was devastated that, even in his death, his spirit wasn't free; even his memories were held to a suffocating standard of expectations.

Oxy's campus went from a safe, loving place to a minefield of memories. Because none of the memorials included his actual body, the way a Buddhist funeral would, I secretly doubted The Dreamer was dead. I spent countless hours trying to decipher a nonexistent code that would lead to the secret life he must be living on an island somewhere, far from the pressures of home. And then, at some point in my barely-expressed grief, I lost my grip on my will to live. The will to stay alive is subtle but it'd always been there. So, when I lost it, it was terrifying. I began wearing only black and smoking cigarette after cigarette, coupled with endless cups of coffee. I barely ate. I whittled down to 120 pounds, which I hadn't weighed since junior high, and everyone started "worrying about me." My mom moved out to L.A. and into my sophomore dorm room to care for me like a small child, cooking and cleaning up after me, encouraging me to go to class and do my homework. In a way that I couldn't even recall from my childhood, she lovingly cared me back to life and quietly shouldered half my hurt so I wouldn't break entirely. It was the most I ever recall needing her in my twenty years as her daughter and I don't think I would have stayed in school without her dedicated support.

The Lover became my only outlet from the pain and giant hole left by The Dreamer's absence from the planet. I started making plans to leave L.A. and, by holiday break, I was back in Paris and back in the tender arms of The Lover, my new safe space, landmine-free and weightless. I let The Lover cook for me, love on me, and shower me with attention and gifts. Eventually, through his care, I began to reconnect with my self-love and find the roots of my will to go on. I began to envision a future again, one filled with happiness and joy, not just constant pain and disappointment.

But, first, I had college to complete, potential to fulfill, and promises to the dead that I intended to keep. So I divided myself in two. My heart would stay with The Lover in Paris, while my mind would pour itself into school in California. Because campus was so painful for me, I crafted an ambitious curriculum that had me studying abroad as much as possible. Whenever possible, I would fly to Paris, meet The Lover, and forget it all. In one year, I maxed out my credit cards flying to Paris seven times, and spent thousands of dollars on long-distance phone bills in between. At school, I became a beast, taking every class on gender and race that I could, eventually majoring in Diplomacy and World Affairs with an emphasis in Comparative Gender Studies. I spent six months in Nepal and India, a semester at the United Nations Headquarters in New York, and won a coveted fellowship to study in London. I took classes on Rastafarianism, pornography, African Dance, and salsa, and I protested when the administration tried to shut down a course on "Whiteness." I even played intramural sports and starred in more than one theatrical play, but I never let myself love anyone in Los Angeles again. The Dreamer's shadow, like an echo that never ends, followed me everywhere.

In the end, I graduated from Oxy with top honors, my senior honor's thesis on the value of gender integration in U.N. peacekeeping operations won an award, and I was nominated to deliver the class graduation speech. I had left the soft and vulnerable parts of me in France and become an academic machine in L.A. Until, finally, upon graduating, I planned to move to Paris and study French Literature at the Sorbonne. And that's when The Lover broke my heart...and like a side-on collision with a semi-truck, I never saw it coming.

She was a Chilean flamenco dancer, which seemed like a plot out of bad daytime television, and The Lover claimed "they were totally in love" after only a few days of knowing one another. I was suddenly "too ambitious," "emotionally unavailable," "unrealistic," and "not feminine enough" for him. I'd spent the past three years pouring all my love, and all my money, into a future with him, and now that dream was dead too. I felt like I had run full-speed into a brick wall and was back at square one in the grieving process. I moved home to Boulder, back in with my parents, and got a temp job ordering office supplies for a tech company. So sure that I was heading to Paris, I had skipped all the job fairs and the resume-building classes for graduating seniors, failed to sign up for the Foreign Service Exam nor the Peace Corps, put all of my eggs in one French basket and ended up back home with yoke on my face.

The Competitor

To say that The Competitor is one person would be untrue. He is more an amalgamation of individuals, an archetype that I fell for time and again. The Competitor is instantly attracted to my independent spirit and intellect. It feels like love, but it's a different type of craving; it's tinged with obsession, driven by a need to dominate. The very thing that attracts The Competitor to a girl like me becomes our eventual undoing. The Competitor is often an Alpha male, accustomed to hearing the sound of his own voice and having his every opinion validated, given ample airtime in our patriarchal society. Maybe it's our animal nature revealing itself, the strong male looking to subdue the independent female, corral her back into her place. Or maybe it's just a load of bullshit we've been trained to mimic. Whatever the reason, I dated—and was damaged by—my fair share of Competitors.

In high school, The Competitor was a semi-professional roller-blader who made sure I never felt too good about myself in his presence. The day I finally got up the nerve to break up with him, he freaked out and begged me to take him back. Once I did, he dumped me the next day, making sure all his friends knew it. Playing with my heart to protect his fragile ego. The Competitors I dated were inferior to me intellectually, and many of them went to great lengths to explain how my overt knowledge of cultures and foreign languages made them feel threatened, making me less attractive in their eyes. Their messages were that I would do better to keep my brain quiet and my makeup fresh if we were to succeed, that all that made me amazing is precisely what they wished I would hide in their presence. Their superiority was predicated on my inferiority and, when I "knew too much," their responses ranged from irritated to infuriated. One Competitor woke me up in the middle of the night to take an IQ test and compare scores; another asked that I not show off by speaking foreign languages around him, as not being in control of the conversation made him insecure.

No matter how many times I fell for, and got burned by, Competitors, it took me a long time to see my pattern. Once I understood the game, I figured out how to stop playing it. I realized that I could spend my entire life trying to win an unwinnable match at home, where all the rules were stacked against me, and end up missing my life's purpose altogether. I began to notice other strong women who had fallen prey to this invisible trap, had gotten stuck trying to prove their worth to the powerful, rather than heed their true calling.

The Competitor seemed like a catch, and he often came in the shiniest package, but I eventually learned to be wary of his attempts to diminish my brilliance so that I never outshone him. The last Competitor I dated ended up breaking into my apartment, the morning after I ended our relationship and ransacking my stuff, which led me to pursue a restraining order. It was the last time I confused a man's obsessive attention with love.

The Friend

Not long after another painful ending with yet another enervated Competitor that I fell for in the The Lover's wake, I reconnected with The Friend. Talking with him was like slipping into a favorite sweater, everything about him reminded me of home and a more innocent time. That's because the first time I "dated" The Friend, we were twelve and it only lasted a week, as junior high romances go. I remember breaking up with him because he had the audacity to try and kiss me after the Friday assembly, in front of all my friends. It took me totally off guard, a tongue-first-surprise-face-attack, and I reacted by ending things immediately.

The second time The Friend and I dated, we were sixteen and in high school. I hadn't met The First yet and was considering The Friend as a possible candidate for receiving my flower. I think I fascinated him more than anything at that age, my home life appearing exotic next to his cookie-cutter American household. I often wished for a mom like his, who cooked and hosted pre-game dinners instead of meditation groups and bizarre parties. When I left high school in the middle of basketball playoffs to study abroad in Bali, The Friend defended me against my angry teammates and promised to write me letters…and he did. He sent newspaper clippings keeping me up to date on the team's progress, all the way to winning the State Championship. But, by then, I had fallen in love with The First, my "good idea," and was busy discovering my wandering spirit.

The last time The Friend and I dated, in the aftermath of The Lover's betrayal, he stepped into my chaotic and confused life, which had been reeling since The Dreamer's death, and provided me some much-needed ground and sound advice.

"I love you," I whispered to The Friend one day, lying in bed.

"No, you don't," he replied courageously, "and that's okay."

He was right. I loved him, but I wasn't in love with him. I don't know what the magic ingredient is that turns a friendship into a romance, but I know it can't be faked. I mean, I could imagine settling into a nice, easy, friendship-based relationship for life with him, but I also knew that we both deserved more. He was one of my best friends and he deserved to hear an "I love you" that he could feel. A few months into our third go at a partnership, I landed my dream job with Urgent Action Fund. It only took a short conversation with The Friend for us to decide I should take the job, and for it to be clear that that decision would take me places I need to go alone. I will forever be grateful that I wasn't tussling with a Competitor when that life-changing career opportunity arose and that The Friend recognized my path before I did, urging me to walk it proudly without him.

Chapter Five

FINDING MY VOICE

When I was eight years old, a new type of computer-based video game was introduced in my elementary school. An educational yet entertaining game that taught geography, wordplay, espionage, and international law. "Where in the World Is Carmen Sandiego" became my obsession. I was allowed to play as much as I wanted, because I was suddenly rattling off facts about foreign capitals, maps, and flags…and winning at Trivial Pursuit on family game night. In the computer game, Carmen Sandiego is a former detective turned international thief who outsmarts all on her trail by using a complex system of disguises and codes…and she always escapes, usually leaving a henchman to take the fall for her. She was the opposite of everything I had been taught about women and the lives they are capable of living.

In the video game, you play a detective trying to capture Carmen by solving a series of riddles and tests; in reality, I never wanted to catch Carmen Sandiego. I wanted to be Carmen Sandiego. She didn't steal for money but, instead, for street cred. It was as if she woke up one day, realized she was smarter than all the male detectives around her, and decided to use her brains to challenge the system and change the world. I played for hours on end, memorizing the names of far-off places like Budapest, Cairo, Kigali, Kathmandu. I began to envision myself in her fabulous hat and mysterious long, red trench coat.

"Kirsten! Get in here!" Grandma Martha yells across the apartment like it's on fire. "Time to stuff the turkey!" Her smile too big, sure I'd been waiting for this moment all day, as she had. My brother, Noah, was allowed to carry on watching TV, oblivious to my penance, his penis excluding him from this particular chore.

"Why do I always have to cook the turkey with you, Grandma?" I complain, "It's creepy the way you take its guts out and stuff it back up with food."

"Because, my dear, someday this will be your job. No one is gonna want to marry a woman who can't cook a Thanksgiving turkey. That, I know, for sure!" She'd state this as if it were written law.

I suppose that's where it began, the earliest roots of my feminism, right there in my Grandma's kitchen. Contrary to her best intentions, my first major act of resistance to the invisible expectations that can cripple girls and exonerate boys, was my resolute aversion to cooking. I subconsciously knew that if "no one wanted to marry a woman without turkey-cooking skills," I could avoid the whole marriage trap by simply avoiding the turkey and the kitchen altogether. The unending work that had bogged down women in my family for generations—our worth intrinsically connected to our ability to feed and clean up after others—was easily solved by refusing to take up the mantle or, in this case, the ladle.

My reluctance to cooking backfired by the time I reached college and could hardly boil water to feed myself. On campus (minus the few months my mom moved in after The Dreamer died), I relied on the campus cafeteria and snack bars, vending machines, and friends willing to share. I developed unhealthy habits, like drinking too much coffee and smoking too many cigarettes, while eating beef jerky and soda for lunch. I learned to ignore my body's basic needs and focus instead on my classes and the mountains of work they required. I wrote throughout the nights and slept until the afternoons. I've always written. Mostly by hand, pencil to paper, left to right. It has been my outlet for processing intense emotions and my vessel for bringing creative visions to life. Writing the stories of the trees along my evening childhood walks put me in the habit of tapping into my pent-up feelings through the physical practice of moving lead across a spiral notebook page. At Oxy, the writing demand was high, and my calloused hands rose to the challenge. Two female professors in the Department of Diplomacy and World Affairs, Dr. Jane Jaquette and Dr. Movindri Reddy, encouraged my writing from day one, showing me how to let my opinions shine in a room full of male voices.

That's how the Politics Department felt, even in 1996. Us girls still stuck out like giant thumbs, some of us in pants, some in skirts, none of us having inherited a clue on how to blend into that male-dominated world. Our very gender felt like a threat to the status quo. The United States' political world was facing its own reckoning with gender, as President Bill Clinton came with a First Lady who also wore pants, kept her hair short, and refused to bake. To compete with the male politics majors, I would have to be smarter and faster, stay one step ahead. Sadly, this did not foster the best environment between us few, competing, females. Thankfully, those of us brave enough to enter this collegiate political arena had a few role-model professors to selflessly lift us up and push us forward.

I marched into Professor Jane Jaquette's office in the first weeks of freshman year, as she was my Academic Advisor, and outlined an ambitious four-year plan to graduation. She looked at me surprisingly and said something along the lines of, "Go for it, girl. I've got your back!" Or at least that's the feeling I left her office with. When The Dreamer died the summer before sophomore year, it was Dr. Jaquette who understood how much I needed to get off campus and pour myself into academic pursuits. She helped me make a plan, stick to it, and achieve it. Without her support, I never would have made it as far.

My first semester abroad was to Kathmandu, Nepal, a place I'd heard stories about from my parent's travels across Asia in the '70s, and a place I'd almost caught Carmen Sandiego in when I was ten. While I was curious about living in a Hindu/Buddhist culture, as I had briefly in Bali, it was also about as far away from Los Angeles—and The Dreamer's ghost—as humanly possible. What I didn't yet know is that you can travel around the entire globe, but your ghosts and your memories still find you. What I could never have prepared for is that Nepal would not only embrace me as a daughter; it would teach me how to finally grieve.

As exchange students, we were fake-adopted into Nepalese families, who gave us each a family name and a place to stay in their homes for the semester. I was fortunate that the family who adopted me included both a ninety-year-old grandmother and a newborn baby. When a Nepalese woman has a baby, she returns to live in her mother's house, called her "Maiti," for a few post-partum months, healing from the birth and learning from older generations how to care for an infant. During this time, the father most likely returns to his mother's house as well or pays a neighbor's wife to cook and clean for him. In all my time in Nepal, I never saw a Nepalese man cook. In my newly-adopted household, men hardly even entered the kitchen.

Like in my Grandma's house, the role of cooking (and cleaning) fell squarely on the women and girls. My host family also had a teenage girl, Pratima, who shared my mischievous spirit, and was constantly nagged by her mother and grandmother to help out in the kitchen after school. She was forever escaping to the roof to show me her latest dance moves, while the older women chased her down and her big brother sat in the living room, watching the only TV set in the entire town, waiting for his food to be served. I was learning that some things in this world are vastly different, while other things are eerily similar.

During my time in Kathmandu, I would walk an hour to school every morning, and Pratima would often walk most of the way with me, off to her own middle-schooling. We would walk and talk, and she would share her hopes and dreams for the future, away from the prying ears of her mom and big sister (who was home with her first baby girl). We became fast friends, Pratima and I, and she reminded me of The Lover's little sister in Paris, who I had also adopted as my own. Pratima helped me navigate the city, the completely foreign customs of her culture, and to see Nepal through her young, optimistic eyes.

One particular custom I was struggling with was around menstruation. Nepalese culture requires women to announce the onset of their menses and are then determined to be *jutho*, or "unclean," and therefore untouchable for three days. Not every Nepalese family practices this custom as strictly, but I was in a high-caste family that adhered to strict codes of conduct. My Western feminist mind could not understand how such a limiting system had survived for centuries, why women hadn't risen up to change it long ago...and then I got my first period in Nepal.

Like Anita Diamant's images from *The Red Tent*, the special women's room in our house is where the magic lived. A few months after arriving, the cycles of all the women living in my house aligned, which is common, and part of the fun. We were five generations of women sitting together for hours, laughing, crying, teaching, learning, and generally letting it all hang out. Pratima said she felt sad thinking that I didn't know when my mother or grandmother were bleeding and, therefore, wouldn't know when to help them a bit more. Here I was, feeling righteous and judgmental about what I had assumed was an archaic social custom when, from my little sister's perspective, we were the ones treating each other in an uncivilized way. I could see how a reserved, all-women venting and support room would have worked wonders for my grandmother and my mother. But it wasn't until I attended my first Nepalese funeral that I understood how truly repressed my American culture was when it came to expressing our feelings.

My adopted Nepalese sister Pratima showing off her latest dance moves, 1998.

My adopted Nepalese grandmother and her newborn great-granddaughter, 1998.

I didn't know the person in our village who'd passed away, but that fact seemed to matter not to the other women in the room. I heard her wails long before she entered the house and, as she drew closer, others in the room began to cry as well. She was the widow; the person recognized as having been closest to the deceased and she was screaming her pain at full throttle. So immersed in her grief that she could hardly stand or walk, and required assistance from other women on all four sides. With her wails, I could feel—the first time in a year since The Dreamer's death—all of the pain still trapped inside of me.

"We believe you have to let all of your hurting into the world. To succumb to the sadness completely while the women around you hold you up." Pratima translated the confusing experience. I could see how the bonds around the widow now, in her darkest hours, had been forged month after month of bleeding and suffering together. I thought of my mom's tribe of healers and soup-makers, helping her fight the cancer. Drawing on their strength, their uncanny and socially-encouraged female web, I found the unique sound of my unexpressed loss and longing. Crying out my suffering with the full capacity of my lungs, the notes blended perfectly with my neighbor's pain, at once foreign and completely recognizable.

That day, in the valley of ancient kings, I finally grieved The Dreamer fully, in my own way. At sunset, my throat screamed dry, I found a roadside barber. He had nothing more than a rusty chair, a pair of scissors, and a small mirror, which was nailed awkwardly to a tree. The barber's face was terrified, and his hands shook when I told him my request, but I was certain enough for the both of us. And I paid him handsomely for his courage. He cut off my shoulder-length locks and using an old comb and scissors, managed to uniformly shape my now pokey hair to within a cm of my scalp. Nepalese women often shave their heads when in mourning, a sign and a reminder, to themselves and society, that their suffering is recent, and it is raw. I swear, with that one bold haircut, I dropped the unbearable weight I'd been carrying and drew my first deep, liberated breath.

Not everything about my immersion into Nepalese culture went so smoothly. One of the big points of contention in my house had to do with Pratima still being in school at age fourteen. I spent long hours chatting with my adoptive father, the decision-maker of the household, improving my Nepali grammar and outlining my arguments for educating girls. He tried to help me understand that, by keeping her in school any longer, he was actively reducing her chances of a good marriage. From his point of view, he was harming her by allowing her to dream such fancies as college and a professional city job. School was hurting her life's résumé, not helping it, and it's impossible to convince a father to harm his children.

Pratima was smart, and one of the reasons we had grown so close was that her English was better than anyone else in the family. She wanted more than an arranged marriage with a boy from her village, the way her mother and her grandmother had done. She wanted to be the Master of Her Own Destiny and I knew exactly how that felt. In the end, after a semester's worth of debate, Pratima's father said that it came down to money, and that high school would cost money they just couldn't spare. Her tears soaked my pillow, as she buried her head in my room and wept for the future she'd never have. If it was simply a matter of money, I decided, that was something I had access to. We didn't have much on a Boulder, Colorado scale but we were beyond wealthy on a Kathmandu, Nepal scale. To Pratima, coming up with an extra $300 for a year of school was an impossibility; to me, it was simply a matter of asking the right people. I got her father to agree—to promise—that, if I found the extra money, she could continue growing that unstoppable brain of hers. It was the first diplomatic solution I had brokered and the first informal grant I ever raised money for and funded. It was also the first time I directly used my access and my privilege to change someone else's life, someone who had everything going for them except their address, and it was addictive.

Figuring out creative, cross-cultural solutions to the overwhelming obstacles that girls and women face became my newest obsession. Thanks to Pratima and her brave father, I began to focus my studies, and my writing, on the oppression of women. When it came time to design an independent study later that semester, I dove headfirst into the brutal, heartbreaking world of sex-trafficking, an epidemic amongst Nepalese girls. The month I spent living in a shelter for former trafficked girls, in a run-down town on the border of Nepal and India, forever changed me. This was the worst of humanity's worst, as far as I could determine. Children sold into sexual slavery, girls as young as five, kept in cages, forced to service grown men, often dozens per day. And, most often, their stories of escape were as terrifying and hard to believe as the stories that trafficked them to India in the first place.

I spent my days at the shelter prepping food, eating, cleaning, making fires, singing "American songs," and interviewing the girls for my research paper. Their stories were horrific, full of unfathomable pain and betrayal, and all I could do was listen. The trees of my youth had taught me that listening in and of itself can be a medicine and that there is healing in simply telling one's truth out loud, no matter how ugly.

"Tell me your story and then let it go." I encouraged them. "Know that I will hold it from now on, that what happened to you is important, but it doesn't have to define the rest of your life." I was ignorant about what the "rest of their lives" would look like, knowing very little about the HIV virus that infected 99 percent of them, nor the Nepalese traditions that would brand them pariahs and ostracize them from mainstream society. I thought that instilling self-love and challenging societal norms were as achievable as convincing decent fathers to send their girls to school.

If I had expected to be inundated with sadness and suffering while living at the shelter, Seema was the unexpected gift, like a lotus flower blooming out of the muck. Her story was a painful as the rest: sold into servitude by her impoverished parents, lied to about factory work and high-paying housecleaning. Once she'd arrived in Delhi, her first time in a metropolis, she was locked inside a house run by a Nepalese "Madame," told she owed an enormous debt for her travel. Seema was eight when she first arrived in the brothels and she spoke about how bravely she fought at the beginning, when she realized what was being asked of her. "The ones who fought were beaten," she explained one day while we were collecting firewood, far from the other girls. "Men will pay double to be with a virgin. They think it will cure them from the sickness, but then they die anyway." Her silence and our shared look spoke volumes about the disease, which she most likely carried, and how quickly it was killing.

The shelter in Bhairahawa was one of several along the India-Nepal border, run by the organization "Maiti Nepal." They worked directly with Indian and Nepalese police to locate and return trafficked girls. Nepalese girls were especially desired in the brothels in India, coveted for their beautiful features and their naiveté. At the time, it was estimated that there were nearly 100,000 Nepalese girls living in India against their will. While sexual slavery is rampant, it is also illegal. A police raid in Mumbai could mean we received a dozen girls in the middle of the night, which is how Seema arrived. A van-full of rescued girls, traumatized and scared, with no one but me (and my flawed Nepali) to greet them and help them make sense of what was happening.

Despite what she'd been through, Seema loved to dance and sing Whitney Houston songs. We had that in common. In the weeks that we lived together, her undiminishable light filled every room. We developed a habit of cleaning the girl's wounds at bedtime, many of whom were suffering from full-blown AIDS lesions, while singing

Whitney's top hits. And, with all of that infectious bravery, Seema became my first example of how we can survive the worst and still maintain places for joy. When I think of all the teachings I have received, it's Seema's unbreakable spirit that inspired me the most.

A week after my arrival and training, the shelter director left for a long bus trip to visit some of the other border shelters and make a supply run to Kathmandu. She left me temporarily in charge, along with two rescued girls who had moved into the shelter permanently and begun working for Maiti. They had no family to return to but, more importantly, they'd begun to play a crucial role in the ongoing fight against trafficking. These two unarmed, unsuspecting teenagers were making a serious dent in the overall trafficking patterns. Maiti struck a deal with the border guards to allow these girls to clandestinely board buses bound for Mumbai and Delhi. Often, they would pose as food-sellers or ticket-takers, while secretly identifying the traffickers and their prey. Each had spent enough time in the Indian brothel culture to be able to spot the type of men who were transporting the girls across the border; and to recognize scared, confused girls, many of whom spoke their tribal languages first over Nepali.

Governments were spending hundreds of thousands of dollars to unsuccessfully stop this particular sex-trade route—the largest in the world—mostly funneling funds into a nationwide education campaign. While here were two, brave, teenaged girls putting their lives on the line to directly intervene and save other girl's lives. It was my first glimpse into how bureaucratic and wasteful large-scale, highly-funded campaigns can be, versus how effective it is to go to the root of the problem and use brave, creative means to confront it. It also became clear that local women had the solution and the chutzpah to change their community's problems directly, if simply given the resources to do so.

I left Nepal an entirely different person than when I'd arrived. I had released my grief and doubled down on my convictions. I flew straight from Kathmandu to Paris to see The Lover over the holiday break between semesters. He was shocked upon seeing me at the arrival gate. I had gained fifteen pounds, cut off all my hair, and smelled like a Himalayan goat, thanks to the hand-knit sweater my Nepalese family had made for my departure.

The Lover and I had our first terrible visit. He rushed me to hair salons and clothing stores, trying to fit the image of me in front of him into a version of my former self. Just like the old pair of jeans I kept at his house, I no longer fit. I fell into a self-conscious, self-deprecating mental state, for the first time in my life. As if society and the person closest to me had just confirmed my worst fear: that, without the makeup and long hair and nice-smelling clothes, my value was greatly diminished. As if the weight of my brains counted for nothing without the fancy packaging. We would continue our international love affair for another year and a half, but The Lover and I would never recover from the chasm that emerged between us after I found my unadorned, unashamed self in Nepal. His grandfather, however, had spent the semester I was away learning some of the Nepali language and planning his own trip there. His friendship during that time buoyed me and helped me to see the value of my inner self.

I returned to Oxy for the spring semester of my junior year and applied for a prestigious summer research fellowship. I had so immersed myself in Nepalese culture, and been so affected by Pratima and Seema, that I designed a research project to study the experiences of South Asian families after migration to the West. I billed myself as an "expert" after my one semester in Nepal, took the fellowship's money, and flew off to London to get to know the Nepalese, Indian, Bengali, and Pakistani communities there. The problem was I had begun reading Edward Said's *Orientalism*, and begun questioning the premise of my research project and, in fact, the entire history of Western sociological study of "others." I was also ignorantly traipsing around London for interviews and getting doors slammed in my face.

At the end of the summer, the only thing I was sure of is that a white girl from Colorado—who spent exactly five months in Nepal—is the least-qualified person to speak on the complex issues of "cultural preservation versus cultural assimilation in South Asian migrant communities in England," as I'd proposed. The difficulty was I had to fly back to Oxy and present my findings to a room full of donors who had given me thousands of dollars to assert quantifiable conclusions.

Back on campus to start my senior year, I stressed about my options, as the fellowship presentation loomed. At some point in my political studies, I had learned about "The Bystander Effect," coined after the brutal rape and murder of Kitty Genovese, which took place in the presence of thirty-eight witnesses. The Bystander Effect is a social phenomenon that states that the more witnesses to an injustice or a crime, the less likely any one person is to intervene. However, if even one person steps up to act, there is a greater likelihood that the rest of the crowd will too. It's just a question of who steps in first. When I learned of it, I thought of Nazi Germany and how many thousands of "good people" did nothing to stop the Holocaust, mostly out of self-preservation, and fear, and waiting for someone else to be the first. It stuck with me, the lesson of this social truth, and I vowed to be that one person who steps up, holding faith in other bystanders to have my back.

When it came time to present to the Fellowship Board, I felt like I was acting as an early bystander to a systemic injustice and, in a room full of mainly white people in positions of power, it was not going to be a popular opinion. I wondered if it would inspire others to speak up too, change the system. With shaking knees and an insecure voice—and with the encouragement of some fierce female anthropology professors, both women of color whose research questioned similar unequal power dynamics and representation—I stood up and criticized the nature of the fellowship itself, admitting the ignorance in my initial proposal, and questioning the history of Western intellectuals studying "others," while simultaneously normalizing and further propagating a self-congratulatory supremacy within its broad "anthropological conclusions." It was the first time that I used my voice and my access to call out institutionalized racism within those institution's halls.

The Fellowship Board was furious afterward, and there was a long talk about my having to pay back the money they'd invested. It was also my first taste of allyship in demanding equal representation and I sensed the responsibility to make uncomfortable waves wherever I had access to oppressive norms. It was simultaneously nauseating and thrilling, as drawing any line can be, using my privilege to call out a flawed system to those who directly benefit from it, including myself. I had taken a brave first step and, even though powerful people were angry with me, I had begun a necessary conversation. Once I began to recognize and leverage my life's unearned advantages that way, it felt impossible to stop.

I left campus again shortly after my one-woman fellowship call-out, much to the relief of certain administrators. I had been accepted into the Oxy-at-the-UN program, a unique internship at the United Nations' Headquarters in New York, the only such program for undergraduate students. The Director of the program had worked in the UN system for decades and had connections in almost every department of the massive organization. I came to him highly recommended because of my stellar grades and was thus given a choice between interning with UNIFEM, the United Nations Development Fund for Women, or filling the one coveted spot in the Department of Political Affairs, Security Council Affairs Branch. I knew that the chances of my landing a job out of an internship with UNIFEM were higher, and that the chances of my being the only female in the DPA office were solid, but I wanted to be in the middle of the political action, where the "war versus peace" decisions were being made. I chose to throw myself into the lion's den, where I imagined I could do the most good.

I donned my fiercest black pantsuit and showed up early for battle. To my surprise, there were already several smart, capable, ferocious women in the mix and they had a lot to teach me.

As much as I thought I would be involved in making a direct impact while interning at the U.N., it is a complex machine of regulations and slow decision-making, and most of my days were spent summarizing meetings into short dispatches for politicians in Washington D.C. But it was also an exciting time to be at the United Nations, as it was the fall of 1999 and Y2K was quickly approaching. The U.N. was introducing new "Millennial Development Goals," boldly laying out a plan to eradicate extreme poverty and hunger, achieve universal primary education, and promote widespread gender equality (as well as five other monster goals) by the year 2015. They were also hosting the largest gathering of Heads of State in history, and, with my high-level security clearance, I had a front-row seat to all the speeches and behind-the-scenes drama.

I was enamored with the culture at the U.N. and began to imagine myself as a career diplomat, working my way up the organizational ladder, mission by mission. My French was improving with each visit to The Lover in Paris, and I could now speak it proficiently enough for work. But my heart was still wrapped up in building a life with The Lover and my evolving plans to attend graduate school at the Sorbonne. I was torn which way to go, and then two things happened that turned me off the U.N. path entirely.

The first thing happened by fluke, as another intern was sick, and I was asked to fill in for her. The absent intern worked for a whip-smart, high-level female staff member with a mountain of fiery red hair whose focus was on conflicts in Francophone Africa. Interns were often asked to attend meetings in a senior staffer's place and to report back, and this day was no different. I sat in the corner of a small, darkened room, not at the large oval conference table full of people in charge, but in the single chair in the corner, a fly on the wall in my boss's stead. We listened collectively, maybe fifteen of us total, as a voice on the other end of the conference call reported on the war breaking out in the Ituri Region of the Democratic Republic of Congo. The voice was shouting and fearful, the French hard to make out, thick and slurred and entirely unlike the Parisian French my ear was used to. The connection kept breaking, but what I understood was horrific and represented a live play-by-play of war breaking out in Eastern DRC, a conflict that would last another five years, cost another 50,000 lives, and displace half a million people. When the line went dead, the room went silent, the glow of the projected map of the DRC reflecting the shocked faces all around.

We stepped out of that room, en masse, into a small press conference with global news agencies. I watched as those in charge reported a milquetoast, revisionist version of what we had just collectively witnessed, using diplomatic vernacular to polish a terrible development in an ongoing, atrocious war. All I could feel was the enormous space between the fear in the voice on the other end of that phone line and the fabrication in the voices that were presenting the DRC conflict in a palatable way for Western audiences. That was the moment I decided I couldn't work for the U.N., that my obsession with truth-telling would only get me in trouble in such a furtive world.

And then the second thing happened, prompting me to write about some uncomfortable truths within the U.N. system itself, another lone bystander calling out a systemic inequality. I came across my senior thesis topic by accident, after a lunchtime comment from a fellow intern who worked in the Department of Peacekeeping Operations. She told me about a recent study outlining the positive effect that female employees have on reducing sexual violence and inappropriate conduct in groups of otherwise only men, like soldiers. The world was still reeling from the discovery of Serbian-led "rape camps" in Bosnia/Herzegovina and U.N. peacekeeper training manuals had yet to include anything specific about responding to sexual violence when responding to a conflict. Reports had emerged of peacekeepers re-raping women and participating in sex-for-food operations. As the U.N. does not have its own army, it relies on donated troops from various member states and, often, these troops are transferred to U.N. missions from other ongoing wars, so peacekeepers come from a variety of cultures and customs when it comes to protecting women's rights. Through my colleague, I gained access to statistics of who had been employed in which peacekeeping operations, and in which positions, throughout history. I analyzed this data to show that the U.N. missions that employed more female peacekeepers, and in higher decision-making positions, had fewer reports of sexual violence by peacekeepers themselves.

My thesis on the topic was a huge success back on Oxy's campus, thanks mostly to the championing of Dr. Roger Boesche, a brilliant professor in the Political Science Department who awarded my research the highest department honors and encouraged my covert plan to send copies to the wives of various ambassadors and diplomats of influence. It was my second, solo, nonviolent direct action, even if I never heard back from any of them.

A few months later, the U.N. passed Resolution #1325, the first legal document that required parties in a conflict to prevent violations of women's rights, to support women's participation in peace negotiations and post-conflict reconstruction, and to protect women and girls from sexual and gender-based violence during armed conflict. Which meant that for the first time since the U.N. was created in 1945, gender-based violence during war was declared illegal and therefore punishable in international courts. It was a major win for women's rights within the context of armed conflict and would soon become one of the primary documents used by human rights advocates seeking to address gender-based violence during war.

I graduated from Oxy in the spring of 2000 at the top of my class, and even received a small cash award for my honors thesis, which I blew on a post-graduation girls' trip to Mexico. The Lover was coming to Boulder for a summer internship in physical therapy and we were finally planning to live together in Paris in the fall. Life was moving firmly in one direction. I had made my choice and registered for classes at the Sorbonne. But then The Lover dropped his bomb on those plans and I ricocheted directly into a life that I thought existed only in childhood video games.

Chapter Six

USING MY VOICE

Once I managed to pick up the pieces of my broken heart, I took a painful look at the missed career opportunities, the blown-off connections with important people, all sacrificed in the pursuit of love. I put a résumé together and sent it out to people I'd met during my time at the U.N., but it'd been months since I'd been one of hundreds of interns. My best friend, Katie—the same Katie I'd dragged across war-torn Cambodia when we were eighteen—stepped in to help me find my ground in the wake of The Lover's life-bomb, and rediscover my confidence as an independent woman with professional goals…all with an impromptu girls' trip to New York City. I had lunch with every contact who'd responded to my inquiries, including, oddly, my cousin's fraternity brother's father, a man who worked on the frontlines of conflict in Eastern Europe and who, alongside his wife, offered to meet me and feed me lunch.

I came away from that trip with two plausible job leads and a whole newfound confidence in myself. I reconnected with The Friend after many years, who was in New York City for work, and he reminded me that I was both desirable and worthy of a love that didn't ask me to change a hair. While our tryst didn't last long, it was exactly what

I needed to get my groove back. Violence had erupted in East Timor, Indonesia, and the U.N. was establishing a peacekeeping mission there. My Indonesian language skills would be a bonus on my application, and my former boss in the Security Council Affairs Branch was "willing to put in a good word." Also, my cousin's connections had turned out to be real gems. A dynamic couple who both worked to better the world. Their relationship gave me hope that there may just be a person out there whose life goals matched mine. They referred me to a new feminist non-governmental organization that "was just getting off the ground and attempting a radical funding model as an emergency response to women's needs in war zones." All they had to say was "feminist," "radical," and "war," and my mind started spinning, as if falling into a vortex or being flushed down a drain. It was a feeling I would later come to recognize and learn to pay close attention to. Like my soul was sensing something my mind couldn't yet see and was thus sending me an urgent message by way of vertigo.

I contacted the number written on the restaurant napkin under the words "Urgent Action Fund for Women's Human Rights" and found myself connected with a woman I'll call The Mountain Goat. Her energy was apparent through the phone in her fast-paced speech and no-nonsense vernacular. I got the feeling I was going to have to work hard to keep up with her, as The Mountain Goat showed no interest in slowing down for anyone. She had been working in feminist philanthropy for years and recognized that the current funding models were limited in their ability—and flexibility—to reach women in crises. Biannual grant cycles, government-directed programing for women's development, and long-term projects only supported what could be planned and predicted. That's not how war works. The reality on the ground in conflict zones, where women need support the most, is that planning is a luxury. Most activists who are organizing on the frontlines are changing strategies daily, thinking on their feet, making last year's program funding stretch to meet this year's unanticipated needs.

The Mountain Goat explained that she'd spent months interviewing hundreds of women activists around the world, asking for their help to design a unique and accessible way of delivering support to the frontlines. They had already made their first few grants, and, at the time, she was Urgent Action Fund's only official employee, working mostly out of her bedroom in the San Francisco Bay Area of California. Then The Mountain Goat said two things that seemed custom-worded for my ears: she was looking to hire their first employee and needed someone who spoke French to help her handle urgent funding requests coming out of Francophone Africa (I flashed to that small room at the U.N. headquarters, the diplomat with the fiery hair, the frantic voice on the other end of the line, desperate for anyone to say or do anything helpful). Then she said that she was "right in the middle of moving Urgent Action Fund's headquarters to a small city in Colorado called Boulder," asking if I'd heard of it.

"Heard of it? I was born and raised there! I'm calling you from New York now but flying home to Boulder tomorrow." She told me where her newly-rented home/office was, and it turned out to be a few blocks from my parent's house, where I'd been crashing in a sea of moving boxes ever since my dreams for a life in Paris had vaporized. The only upside to my unplanned stay at home had been reconnecting with Grandma Martha, who'd just turned ninety and was still living competently on her own in Boulder. Our bond had remained tight during my years away, as she was an avid letter writer, and now my career and my family were aligning in the same place. When life sends you a sign like that, you follow.

The Mountain Goat and I met a few days later in Boulder, over a cup of tea. I would soon learn that she only really stopped moving for tea breaks. She was a warrior woman in the most compact body I'd ever seen—"small yet mighty," Shakespeare would say—and she didn't mince words when talking about the severity of UAF's work, the need for absolute confidentiality, total availability, and intense commitment. She presented the work like she was presenting a secret mission, lives hanging in the balance of every decision. The Carmen Sandiego inside of me was instantly awoken. Secret missions into foreign lands to help weave a web of feminist funding networks and distribute wealth where it was needed most? I couldn't have dreamt up a more perfect job to throw myself into.

The Mountain Goat offered me ten hours a week of French translation work, saying she would take me on for a "trial basis," and would only need me as requests for funding came in, adding that, "when she called, I'd better answer." She didn't yet know how indispensable I could make myself when I set my mind to something, nor how determined I was to turn Urgent Action Fund's bold vision into an global force for change. I also didn't read nor write French very well, though I spoke it quite well. I had maintained a connection with The Lover's younger sister in Paris, and our friendship grew as she translated written material for me behind the scenes, helping me secure a full-time job with UAF. In many ways, The Lover's parting gift to me was his non-interference in the friendships I maintained with his sister, mother, and grandparents, all of whom refused to let the breakup end our relationships.

The Mountain Goat did not start Urgent Action Fund alone, and she relied on key decision-making support from an eclectic and powerful board of directors, which grew exponentially in size during my first few years with UAF, growing naturally into a global family of mentors. The other two founding board members, along with the Mountain Goat herself, I will call The Tortoise and The Groundhog. They were the ones to sign off on hiring me as UAF's first full-time employee a few months after my trial period ended. By then, I was pouring more than forty hours a week into expanding and translating UAF's mission and soaking up everything The Mountain Goat had to teach me. Her fundamental lesson, which she would repeat over and again in various ways throughout the years, was that our role as Western feminists and outside funders was to get resources into the hands of the women who had requested them from the frontlines and then disappear. Remain anonymous; get in and get out, and never, at any time, take credit for the work on the ground. If we went into a country, it was because we had been invited in by local feminists, and we were there to deliver funding, spread resources, and—when necessary—leave with confidential documentation for later use in international prosecution of war crimes.

Wise, well beyond her human years, The Tortoise's energy and advice were reminiscent of Morla, The Ancient One, a character from *The Neverending Story* who infused my childhood dreams. When The Tortoise spoke, everyone paid attention. Her thick French accent and tendency to insert random French words—or even made-up English words—into conversation, with little pause or care for your understanding, made her impossible to ignore, lest you lose the plot all together. When The Tortoise had a strong opinion around an issue, it was immoveable. Both The Mountain Goat and The Groundhog deferred to her final decision to end any disagreements, though the three of them seemed to move along the same lines of thinking most of the time. The Tortoise was also the first unapologetically lesbian activist I'd worked with and, like me, a lover of books. The Tortoise had started the first feminist bookstore in Montreal, Canada and she lined the walls of her home with bookshelves. She held a high-level position within the Canadian government's Rights & Democracy, and as the coordinator of the Women's Rights Program had deep connections everywhere. Simply dropping her name into conversation opened doors (and checkbooks), allowing UAF's work to flourish.

It was The Tortoise that provided the ultimate vision for where UAF needed to be and when. She had a widespread knowledge of conflict and how it arose, and could see where moments of opportunity lay for us to step in and be helpful. She challenged me on every level to be smarter, one step further than others, and to rise above the divisiveness and pettiness that can submerge small groups of caregivers. She was, at once, radical and unradicalized in any way. She taught me, from the beginning, to question all of my assumptions, to challenge my feminism, to see beyond the borders of my white, heterosexual American lens. And, for as gruff as The Tortoise could be, she was the most inclusive and generous with her wisdom of any of my mentors, as if the search for comradeship, or perhaps a personal struggle against loneliness, was also at the root of her activism. Like an actual tortoise, she was hard on the outside and soft on the inside. Once you got past her shell, you had the feeling of being part of her family for life.

The Groundhog was more elusive. During my five years working for UAF, I only met her in person once or twice, though we spoke on the phone, from time to time. She represented a key force in what UAF was attempting to do and was the first person introduced by The Mountain Goat as a "donor activist." Up until then, I had envisioned an "activist" as someone on the streets, confronting oppression head-on, megaphone blaring. But here was an entirely different—and arguably more effective—approach to activism. The Groundhog represented an underground network of wealth; women coming together, trusting each other, and using their money to fund radical change. A community of women donors, mostly anonymous, who didn't need anyone's permission to move their money around, and, without whom, none of our work would have been possible. I left it to The Mountain Goat to confer with The Groundhog most of the time but always carried her quiet, graceful spirit with me. True altruism is giving up the need for recognition, and I learned that from her steady, silent support.

At the end of the day, although I had little money in my bank account, all of us working at UAF were donor activists. When I went into the field, I represented access, financial power, and an outlet for the truth to find its way to a place where the truth still mattered, at least to some people. Like The Groundhog, I remained as behind-the-scenes to our public work as was possible. The mission was clear: get funding and resources into the hands of women on the frontlines, as quickly as possible, and let them lead. My job was to hide in plain sight, to use the travel access my passport provided, the innocence my blonde hair and fair skin projected, in order to transport cash and information across borders that others could not cross.

Oftentimes, our "Rapid Response Grants" could be sent via bank wire transfer or, if the banks were already frozen, by Western Union or another money transfer service. Sometimes, activists on the ground could cross into neighboring countries to pick up "pass-through funds" via other trusted women's groups. Occasionally, however, grantees were completely cut off by war and had lost all access to our granted funds. In that case, I would go in instead, bringing the cash to them.

The Mountain Goat and I, in counsel with The Tortoise, began to identify areas in the world that were not yet at war but were teetering on the brink, political tensions rising, fragile peace treaties breaking down. We developed a plan to send me in early to develop direct relationships of trust with activists on the ground and open lines of communication. The year was 2001, and the world was mainly communicating through email, with analog cellphones and SMS just beginning to infect the masses. I bought The Mountain Goat her first cell phone that year, and we entered the information from her paper Rolodex into it, name by name. She eventually got the hang of it, but the Rolodex stayed on her desk long after I stopped working for UAF in 2005, "just in case." The Mountain Goat was raised in a military family and was born in Guantanamo Bay. "Just in case" was in her blood.

UAF had developed a revolutionary model of grantmaking that could accept requests in any language, respond within seventy-two hours, and get money on the ground in a week or less. For us, that meant checking email around the clock, sending wire transfers in the middle of the night, and being prepared to travel at a moment's notice. The Mountain Goat had insatiable morning energy and would begin emailing me at 6:00 a.m., after she'd returned from her morning hike. She'd had polio as a child and had been wheelchair-bound for some time. She told me that, once she regained use of her legs, she never stopped moving for long again. We worked together well, as I got my initial wind of energy around 3 p.m. and could work well into the night. Between the two of us, we were available and responding to urgent requests from women all over the world for twenty out of the day's twenty-four hours.

I became an expert on the visa application process country-by-country, kept a to-go bag packed at home, and never strayed far from my laptop or cell phone. In some ways, it was reminiscent of my childhood playing *Where in the World Is Carmen Sandiego?* I spent my days solving international travel puzzles, decrypting messages in foreign languages, trying to outsmart an invisible foe, and clandestinely slipping across borders to plant seeds of change. The work allowed me to go to places few other travelers had ever seen and to show up with resources to help. I was becoming the person I had been wishing for during those painful days at the shelter for trafficked girls in Nepal. Back then, I would daydream about an army of resourced, powerful women arriving to put an end to such immense and senseless suffering. With UAF at my back, I got to represent such an armada. I always felt that, if The Mountain Goat was the brains behind UAF, then The Tortoise was the heart, The Groundhog the backbone, and I was lucky enough to become the legs that took UAF off and running around the globe.

Shockingly, my first solo outreach mission for UAF, after nine months of training, wasn't to a faraway war zone, but to Washington D.C. in response to the plane-bombing of the World Trade Center and the Pentagon on September 11th, 2001. We were a rapid-response feminist fund designed to respond to unanticipated violence that threatened women everywhere, and most of our requests for support that week came from Muslim-American organizations and Muslim community centers that were being targeted by ignorant, racist Americans who were wrongly blaming them for the plane attacks. Most of our resources went to provide employee protection and promote awareness around the difference between Muslim-American communities and the terrorists who had hijacked the planes. The drums of war had already begun to beat in George W. Bush's cabinet, and many people were going to pay the price for such a monumental assault on U.S. soil. No one knew yet that the punishment would include the deaths of millions and last eight brutal years, resulting in little more than increased global resentment towards America, and thousands of U.S. soldiers suffering from PTSD.

My second mission was shortly thereafter, even before U.S. Congress gave President Bush the green light to invade Iraq. The civil war in Nepal had already begun in 1998 when I was an exchange student but, now, in 2002, the fighting had reached an all-time high, and the Maoist rebels (with financial and military support from China) threatened the major cities and the Nepalese monarchy. The royal family had ruled Nepal for 233 years, enjoying the financial and military support of the U.S., the U.K., and India. As prime territory between India and China and the access point to the Himalayas, Nepal represents a strategic geopolitical ally. Both China and the West have been vying for influence there for decades.

My assignment was to meet The Fox in Mumbai, a brilliant, young, Indian human rights lawyer who had recently joined UAF's board of directors, who I hadn't yet met face-to-face. She and I would travel together from there to Kathmandu, Nepal, where The Elephant and The Bear were already preparing a groundbreaking peace conference. The Elephant was outwardly empathetic, exuding kindness through her eyes. She had spent most of her life as an outspoken widow, her late husband a member of the Nepalese royal family. In a culture where widows are expected to remain silent and hidden, The Elephant had used her privilege and wealth to challenge that status quo. Her reputation opened doors, and she used it to her full advantage to move the needle on Nepalese women's rights. I admired her deeply.

The Elephant had sent for The Bear's help when the civil war in Nepal escalated. The Bear, a long-time human rights activist from Sri Lanka (whose white streak through her dark hair suggested she may have had some polar bear in her), was an expert in "conflict transformation," a term I had never heard before meeting her. Using The Elephant's vast influence and networks throughout Nepal, they had designed a historic peace conference, gathering major decision-makers from both sides of the conflict to work together to forge a communal solution to the violence. It was tricky work that required careful diplomacy and skillful mediation.

On the first day of the conference, I watched from the sidelines as the room erupted in argument, participants lobbing insults and blame toward one another. By the last day, I sat stunned, as pairs from both sides of the conflict sat down together and mapped out their "hopes and dreams for Nepal" on construction paper. Watching The Bear work was like taking an advanced class in peacemaking and I spent those days in awe of her quiet talents, taking notes.

I thought a lot about the mock battlefields of my youth, the training we'd received from Chögyam Trungpa Rinpoche about coming up against our enemies, seeing ourselves in their passion and anger, and finding another way through, a third choice when at first there only seemed to be two, a trap door to the seemingly unsolvable cycle of war. The Bear naturally saw that trap door and helped guide folks to see it too, and then gently encouraged them to open it and walk through. In this context, she appeared to wield magic, to conjure up an antidote, to offer all of humanity another way forward.

Near the end of the conference, The Bear received word that one of her children in Sri Lanka had committed suicide. I was in the room when she got the news and watched her face steel against the overwhelming pain, her hands moving quickly, making accommodations to return home. She never cried nor broke down; she simply shared the news with us from a deep, impenetrable ocean of sadness, a place beyond tears. The boy who died had been orphaned by the war and had been adopted by her family. She, like many women activists in war, had taken in several children over the years. Before The Bear left Nepal, she said something along the lines of, "Too many have died in my country, in my family, in my heart. We have shed all of our tears and still we must put the pieces back together and carry on with what work we can do. Don't let Nepal go into a decades-long war, as my country has endured. Find your common ground and make your compromises. Save your children from the same fate as ours." And, with that, she left for the airport, leaving The Elephant, The Fox, and me to conclude the conference without her. The Fox and I had plans to meet up with The Bear the following week in Sri Lanka, but it would never come to pass. In fact, it would be years before I laid eyes on The Bear again and, by that time, she too had joined the board of directors for UAF.

Just as the conference was ending, I made one of the most embarrassing mistakes of my career. Before leaving Colorado for South Asia, my first official solo trip abroad on behalf of UAF, I emailed back and forth a bunch with the Nepalese staff of Tewa, the foundation started by The Elephant that was hosting the peace conference. The Mountain Goat, visibly nervous about my representing UAF on this scale without her, suggested I bring small, Colorado-esque gifts for the Tewa staff who had helped arrange our travel and accommodations. Without much thought, I made the executive decision to bring the staff the amount of cash the gifts would have cost instead, knowing how far the American dollar goes in Nepal. I was thinking of my adopted Nepalese family and how much more they would appreciate cash over a Colorado calendar or snow globe. I went even further and decided that some folks who I'd worked with more deserved more cash than others, and I made cute little envelopes with their names on them. I then doubled down on my ignorance and presented the envelopes as "thank yous" from UAF, in front of the entire Tewa staff, praising some people and not others.

The look on The Fox's face should've been my first clue, but it was the ferocity of The Elephant's words that snapped me wide awake, not unlike the way a real elephant's trumpet stops time and forces everyone's attention. While these are not the exact words she spoke, her public chastising went something like this: "You ignorant little American girl. What do you think you're doing? Have you no respect for me? Have you no respect for my staff? Have you learned nothing in all the time you've spent in Nepal?" The Elephant spoke in English to make sure her words were clear, the staff around us bowing their heads, her tone needing no translation. I had insulted most of them already, randomly deciding who deserved how much money...based on what? The name signed at the end of emails we'd exchanged? I had undermined The Elephant's authority by not talking to her about it and I had unknowingly included as much as one month's salary for some of the staff. Some were worried I was trying to bribe them for future favors. I was mortified and, at first, I thought of trying to explain that $500 USD, split between ten staff members, wasn't a lot of money to me. But, no matter how I tried to word that in my head, it only made my mistake sound more insulting, privileged, and profoundly ignorant.

I said nothing and instead bowed my head, hoping no one saw the tears welling up. There's nothing more painful than realizing you've made a hurtful mistake that you can't take back. I was glad The Bear wasn't there to witness it and hoping The Fox didn't hate me for it. I spent that evening crying alone in my hotel room and writing out an apology. I later learned that The Fox and The Elephant went for a private dinner out and hadn't extended an invitation my way. The snub stung, and that sharpness was a potent lesson about making assumptions and checking my entitled behavior…especially when it came to money, which is what I represented. With The Fox and I heading to Sri Lanka in a few days, I was going to have to pull myself together and face my blunder head-on, take accountability, and learn from it. As painful as it was, The Elephant's public takedown was one of the most humbling, transformative lessons in my life, and I have often recalled it when working across cultures, customs, and currencies. If we only see our clouded intentions and don't consider the impact of our actions, that's when helping can actually make matters worse. Painful as it was, The Elephant had offered me a gift and I intended to carry it with me forever.

The Fox and I flew to Sri Lanka shortly afterwards to interview activists about the funding needs and strategies of women on the frontlines. The Bear was too occupied with tragedy and grief to meet with us, but she set up appointments for us with the top women's rights advocates in the country. We spent several days interviewing women in Colombo and then took an ancient train through the mountains to Kandy to meet with more women activists there. Story after story was heartbreaking, both sides having lost so much in the nearly four decades of war. Mothers of Sri Lankan soldiers who have disappeared, still unaccounted for. Mothers of Tamil fighters, trying to make sense of so much endless violence. It was the first war I had witnessed that used Buddha, the epitome of nonviolence and pacifism, as a justification for killing others.

I listened and took notes, becoming more and more aware of how sharing one's story can be a healing in itself. By the end of the week of interviews, an unpleasant vein of feedback had emerged, one that would require UAF to look at its own funding models in the mirror. It came down to this: the women of Sri Lanka were sick of being interviewed and studied by Westerners. It took up valuable time and resources that they didn't have and amounted to no support for their work in the end. If they were being asked to participate, as we were asking, they wanted us to know that the least funders could do was to pay for their time and transportation, while providing food and childcare at the meetings they request. It was critical and honest feedback for UAF to take in and apply. I was reminded of my time at Oxy and going before the Fellowship Board to tell them that their entire approach was faulty, that they were the ones perpetuating cycles of harm, that they needed some systemic change. Now UAF would have to consider its approach differently too, to reconcile with its assumptions and mistakes, the way I was doing personally after Nepal, the way we all should have the courage and fortitude to do.

The Fox left me in Colombo and returned to Mumbai, but not before we shared a last, poignant dinner together. We talked openly about my error in Kathmandu, and she encouraged me to own it and to share the lesson with others back home, for it was an important one and painfully gained. And then we talked about motherhood, of all things, and everything that the role meant for strong, independent women like us. The Fox was getting closer in age to having to make a decision about having children naturally, while I had just turned twenty-five and was adamantly *not* having kids. She mentioned that she may, one day, decide to adopt a child instead, as there are many in need in India, and we agreed that it was a blessing to have the choice about how, and if, we wanted to create and raise another human being; that the world would be a much better place if all women simply had that option.

I didn't want to burden The Bear with my trivial needs, not with all she was going through, and yet I found myself with a few days off before the long trek home to Colorado. I made an impromptu decision to take the train south to Unawatuna Beach, a place my parents had partied in their hippy days, and thus a name that had entered my childhood fantasies. I thought I was being brave and self-reliant but, it turns out, I was making another crucially-ignorant mistake and this one almost cost me everything.

▪ ▪ ▪

The train ride south should have been my first indicator that this wasn't going to be the relaxing beach holiday I'd envisioned. I had already made two crucial errors before I even boarded the train: first, I didn't exactly know where I was going, and no one was expecting me, and, second, I didn't tell anyone where I was going (because not even I knew). It was the kind of mistake born out of a life built on safety and trust, an American white-girl mistake, full of ignorance and hubris.

The train car was packed tight, every seat occupied, men sitting on armrests, windowsills, and any square inch where one could balance. I say men because that's all there were. As a woman, traveling alone makes me an anomaly…never mind my foreign features and clothing. I knew enough to cover my arms and legs, but not enough to book a first-class ticket where the other females ride, a fact that I would learn too late. I had left most of my luggage and work clothes in storage at the hotel in Colombo, packing a small backpack for the weekend sojourn. I clutched that pack tight to my chest, tucking my arms around it and myself, making my overall imprint smaller. The train car filled with more bodies, although there was no visible room for them, and we all continually adjusted and jostled to hold our ground. As we swayed, the train car began to move and men from all sides pushed closer into my body, some touching me accidentally, some obviously on purpose. I made eye contact with one man who licked his lips and grabbed his crotch. I felt unsafe but there was nothing I could do; the train was moving faster and faster, there was no way out now.

My backpack smelled like home to my squished nose as I attempted to turtle my body, hiding my belongings and my most vulnerable body parts in the center of my bent-over form. I began to rock back and forth and twitch, talking to myself loudly in English, the way my mom taught me to do when I am scared of being attacked. It worked for a short while, but then a hand stroked my back intentionally and I reacted immediately, jumping upright, causing a scene. I locked my hands and thrusted my elbows outward, widening my stance to take up more personal space and balance with the swaying train. My reaction was strong enough that no one tried to touch me again, though most of the train stared at me as I stood for the entire two-hour ride to Unawatuna, elbows out, heart racing, eyes alert. *What was I thinking traveling alone without a plan?*

I was chastising myself for knowing better as the train arrived at the station and I pushed my way towards the exit, a random hand grabbing my ass on the way out. I wanted to put as much distance between myself and that train-car-mistake as quickly as possible. Maybe that's why I walked straight into a second, much larger mistake, one of the biggest of my life, breaking the one cardinal rule of travel from a scared, desperate mental space. I didn't think it through clearly and didn't listen to my wits' warning when the smiling taxi driver approached me, pointing to his tuk tuk and asking my destination.

"Unawatuna," I replied.

He responded with an even bigger smile and something like, "Yes, yes ma'am. Not far from here." My golden rule is to never accept a ride from someone who approaches me, which I had learned the hard way as a teenager in Thailand. Or maybe it was on the streets of New York City as a child, my parents teaching me that scammers and Con Men are the ones up and out, looking for their mark. When someone approaches you with all the right answers to your questions, it's best to walk away and look for your own ride. I'd stuck to that rule for most of my life but, now, with little second thought or much concern, I agreed to the offered ride and got in the three-wheeled taxi.

Nine times out of ten, this type of error would have meant paying more than usual or being taken to some tourist trap to buy trinkets from the driver's friend along the way. But I had never vacationed in a war zone before and I didn't know squat about how bad things had been for the people of Sri Lanka, nor for how long they'd suffered.

Initial alarm bells started softly ringing when the Smiley Man got into the back of the trishaw taxi with me, while another man climbed into the driver seat. He was talking away, pointing out roads that lead to various tourist sites. The problem was, I hadn't looked at a map and didn't know the correct way to the beach, so I was placing all of my trust in him. Even more stupidly, I told him I wasn't sure where I was staying that night. The alarm bells started clanging when we stopped by the side of the road and another man, squinty-eyed and quiet, got in the taxi, on the opposite side of Smiley Man, making me the sandwich meat. Smiley Man asked if I minded giving "his friend a ride to the next town."

I played it cool and nodded and then said, "I thought Unawatuna was close by, but we've been driving for twenty minutes."

His tone was appeasing and ominous when he replied, "Yes, yes, madam. Unawatuna soon, very soon."

But it was not very soon, and we did not drop his Squinty Friend in the next town. Instead, we pulled off the main road and into the jungle, as Smiley Man explained that he knew of a "very nice hotel with lots of foreign visitors," and we approached what looked like a hotel or guesthouse.

I was more annoyed than concerned at this point, and I asked, "Is this Unawatuna Beach?"

"Yes, Yes." Smiley smiled. But it wasn't the picturesque horseshoe bay with luxury hotels that I'd seen online; it looked more like a run-down, shitty hostel for backpackers. The registration book at the front showed the names and nationalities of past guests with "Sweden," "Israel," "England" written next to their names, and so I started to relax a bit, thinking maybe the main beach wasn't yet visible. But I failed to notice that there were no check-in dates next to the names, nor that Squinty Man and The Driver followed Smiley Man and me as we went into the jungle to take a look at one of the available rooms. In fact, I didn't fully realize I was in trouble until I was inside said room, with three strange men, and one of them locked the door. The way he did it was so terrifying that my throat closed up, like something out of a horror movie. He was joyfully showing me how the door had good security when he clicked the deadbolt shut, then open, then shut, then open, then shut. The missing sound of the next click open hanging in the room like a death toll; Smiley's smile now faded into a sinister line across his face. His eyes shifted to the other two men and they all approached me at once, my back to the back of the shack. Not-So-Smiley-Now reached me first saying something like, "We have ideas for how to have fun. Do you like to party?" Though the actual words he spoke are lost in the void of trauma.

When terrified, the body has two natural responses. One is to fight and the other, much more powerful and hard to resist, is to freeze. I don't remember how long I stayed frozen, but I do recall how time stood still—like the day on my living room couch when my mom told me she was sick—and how that slowing effect felt like a blessing, a gift to my psyche, and I used that minute opportunity to assess my situation. I was locked in a wooden shack, in the middle of the Sri Lankan jungle, with three men who most likely intended to harm me…and not one other person in the world knew where I was. Not only did I know that I was fucked, I knew that it was up to me alone to get myself free.

I considered fighting back but, at 150 pounds, all my years of athleticism and martial arts training taught me enough to know I was outmatched. Then I thought of the World War I spy Mata Hari, who I'd learned about as a teenager in Indonesia. She had used her belly dancing skills and her sexual wiles to convince men to do almost anything. I had to make a choice. I could either fight what was happening or I could regain control by convincing them I was theirs. I had to de-escalate the situation, or I was going to lose badly.

I threw my backpack on the bed and proclaimed, "I love it! This is just what I was looking for." Then added, "And yes, I do like to party." The three male forms physically relaxed as I moved around them slowly, plopped onto the bed seductively, and asked them if they had any alcohol or pot.

"Yes," Smiley Man's smile returned. "We will be right back!"

"Great. I'm gonna take a shower and get ready for the fun!" I giggled and maybe even winked, making my way towards the bathroom. In my mind, I was really putting it on and winding them up. Smiley and Squinty left, saying they'd be right back, while The Driver sat on the porch and watched the front door from the outside.

I grabbed my backpack and went into the bathroom, locking the door. Miraculously, the bathroom had a window and, even more miraculously, I fit through it. I steadied myself for the fall. *I was fucking Carmen Sandiego and I was not gonna be caught by these goons*! I had to at least try and escape.

I dropped to the ground with a loud thud, backpack strapped to me, and, worried The Driver would have heard my fall, started running through the jungle back in the direction of the road we'd come in on. I was sure I was being chased, but, when I finally turned around, all I could see were trees. Thickly-rooted, viney and endless, the trees would be my cover and my salvation…once again.

In a few short minutes, I reached a hill and started climbing, hoping for a better vantage point. At the top of the hill, in what seemed like a third miracle in as many minutes, I came to the paved highway road we'd come in on. I sat on my backpack, catching my breath, and looking for signs of The Driver from the direction I'd come. My leg was bleeding from something having scratched me on the fall, but it was surface-deep. And then I heard a car engine approaching and rose to meet it. Flagging down the driver, I took out my wallet, flashed some money and said, "Unawatuna Beach?"

He nodded and I got in, exhaling deeply, grateful for each minute we added pavement between those men and me.

It took another twenty minutes to reach the beach I was originally aiming for, and I asked the driver to stop at the first fancy hotel I saw, overpaying him for the ride. Walking into the marble-floored, decadent hotel lobby, I saw the first other foreigners since leaving Colombo, sitting in the hotel restaurant, laughing and fine-breakfast dining. I approached the ornate reception desk, met the warm smile on the receptionist's face, and burst into tears saying, "Do you have a room? I think some men just tried to kidnap me!"

I sat in my fancy hotel room, door locked, chair lodged under the door handle, thinking of all the ways that could have gone, my heart still overbeating, my ears still ringing from the adrenalized mind bells I'd ignored. I got under the bed covers completely and curled into a fetal position. I touched my toes and my elbows, my stomach, and my face. The way a mother inspects a newborn, in awe of all the intact, working parts, wide-aware of the miracle of human life. I'd almost lost mine, at least in my worst versions of *what if*, stupidly thrown away my insanely-advantaged and well-trained life for nothing. I was behaving recklessly and tempting fate. If I was going to give my life up for something, it sure as shit wasn't going to be a beach vacation.

Part of me wanted to stay in that comforter-womb forever and part of me felt that, if I didn't get up and back into the world soon, I might not have the strength to get up at all. I looked out the window and saw people down on the beach, a foreign couple laughing and enjoying themselves and I tried to remind my fragile mind that not everyone was out to get me. The ocean was azure blue and inviting and I mustered up all my courage to change into a swimsuit and head down through the hotel's private beach entrance. I had seen a couple sitting close to the hotel but, by the time I arrived, the man was out swimming while the woman sunbathed alone.

I set up my towel near her and put on my friendliest face. It wasn't long before we were chatting, and I learned that she and her swimming boyfriend were living in the area, he working as a personal trainer in one of the five-star resorts. They were both Australian-born but had been living and working in Sri Lanka for years. I decided to take a chance and trust her enough to tell her about my experience from a few hours earlier. She was shocked and sympathetic and also wondering why the fuck I was traveling alone. "Did you not know that Sri Lanka is at war?" she asked. Not only did I know it, I was there because of it. I felt like a complete idiot.

No sooner had I told her what happened when Smiley Man, Squinty Man, and The Driver come storming up the beach in our direction, yelling and angry-faced. My beach-blanket buddy seems confused until I explain that these are the men who locked me in a shack, at which point she starts yelling in her boyfriend's direction. I am on my feet and in a fighting stance, my anger exceeding my fear, drawing strength from being in a public place, drawing more attention our way. Like a scene out of a movie—an embarrassingly-clichéd damsel-in-distress movie—The Boyfriend comes running out of the water in our direction and "he's built like a Greek god" (as that movie's subtitles would inevitably read). He's also shouting back in Sinhalese, which turns the three goons' attention towards him, just as he puffs up like a cobra.

In the most bizarre turn of events, I get to see the look on the faces of my three captors, as they cower in fear, outmatched. The Boyfriend turns to me and says, "These men claim you owe them cab fare and reimbursement for the alcohol you ordered." For a moment, I wondered if I had totally misread the situation. Then I remembered the fear I felt when they locked the door. I explained that they had taken me to a place I didn't ask to go and locked me in a room. That I had asked for alcohol to get them to leave, which was when I ran away. The three now wreaked of grain alcohol and, eventually, after The

Boyfriend threatened to call the police, they left empty-handed and angry. The Boyfriend explained that they most likely thought I was a prostitute when they saw me get off the train alone and took advantage of my ignorance. I blamed myself. For not being better informed, for knowing better, for ignoring the bells.

I spent the next day, the last of my relaxing weekend getaway, walking the beach and thinking about war and what it does to a place and to its people. These huge, fancy hotels sat now mostly empty, as shrines to a simpler time. Though I eventually found a couple of women traveling for fun, I seemed to be one of the only guests there for vacation and not for work. The traveling duo I met were also returning to Colombo the next day by train and invited me to join them after hearing about my terrible journey down. It appears I had naively booked tickets in the working-class section of the train where women rarely traveled, and they were surprised that it hadn't been worse.

I sent a quick email home before leaving Unawatuna, not realizing in my traumatized mental state that mentioning, off the cuff, that "I'd had a brief encounter with some bad men who locked me in a shack but that everything was fine now," would throw my family and friends, not to mention The Mountain Goat, into a tizzy back home. During that time, I had begun the long trek back to Boulder by heading first to the train station with The Traveling Duo. Not two minutes after our arrival, and The Three Goons are there, having spotted my blonde hair. I stamp my ticket and enter a part of the station they cannot reach but they are yelling and spitting in my direction. I do my best to ignore them and board the train early.

Even in the upper-class car, it's crowded and smells of too many bodies in too-little space. One of the Traveling Duo is a no-nonsense Brit who has been teaching English in Iran for many years. She elbows and pushes us into three seats, eyeing me sideways. "What are you doing?!" she finally spits out.

"Me?" I ask, unsure of what she's referring to.

"Yes, you, child," she snips. "You need to take up more room!"

"I'm trying to be polite," I contend.

"Well, if you're gonna make it in this dog-eat-dog world, you're gonna have to stop being fucking polite and learn to take up more space." And, with that, she turns to a skinny man who has just decided to sit down on her chair's armrest and, with the commanding authority of a general, shouts, "BACK OFF! THAT'S MY SPACE!" at which the skinny man shrinks back into the masses to crowd someone else's seat. "Like that," she adds definitively. I feel like a child pretending to be an adult.

My last night in Colombo, I tell two more people what happened in the south. The Mongoose, a young Sri Lankan-Canadian activist working for Oxfam, says little in response save for, "I'm very sorry that happened to you." The Bear, however, says exactly what's on her mind (and what I later imagine The Mongoose would have said, had we known each other better).

"You silly girl." The Bear growls into the phone and I feel fortunate we are not meeting in person. "What would have happened if you were killed? Raped and left for dead? With no one knowing where you went!" She has obviously received an email from The Mountain Goat, whose anger and confusion are amping up her response. "I would be the one to blame, the one to answer to your mother. Do you think I need to mourn another child right now? To have to explain to The Mountain Goat and The Tortoise your ignorant, entitled decisions? Do you think this work is a game? That it is fun to visit a war zone and then do whatever you like?"

Her honesty is a cutting blow to my ego, gutting me. The girl on the beach, the woman on the train, The Mongoose, they had all been thinking the same thing. And, maybe, in my mind, I *was* still playing a game. Still pretending to be Carmen Sandiego, who always comes out safe in the end. If my first international mission for UAF had taught me anything (and I thought I'd learnt my toughest lesson in Nepal), it was that I wasn't acting smart enough or aware enough for this level of human rights work; that the real winners in the reality of war are those humble enough to learn from their mistakes and take such painful lessons deeply to heart.

I hadn't died in Sri Lanka, but part of my naiveté had. I left the island feeling harder and sharper than when I arrived…if a little scarred up by The Bear's claws.

Chapter Seven

WHAT MAKES YOU HISTORIC?

Shortly after I returned from Sri Lanka, I attended the Association for Women in Development's "Forum," the largest gathering of feminist activists in the world, held in a different location every three years. I was there representing UAF, talking about and networking around our unique funding model, and it was an old dream realized. Three years earlier, as a senior at Occidental College, I had attended the Forum with the encouragement and financial support of Professor Jaquette, and a few of us Oxy senior women made the trip down from our internships in New York to the conference being held that year in Washington, D.C. I remember being enthralled, overwhelmed, and dwarfed by the size of the women's human rights movement globally. I set my mind to one day attend the Forum not as a student, but in an official capacity.

By the next Forum gathering, I was there in Guadalajara, Mexico, representing UAF, something significant to add to the conversation around advancing and protecting women's human rights. The Tortoise was there too, speaking in the opening plenary in front of thousands. That was the moment I knew I had made it to a place I was always destined to be, that I was learning from the best, and that there was nowhere else in the world I would rather work and grow.

I flew from Guadalajara straight to Bogotá, Colombia, where I had an outreach trip planned. Fighting in the decades-old Colombian war had intensified, and women activists were being targeted specifically. One of the areas Urgent Action Fund had begun to fund was the security and evacuation of key activists whose lives were in imminent danger. The country from which we were receiving the most security requests at that time was Colombia, and our main contact in Colombia was The Pelican. I was grateful for the week in Mexico to practice my Spanish, which was rusty at best, and happy to have The Pelican with me to translate UAF's message. I had taken a lot from the teachings of The Elephant and The Bear—harsh as they felt at the time—and spent time in contemplation around my actions and choices, recognizing the gifts their lessons were. I was prepared to go in lightly and let The Pelican lead.

But The Pelican was unlike any activist I'd met before, just as Colombia was unlike any war I'd witnessed before. The Pelican was born in Canada and her skin was as fair as mine, her hair blonder, which is part of the reason she was still alive. She had flown back North to Canada for a while when the death threats against her grew too real and too many of her colleagues had disappeared. But her talents were needed on the frontlines and her heart was rooted in Colombia. She was a brave survivor, speaking the truth, refusing to be cowed…like an actual pelican, which can fly up to 10,000 feet and subsist on nothing but seawater.

One of the main ways The Pelican was able to assist the Colombian women's peace movement was as an international witness. Because of her Canadian citizenship, her ability to speak Spanish and English fluently, and the privileged color of her skin, Canadian officials cared about her opinion and valued her life. The Pelican was the first to show me how to use such a privileged existence for good. She was an amplifier, a translator of suffering from the silenced to the conscientious in the global North, where the realities faced by Colombian women were otherwise unfathomable.

We spent a week together, The Pelican and me, spreading the word about UAF in Spanish and hearing about the specific needs of the Colombian women's movements. The Colombia women we met were creative and loud and brave. Like the Sri Lankans, they had endured generations of war. One group we met with, "La Ruta Pacífica," had designed elaborate peace caravans that drove across Colombia connecting peace activists and uniting the movement to end the war. One group had watched their women's community center destroyed, burnt to the ground. They organized a march, single file, a massive rebuild project wherein thousands of women walked from town to town, a single brick in their hands, until they reached the burned-down building...they then resurrected it, brick by painfully-carried brick, two hands at a time, until they had built a center again. Their sheer numbers didn't allow for any blame to fall on one woman's shoulders.

I learned from The Colombians that our real strength, when the pavement hits the rocks, lays in combining our numbers and in raising a collective voice. The Pelican showed me what it looked like to be an ally and to leverage one's advantages to lift others up and strengthen their messages. She also learned my speech about UAF's grantmaking program by heart and, before long, began to pass word around Colombia like an actual pelican, with a network that spreads far and wide. Soon, my presence was no longer needed, but our friendship was forever cemented in our mutual admiration and recognition.

▪ ▪ ▪

I returned from Colombia and had a hard time blending back into life in Boulder. Compared to what I'd witnessed in Bogotá and Sri Lanka, nothing about daily Boulder problems seemed important. I was repulsed by the excess, infuriated by the apathy, bored with the narcissism, and confused about how I could possibly live in both extremes. I was also having nightmares about the shack in Sri Lanka. I went to a party at Katie's house and had a teary meltdown about the amount of chapstick and lip stuff she had in her bathroom alone, shouting, "Who could possibly need that much chapstick?" raging at the materialism that leads us Westerners to think we need so much, my mind replaying images of refugee children's over-chapped lips, no balm in sight. *How can anyone stockpile resources while leaving others hungry and sick? How has humanity gotten to this awful point?* I was spinning. I was difficult to be around, and I found it difficult to be around others. People asked what I'd been up to, in a polite way, and when I told them 15 percent of what I'd been doing, I felt like I'd ruined their whole day. Their willful blindness to the calamities plaguing the world was a reward for their unearned privilege and they preferred to "stay positive" rather than consider the suffering of others.

During this same time, I ended my brief affair with The Friend, crashed into yet another volatile Competitor (who I knew was bad for me the moment we met) and had a fleeting tryst with a woman, whose heart wasn't in it and neither was mine. My heart, it seemed, had crawled deep into a cave and was unavailable for "feelings." Try as I did, I felt nothing except sadness…and fear during the middle-of-the-night-mares.

The Mountain Goat was moving faster than ever, expanding the vision of UAF, expanding the board of directors and the newly-formed advisory board, helping us field the dozens of grant requests we were receiving daily. Together with The Tortoise, they were always pushing the scope of where and how we reached women on the frontlines. They had begun to design the prototype for what we were calling "Rapid Response Teams" (RRT), which would take the rapid-response funding model UAF had developed and expand it beyond financial help to include specially-trained legal and technical teams who could travel at a moment's notice. They were planning the initial feasibility/brainstorming meeting on the RRTs that winter in London but, first, I was heading to Nairobi, Kenya, where UAF's newest board member, The Eagle, lived and worked.

I stood on the edge of the hanging walkway that led to the plane, staring at the small crack between the smooth outer shell of the airplane and the threshold of the elevated hallway. This particular airplane was heading to London, a place I know well. But the final destination of my trip is what's giving me pause, or more like freezing my feet in place. "Africa." The name alone conjures images of bushmen and wild animals and the unknown. A subtle, global racism that allows us in the West to refer to an entire continent of fifty-four countries as if it were one giant, savage place. "Will you be sleeping in huts or in trees?" more than one ignorant friend asked me before the trip. The truth is I don't know where I am going to be sleeping or what I am going to see. That same force of Western racism had ensured that I'd never seen images of modern-day African cities, nor had a clue what daily life was like for the millions of Nairobians who make up the bustling epicenter of East Africa. As soon as I stepped over that crack and onto the plane, I was stepping toward the completely unfamiliar, and I was scared.

As unfounded as my fears turned out to be, I was feeling the hesitation and anxiety that comes with doing something new, and I was grappling with the apprehension and fright that much of the "modern world" associates with "Africa." I had recently read Joseph Conrad's *Heart of Darkness* and I remember thinking afterwards that that one book founded the collective Western consciousness' fear of Africa, and therefore of darker-skinned people, and it was that fear that justified colonization, slavery, and genocide. As much as I didn't want to feel that fear, or even name it, it was right there, rising up in me, solidifying my steps. I reminded myself that I wasn't actually afraid of Africa, but that I had been taught to be afraid of Africa...and that those two were not the same thing. I was afraid of a myth, a ghost story, and now I had a chance to see if that story was true or false. I looked my racism right in the face, painful as it was to recognize it, and told it, directly, "I don't believe you." Then I took a deep breath and stepped onto the plane.

If touching the earth in Nepal had felt new and exciting and full, touching down in Kenya felt old, and wise, and welcoming, like the embrace of a mother or the reassuring smell of a lover's left-behind shirt. It was intoxicating. The land itself had a story as old as mankind and there was an overwhelming sense of coming back to a place I'd never known. All of my preconceived notions and stereotypes fell apart as I was embraced by people who felt like they had much to show me and were so happy I'd come.

The Eagle and I would be traveling together through Uganda, Tanzania, Kenya, Zanzibar, and Ethiopia before she hosted UAF's first board meeting in Nairobi. George W. Bush and Colin Powell had almost convinced the U.S. Congress and its allies to give them the green light to bomb Baghdad, and UAF was exploring new visions of how to grow our work, including starting independent sister funds around the world. The board was beginning to talk about establishing a UAF-Africa, to be run by The Eagle out of Nairobi. She would recruit her own Pan-African board of directors to support her and her colleagues to rapidly fund and promote African women's rights, under the leadership of African activists. Funding for their work would no longer funnel through the United States, where the Bush administration was cracking down on the flow of money supporting international human rights work.

Under broad "anti-terrorism" legislation, they had already reimposed the "global gag rule" on U.S. funders, trying to prevent support for reproductive rights and access, and now they were investigating foundations like UAF, which were moving money around the world quickly, often to fund "anti-government" activities. Prominent and outspoken women leaders were put on "no-fly lists" and named "terrorists" by authoritarian governments who used the moment to crack down on dissidents. It was a precarious time to be funding radical work, and we all had a sense that we needed to de-centralize (our money and our decision-making), and to grow in a more organic and feminist way than a traditional NGO. Also, most of our board members at that point were unwilling to travel to the United States given the abuse and interrogation they'd been subjected to at the borders since 9/11. We collectively decided that, for the time being, we would only meet outside of the U.S., especially given how much easier it was for those of us from the U.S. to obtain visas to almost anywhere in the world.

I met The Eagle at her stunning country home on the outskirts of Nairobi. She was regal in appearance and mannerisms, at 7:00 a.m. or 11:00 p.m., I would soon learn. She usually wrapped her locks in brightly-colored fabrics, patterned and carefully selected to match her classic Kenyan dresses. She often wore jewelry fit for a queen. In many ways, she was Kenyan royalty, married to a prominent and respected member of Kenyan Parliament and her upbringing represented the best that Kenya and its British colonizers had to offer. As one of the top human rights lawyers in the region, The Eagle's reputation preceded her and her efforts to include violence against women in the International Criminal Tribunal for Rwanda were historic.

The Eagle had a knowing demeanor and a voice that captivated a room. Not the way The Bear had in Nepal, which was like a headmistress, but more the way a sound can seduce you into listening, as if revealing a secret. To me, she was warm, generous, and open to all my ignorant questions about her life and about Kenya in general. I wanted to stay in her presence and learn everything she was willing to teach, which is likely why, by the time our travel together ended, I volunteered to move to Nairobi and help her start UAF-Africa's grantmaking program.

Nairobi was the opposite of everything I had expected to see in "Africa." A major metropolis with shopping centers, world-class restaurants, skyscrapers, and a nightlife that rivaled New York City, surrounded me. I wondered why the media back home didn't show us *this* "Africa?" Why do we only see images of war and poverty, indigenous lifestyles, and wild animals on this vast continent? The West's hidden conspiracy to hide the success of Africans. From its impressive universities and halls of government, to its thriving centers of industry and creativity, I realized that the contributions of Africans have been pigeonholed and ignored in the West. I was ashamed to have been complicit in that cover up.

Once the idea of my moving to Nairobi was raised in the board meeting, I had already spent a few weeks in The Eagle's presence and I knew I wanted much more time under her comforting wings. And my soul started to whirl at the thought of it, that familiar vortex feeling telling me that this was my path to walk, that Kenya had much more to show me. It was as if I'd finally been let into the section of humanity's library where they keep the suppressed information on the history of mankind, and I did not want to leave. *How could I have waited until I was twenty-five to see this part of the world? How is it possible that this land is where all humans emerged from and yet I know almost nothing about it?* Nothing except that it was home to stolen slaves for hundreds of years and that white men had slaughtered and dissected it for their own exploitation. I had read Jared Diamond's *Guns, Germs, and Steel* and so I understood the Western version of how the world was colonized but, once I met The Eagle, it was clear that I didn't know squat.

After our meeting, I went on my first safari alone, courtesy of The Eagle and her unending generosity. Seeing African elephants bathing at sunset or African giraffes running across the Serengeti, one can never go to a zoo again without feeling an overwhelming sadness that they are not in their natural habitat. After my time traveling around East Africa, I could never talk about "Africa" again as if it were one homogenous place and not thousands of cultures, older and more sophisticated than much of the West. The Eagle's first hire was an office manager named Maki, who was closer to my age. She and her family took me in as one of their own, forgiving all of my obliviousness and patiently teaching me about the rich Kenyan cultures that my education had failed to include. I left Kenya with an entirely new perspective on the world, a group of dear friends, and promises to return soon.

Me and new friends "Maki" and "Lorna" out in Nairobi.

■ ■ ■

Not long after my trip to East Africa, the first meeting on the creation of UAF's Rapid Response Teams took place in London. The Mountain Goat, The Tortoise, The Eagle, The Pelican, plus The Butterfly, The Meerkat, The Raven, The Koala, and several other prominent women's human rights activists, flew in for the occasion. The Meerkat had replaced The Groundhog (whose health would not allow her to travel anymore) as the principle donor activist on UAF's board of directors. She connected us all to an underground network of supporters that was the lifeline to UAF's success. Like an actual Meerkat, she popped up from time to time, listening and passing along crucial information to that essential network.

What made the gathering truly unique was not just the powerful cast of characters in the room, but the interests they represented. One woman was from Serbia, one activist from Kosovo. One person from Israel and one representing Palestine. Several devout Muslims, a few church-attending Christians, a handful of Jews, and a couple of us who follow the teachings of Buddha. Each woman with families, histories, and livelihoods at stake in these conflicts; each coming to the table to dream and invent a new way forward together. Collectively, the women in the room had founded massive movements and effectively changed the thoughts and actions of millions. The Tortoise said it best at the meeting's opening when she declared, "If we are going to meet the needs of women on both sides of conflict, then we are going to have to start with both sides of the conflict at the table."

None of the conversations in the days to follow were easy, nor were the solutions simple. But the vision felt hopeful and even possible, which, for many in the room, was novel in itself. No one at the meeting was as hopeful as The Butterfly, even if she came from a country teetering on civil war and widespread famine. The Butterfly was hard to pin down, elusively absent from most group photos. In her home country of Zimbabwe, she enacted change, one imperceptible step at a time. Her country had recently fallen into severe poverty and widespread food shortages after their longstanding president expelled all the white landowners from their farms, reclaiming the land that had been colonized in the first place. It was a bold and controversial move, but his government also failed to utilize those farms to produce the food they had once provided, and much of the country was now starving. The Butterfly talked about waiting in line for days to get a loaf of bread and then dividing that bread too many ways to fill any one stomach. It was hard for her to be in London, to see the gluttony and waste of the West while her countrymen were dying for scraps. She could barely explain to us, her feminist community, what she needed, nor determine a way to meet the massive need. *How does one witness such massive inequality and still maintain hope?* She was a testament to the spirit's ability to withstand incredible hardship and to rise still and keep fighting.

Like an actual butterfly, she left little trace of her activism, her very survival dependent on the fact that change, for her, arrived as a whisper and mountains moved one grain of dirt at a time. I later learned that she enacted her activism between the hours of 2 and 4 a.m., when prying eyes and ears slept; that few at home even knew what she did, famous as she was in the global women's human rights movement. I thought of the access and the voice I had, the protected right to express my political opinions freely. *Would I be so bold if I knew that persecution, prison, or death was on the line?* Of all the mentors I'd had so far, none was braver than The Butterfly with her gentle, yet thunderous and unending actions for peace.

The Tortoise was annoyed with me, judging by her tone, and she spared no gentleness in telling me that my report from my recent mission to Colombia lacked depth of analysis and was "sophomoric." No one could make me feel smaller than The Tortoise; she was also right. I was exhausted. Having been to South Asia, South America, and East Africa in the past few months, I was barely in my body, hardly aware of where I was in the world, grasping for ground and a solid time zone. I had only been working for UAF for two years and I was already showing signs of burnout, recognizing symptoms of PTSD from Sri Lanka, and barely able to handle the ever-expanding workload. That year alone, The Mountain Goat and I had made nearly a hundred separate grants, giving out nearly $500,000 in $5,000 chunks. As an organization, we were growing faster than our capacity, even though we now had three additional full-time employees working out of our headquarter offices in Boulder. Brave, intelligent women had joined The Mountain Goat and me, taking UAF from a chaotic operation of two into a well-oiled operation. I was training my replacement there, another Boulderite who grew up in the same Buddhist community as I did, whose dedication to human rights mirrored mine, who I'll call The Sparrow. Meanwhile, I was planning to move to Nairobi in a few months' time to work with The Eagle. It was thrilling and overwhelming and more than a little intimidating.

I was surprised when The Tortoise stopped by my hotel room and invited me to join her and some of the others out for a drink. But that's how The Tortoise was: cutting but kind.

"What makes you historic?" The Raven asked to a silent, listening room. We were in an underground lesbian bar, located under a Tube stop, which required a password to enter...of course, The Tortoise knew it. The drinks were stiff, the tables and lights were low, and the air smelled like collusion. It was one of the coolest places I'd ever been, and I kept looking around to see if anyone noticed how awkward I felt or pointed out how much I didn't belong. We'd all been getting drinks and making small talk, me about the giant, fuzzy, purple hat I'd bought earlier that day in Piccadilly Circus, when The Raven—a pioneer in the Serbian women's rights movement—silenced the room. Looking around, I see that I am the youngest by at least twenty years, and the question floating in the air makes me feel even younger and more out of place. It was posed more like a challenge than a simple inquiry, like a gauntlet waiting to be picked up, and makes me want to crab-walk right out of there.

At first, no one moves. Then The Koala—an Israeli activist who founded a worldwide movement called Women in Black—begins to speak about the children she raised and what incredible people they are in the world because of her commitment not to raise them in anger but in love, even during war. Her answer strikes me as a bit trite, compared to what I know her activism has accomplished in the world. Then, The Meerkat speaks up uncharacteristically. "What makes me historic? My daughter. I brought her into this world on my own terms, and she is growing into a powerful young woman in the world." She goes on to share the story of deciding that she was ready to be a mother and, since she didn't have a partner at the time, went down to the sperm bank and picked out "some good Jewish sperm" (as was important to her) and got pregnant by herself using a turkey baster. While her story is unique, and shocks some of the other activists, I am surprised that she doesn't mention all the causes she's supported or the films she's produced.

The Tortoise's reply shocks me the most. Instead of mentioning the incredible impact she's had on women's rights development and funding in Canada, she talks about the children she helped raise in a women's collective and the feminist bookstore she started. She shares about the pride and accomplishment she felt when one of her children stood up on graduation day and recognized the five mothers who had collectively raised her. The Tortoise fails to mention the groundbreaking human rights works she is credited with, nor the creation of UAF itself. Each woman present had played a significant role in the advancement of women's rights globally and yet, when thinking about their legacy, each person talked about their tribes instead. Their families, their adopted and created children, whose lives were a testament to their commitment to humanity's future, is what made them feel historic. It was also a testament to how women activists often work, sharing credit or remaining anonymous, protecting one another's security, and advancing change collectively rather than as individuals.

It occurred to me, in that moment, that I had been looking at life backwards; staring out the front windshield of my vehicle and never, not even once, looking in the rearview. I was thinking about my life's achievements solely in terms of me and what I was contributing to the world. Yet in front of me were women who had done more for gender equality than I could ever dream, telling me that it was the love they sowed, often against all odds and with war as their backdrop, that made them historic. It wasn't the work itself, the recognition for which they each readily shared, but the reasons behind the work that made it worth the struggle. At the end of the day, I was young and self-centered and I had no idea what sacrifice looked like nor what building community took.

"And you?" The Raven turns the dark room's attention on me and my shrinking confidence.

"Oh, I'm not historic. Pass." I murmur with a dismissive wave to the next person.

"Of course, you are!" She shouts. "Even if you don't know it yet." Then adds, "Listen to these women around you, really listen to their stories, let them guide you because they have already been you," which barely makes sense to my young mind, but lodges itself deeply into my young heart.

Before leaving London, I find a small gift outside my hotel room door with a note from The Butterfly, who has already flown away. "Never lose your color, it's what makes you uniquely you. Never dull that for anyone or anything," it reads. I have always kept my hair funky colors and cuts and worn bright, optimistic, colorful clothing. Lately, I had been toning it down, dressing more somber, my appearance beginning to reflect my worn-down insides. The Butterfly was right; I had a choice to make. I could let the stress and sadness get me down and envelop my fighting spirit or I could choose, every day, to shine my bright and colorful light anywhere I could. From that moment on, whenever I felt overcome by the vast amount of pain and suffering we were confronting, I would think of The Butterfly's words and the powerful messages from the women at the underground bar and focus on the love I was creating in my wake, and not just the endless battles that lay ahead.

Chapter Eight

INTO THE HEART OF DARKNESS

Not long after our meeting in London—the excitement around the Rapid Response Teams buzzing in the office air—UAF learned about the very first gathering of women activists from the Eastern Democratic Republic of the Congo (DRC). The DRC was experiencing their first lull in fighting for many years, partly due to the recent eruption of Mount Nyiragongo, which took out half of the major eastern city of Goma, which is also where the meeting was to be held. It was an unanticipated and unprecedented opportunity to connect with Congolese activists and spread the word about UAF's rapid-response funding. The Eagle agreed that UAF should be there but, as she was unable to attend, she suggested I go in her place. The big challenge was that the meeting was taking place in little over a week, which meant we needed to decide quickly, expedite travel visas, and trust our local contacts to provide all the last-minute logistics. This was my chance to be physically on the other end of that U.N. phone line; to stop hiding behind my citizenship and my over-advantages and join women bravely holding the frontline.

This time, my feet didn't hesitate to jump onto the first of four planes that would take me to Kigali, Rwanda. From there, my contact, The Rhino, would escort me across the border and into the DRC. While there wasn't a recognized government operating in eastern DRC, per se, the rebel faction that held Goma had agreed to talks and a cease-fire and had opened the border. Initially, they let in aid workers to assess the damages and needs cause by the volcanic eruption, which had sent rivers of burning lava straight through Goma and into Lake Kivu.

The Rhino met me at the airport with a suspicious look, my too-big smile failing to turn hers even slightly upward. I'd had a long layover in Kenya and met Maki and friends at the beach for a day, which saw me arriving jet-lagged, hung-over, sunburnt, and smelling like the ocean. I'm sure I looked a far cry from who she'd expected to find representing UAF. Or maybe she was insulted that The Eagle or The Mountain Goat hadn't come. Most likely, she didn't feel like there was much to smile about when her people were dying at alarming rates while most of the world refused to pay attention…and chances are she didn't have time for a bubbly American girl who'd had a few too many cocktails on a quick vacation and showed up with sand between her flip-flopped toes.

I got my bags and took a moment to change in the airport bathroom, steadying my nerves and lacing up my good running shoes. We drove the hours to the border in a taxi in silence, each lost in our own thought bubbles. Mine said, "Freaking the fuck out! Trying not to show it." I wish I knew what The Rhino's said. The Rwandan countryside is breathtaking. Rolling, lush, emerald hills fill in the horizon line, giving this magnificent country the tagline "land of a thousand hills." People walk along the roadside carrying full baskets on their heads and small children bound to their backs. Every road we drive is lined with people walking, working, living. Rwanda still sits in humanity's collective consciousness like a warning sign, evidence of what can happen if divisiveness, fundamentalism, and tribalism take over our connection to our shared humanity and eclipse basic empathy. The genocide was still evidenced across Rwanda, like a weeping wound, bleeding still, now eight years later. The impact of such horrendous communal violence takes generations to overcome.

And yet, just across the border, it is happening again. Mass murder for the sake of deluded allegiance and greed. In the case of the DRC, many different allegiances, almost too many factions to count and keep track of, with seven different African nations currently stationing soldiers there as well, protecting their assets. Throughout time, as far back as we have recorded, mankind has killed each other over disagreements; clashes in philosophies, religions, cultures, languages, skin color, and a million other made-up allegiances. At times, that divisiveness and ignorance lead to mass murder, a genocide against a specifically-identified group of "others." We saw this with the genocide of the Native American tribes in North America and the Aboriginal tribes in Australia. We saw it happen with the Nazi Holocaust targeting the Jewish race, and the pogroms against intellectuals in communist Russia, China, and Cambodia. And now we've seen it happen, in my lifetime, here in Rwanda, where 800,000 people were killed in a matter of 100 days, turning neighbors, colleagues, and families against each other.

For a short time, it seems humanity learns from such grotesque waves of misdirected violence, holding perpetrators accountable and dissecting how we arrived at such breaking points of murderous rage. But then it seems a collective amnesia washes over, no matter how many movies are made, nor books written, and it becomes too painful to look at, so we turn away. In that collective blindness, it happens again. We step out of our human family, identify with a self-serving ideology, and justify murdering other human beings to protect ourselves from a perceived threat. It's like a bad glitch in our wiring, left over from our cave-dwelling ancestors. Even if we know that there are enough resources to go around, once we are convinced that someone is going to take from us or harm us, we are willing (and quite able) to kill, rather than simply adjust or learn to share.

We make sure our kindergarteners know how to share, yet we don't hold adults accountable for individual hoarding. In fact, we usually praise it as "success." No wonder all it takes is one, charismatic, outspoken leader to convince us we are in danger and to identify a supposed enemy, and we willingly become animals. If we believe it is kill or be killed, we are programmed to destroy. In reality, there's plenty of land, food, and resources to go around, and there always has been. If humanity is going to evolve past the cycle of endless war, we are going to have to think and act collectively. A life in Rwanda is going to have to be equally valued to a life in the United States. As we drive across Rwanda, more than a million people are dead or displaced by the war in the DRC, while few people back home are aware a country called the DRC exists. Right now, if I were to be harmed or disappear, my single, solitary life would be more newsworthy to the West than the death of a thousand innocent Congolese. That double standard and Western supremacy is not only staggering to acknowledge and take in, it is also a unique advantage to be leveraged when the time is right.

Eventually, the taxi comes to a stop at a small clearing with a low, cement building and a large tree trunk blocking the road. "We get out here," The Rhino says stoically, motioning with her hands in the direction of the cement building. I've crossed many borders before but this one feels both arbitrary and dangerous. I am going to have to walk this line very carefully, defer to The Rhino, and use all of my charm to talk my way into the Congo. What I haven't told anyone, not even The Rhino, is that I have a large sum of cash taped to my stomach, intended for grantees on the other side. I was too nervous to put that much cash in my bag, where it could be discovered or stolen, and knew that the last place they would search would be my mid-section. In the same way that brown and black women's bodies have been subjected to the violent control of white men with guns, white women's bodies are often held sacredly off-limits. That made my mid-section like a kangaroo's secret pouch, the perfect hiding spot. As many times as I had been physically searched by male guards and soldiers, none of them had ever touched my stomach or breasts. My bra was therefore a super-secret vault, perfect for smuggling memory cards and messages.

I didn't tell The Rhino about the money, so she could maintain innocence if I was caught with it, but also because my work was strictly confidential, and she didn't know about all of our grantees coming to the meeting, or at least she wouldn't find out from me. Building that trust was crucial to our success as frontline funders.

I put on my most innocent, girly, American-accented French and got my eyelashes batting, explaining to the border officials that I was simply there to work with the suffering women and children and would only be staying a few days. They did not represent an officially-recognized government, still in peace talks with the official government in Kinshasa, 1,500 miles away, but they were clearly in charge of who crossed the fallen tree and who didn't…even if just by the amount of AK-47s their soldiers were holding.

The men inside seem to know and respect The Rhino and she speaks with them in a language I can't translate. In a few minutes, they've slipped a passport-sized piece of paper into my actual passport and stamped it with their faction's initials. We step outside to head across the border by foot and I march in lockstep behind The Rhino, following her lead, keeping my eyes low.

The soldiers sitting on the tree trunk are also young, vacant-eyed, traumatized boys; barely teenagers who have survived years of unthinkable violence and loss and yet have come out guarding a fallen tree and an arbitrary border. They stare at my alien image through bloodshot eyes and hold tight to their guns the ways a teen back home might cling to a video game controller. One of them, older than the rest, shouts a command and they all jump up and begin the collective work of lifting the tree trunk so that we may pass through. In reality, we could have walked around but, in their world, this was their main duty, and they were calling the shots. They never remove their eyes from us as we walk slowly to another car that The Rhino has arranged, waiting. "No sudden movements" was the only advice The Rhino offered me during the twenty minutes it took to cross into the Congo, into Western consciousness's *Heart of Darkness.*

And then we are in. I am finally on the other end of the phone call. I have been in several countries at war before, a conflict raging within their borders, but that wasn't the same thing as entering an active war zone with a tentative cease-fire. My guard stays up and my senses begin working overtime ferreting out my surroundings. I study faces and patterns and try to memorize the path our taxi takes through the city so I know which way Rwanda lies. But the city itself is divided by blackened and makeshift passageways of lava, many of the streets and navigation signs long-destroyed. Barefooted children are scavenging the lava piles for unburned goods, smoke still rising from leveled buildings. A people ravaged by war, felled by natural disaster, and forgotten by the modern world, the Congolese have survived against the odds.

Driving across Goma, it made sense then why The Rhino didn't have any smiles to give away. We belonged to two different realities; I the one where hope and laughter were abundant, she the one where massive suffering and endless deaths fill one's days, where even a smile was an affront, a blindness to what was taking place. I thought of my bright, bubbly greeting in Kigali, talking about my vacation, and how that now felt insulting. I needed to bring my colorful, loud spirit to the table, but I also had to check myself and recognize when my positivity was offensive. The Elephant's words, mixed with still-painful lessons from The Bear, traveled with me, reminding me to listen and absorb what the Congolese women had to teach...and to know when to shut my mouth.

We arrive at the only hotel in Goma where foreigners are allowed to stay, which is buzzing with women, greeting one another after long days of travel. The Rhino seems to know everyone and leaves me to check in while she mingles and welcomes. It is a side of her I have not yet seen. I am the only non-African in the lobby, and most of the other women are looking at me sideways, curious but untrusting. In a country once ravaged by Dutch colonists and then actively underdeveloped by people who looked and talked like me, the lack of trust and long stares are understandable. I am going to have to come to the meeting tomorrow with buckets of humility and apply all of my studied diplomacy skills, hoping they can see past the color of my skin and give me a chance to work with them.

It helped that I was coming to the conference full-handed, presenting a whole new approach to funding, one that was created by activists, for activists, and one that operated in their native language, not mine. They wouldn't have to fill out long, confusing forms in English, nor wait months for funding cycles to come around. I was excited to present UAF to these activists tomorrow, many of whom had traveled for days, by bus, car, plane, and foot, to be there. But I wouldn't get the chance to present UAF the way I'd meticulously prepared (this being the first time I was publicly presenting the Fund in French, I'd practiced the entire flight from London to Nairobi), nor would anything about my time in Goma go as planned.

The opening dinner took place that night at the hotel's attached restaurant, buffet-style. At least sixty women were present, each wearing multicolored dresses and matching head wraps, speaking dozens of dialects that fell dissonant on my ear. The packed room moved like a kaleidoscope and sounded like a handful of songs being sung at once, none of which I recognized. The Rhino barely acknowledged my presence, caught in some pressing conversation, surrounded by her most-trusted. I got some food, most of which I didn't recognize, and took an empty seat, flashing a subtle smile to anyone willing to look my way. At first, I sat alone, as table after table filled up, but, eventually, someone approached the table I was at and said, "Bonsoir. . . ."

I was just starting to feel comfortable and that my French was being understood when it started to rain. Not a small, whispering rain. Within minutes, a pounding, driving rain. The corrugated roofing became a discordant drum, the swinging beaded curtains bizarre castanets. I looked around the room wide-eyed, all conversation stifled by the cacophony, the faces of dozens of shocked women staring upward in the same state of amazement. As if a marching band had suddenly struck up a song at full volume. And then, just as shockingly, the lights went out.

It was pitch-black, the rooftop concert approaching a crescendo, and I couldn't find my hand in front of my face. I thought I might start screaming, the fear of being alone in the dark with so many strangers threatening to loosen my vocal cords, when someone else, at that exact moment, started singing. And then, within seconds, as if everyone received a message but me, the entire room started singing. I'd never heard the melody with my ears, but my heart recognized it. Since no one could see me and, over the rain, no one could hear me, I joined in the song, making up my own words. The notes spoke to me of community and struggle and courage, of many voices rising up to form a revolution of defiance, even in total darkness.

The room sang until the lights came back on. Faces reappeared full of delight and joy. In the span of a few minutes, all the awkwardness and tension had been chased away by rain and song, each of us lightened by the incredible interruption. The way a thunderclap can wake you up to the present moment and place all of your problems into a different perspective. Someone reached out and put her arm around me reassuringly, as the songbird conversations recommenced. I smiled honestly and gratefully at the stranger, closer to her for having come through the dark together.

■ ■ ■

That same night, as I was preparing for sleep and finally washing the Kenyan sand from between my toes, I received terrible news. Grandma Martha, the woman who had raised my mother and my aunts, and then spent so much time and money raising me, had passed away peacefully at the age of ninety-three. The pain cut into my heart, flaying me open. Not the way that death had surprised me with The Dreamer's sudden passing but more like the inevitable ending to a story you've been reading your entire life. The finality of losing a parent figure meant the ground was less stable and, although she had lived a long and fruitful life, her death devastated me. My mom's voice over the phone was filled with sadness and yet marked with the slight relief that comes from watching a loved one release their pain.

Grandma Martha and Baby Kiri, 1978.

Grandma Martha was suffering from advanced dementia at that point, and a broken hip had bound her to her final bed. When I last saw her, just before leaving Boulder, I said my final goodbyes…but I had also hoped I would see her again, having the chance to share with her all that I'd seen and learned on this trip. She was a high school dropout who had taught herself to survive through the Great Depression, but who had never seen or heard much about the DRC. The Rhino, no stranger to grief, held me while I sobbed, all the remaining distance between us melting. Death is a language spoken by all.

By the time dawn arrived, I'd barely slept and looked like a puffy-eyed mess. I had no idea where I was going to find the strength to present in front of dozens of strangers. I didn't want to add my pain to a room filled with painful stories, and yet I wasn't sure I was strong enough to hold back the tears. I hadn't managed to make them stop all night. I'd considered going home but, even if I moved mountains, it was still a three-day trip back to Colorado and I would miss the funeral. Not to mention, my leaving now would jeopardize all of the work and money that was invested in getting me here, all to deliver this very important presentation. There was no option. I was going to have to find the strength to grieve the biggest loss of my life and publicly represent UAF at the same time.

I enter the already-full conference room carefully, stepping lightly, though, as soon as I do, most faces turned towards me. Instead of the untrusting looks I'd gotten earlier, I find expressions of kindness mixed with a knowing sadness. The Rhino, it seems, has told them of my loss, and word has spread. Several women approach me with open arms, which catch me and my newly bottled-up tears off guard. I choke them back and try to draw on my grandma's strength to stay standing firmly upright. I have a job to do, and there is no point in wallowing now. I can almost hear Grandma Martha's voice saying, "Can't complain," when asked how she was doing—even if she had a broken limb at the time. Or her questioning, "What are you made of, sugar?" as she encouraged me and my brother to play outside in the rain and get soaking wet. I was going to have to draw from that well of stoicism and practicality if I was going to get through the next few hours.

I take a deep breath and look around the room slowly before I began, recognizing my pain on so many of their faces. But this isn't about me and my pain, this is about delivering a message I have come a long way and risked a lot to impart. I am going to have to push my pain aside and focus on the work at hand. But that was not the Congolese way, as I was about to learn.

As soon as I started talking about our new funding strategy, a hand went up in the crowd. Assuming it was a clarification on my French, which was Parisian and not Congolese, I stopped and motioned for the owner of the hand to speak. "Dit nous de ta grand'mere. Quelle age etait elle?" *Tell us about your grandmother. What age was she?* Stunned, I tripped on my words, unprepared to talk about her in any language, but ashamed not to at this point. I stammered on and dropped all my notes and carefully-translated text, doing my best to translate the life of a woman who simply never quit. Once I started, the tears came and went, and I just continued to talk through them, finding comfort in conjuring up her spirit. Many were shocked at her age and, for some, it was their first time learning that humans will die of "old age" even if nothing else kills us. In the DRC, the life expectancy is fifty-two. It struck me, for the first time, what an incredible privilege it is to grow old, and to count on probably growing old. How most of the world's population could not count on that basic facet of my life; how most of the people I knew back home believed they would live for eighty or ninety years. How much differently would we Westerners lead our lives if we thought we only had forty to fifty years to live it?

I talked about the Great Depression, which hit in 1929 when Grandma Martha was nineteen, and left much of the United States in extreme poverty. I explained how she'd survived by cooking, how feeding people became the way she healed people and how she brought people together. Then—in a way that I could have never predicted nor planned—the participants began to talk about their recent losses, many of them parents, and how they'd barely survived when the war began and the bottom dropped out on their lives.

If I'd entered this conference room as planned, as a well-put-together "professional funder," I may have made some contacts but I never would have made any friends. Sobbing mess that I was, it was my pain and honesty that endeared the others to me, and all the once-stark differences between us paled in light of our similarities. If only the entire world could grieve each other's losses this way, focus on our shared experience as humans instead of the false allegiances we hold; maybe that level of empathy is the key to ending the insane cycle of war.

Here I am presenting at the first major gathering of women activists in Goma, DRC, the morning after losing Grandma Martha, 2003.

It was the same lesson from the mock battlefields of my youth, where the end goal is not to destroy the perceived enemy but, in recognizing that the enemy is you, to be brave enough to turn and destroy the conflict instead. "Victory over war," lies in seeing ourselves in others and feeling their pain as our own. The Congolese women surrounding me only opened up to me about their pain because I showed my most vulnerable self to them...and, once we bonded over death, I never felt alone again. Two Congolese girls moved into my hotel room that afternoon, explaining matter-of-factly, "We don't let people grieve alone," as if that one small rule couldn't transform the entire trajectory of humanity. I had so much to learn from these warriors, not just about survival but about sisterhood and showing up. I thought of all the people in my life who had lost someone and how I didn't know how to respond to their pain. I thought of how alone and confused I felt when The Dreamer died, as if a chasm had opened between the world and me, and no one wanted to acknowledge it, as if Death had cooties. I felt blessed to have found myself around Congolese women when my grandmother died and wished everyone could be so lucky when death comes knocking unannounced. I said a silent "thank you" to Grandma Martha for leaving her body at a time when I was so well held.

I left the DRC a day later, my new friends remaining with me until it was time to check out and escorting me all the way to the Rwandan border. Gifts for my mother "who had lost her mother" filled my bags and a warm sense of confidence and joy filled my heart. The Congo had given me a heart of lightness. I had come all this way thinking I was bringing something to the Congolese, that I was there to help them, and I was leaving having depended on and been helped by them instead. And I had a sense that the whole world needed their wisdom, that, if war ever does come to the over-advantaged shores of the West, we would do best to study the Congolese women to help us through. It was a humbling experience, and, when I talked to The Eagle about it on my way home, back through Nairobi, she shared a quote with me from an African activist that summed it up: "If you've come here to help me, you are wasting your time. If you've come because you know that your liberation is linked with mine, then roll up your sleeves and join us." And that was basically what I'd learned in just three days with Congolese activists, that my freedom and my future were inextricably linked to theirs and that—contrary to what I had believed before—they were going to be the ones to lead us out of this global human mess. When the shit hits the fan for the world's over-privileged, it will be African freedom fighters who we will need to turn to for help, not the other way around.

Chapter Nine

FORTUNE FAVORS THE BRAVE

I returned to Boulder, bags heavy with gifted wooden masks and beaded sandals, heart heavy with the loss my family had suffered, which I'd been absent for. I was worried about my brother, Noah, who had dealt with more than his fair share of death and loss by then; and I was worried about my mom, who had depended on her mother for almost six decades. I tried to carry the Congolese women's spirit with me, but it was hard to translate across the oceans. Katie had gone to the funeral in my place and said a few words but, try as she did to paint the picture for me, my mind could not grasp that fact that Grandma Martha was gone. I had things to tell her and she would never be able to hear them nor respond. I felt deeply untethered, floating outside of my lived experience, sure she would reappear for that last conversation. I hadn't seen the body burn, the way my family had, and I was having trouble grasping the reality of her death.

Katie and I had been talking about getting a tattoo together since we were travelling teenagers. We had tried once in Bangkok, but both chickened out at the last minute. Katie had been waiting tables all year at a café in Boulder and knew of a tattoo artist who came in regularly, ordered the catfish sandwich, and left a huge tip. "All the waitresses argue over who gets to serve him and he just seems like a really nice guy." She was suggesting I get a memorial tattoo for Grandma, something to make the loss feel permanent and real and also suggesting that her big-tipping, nice-guy customer was just the artist to do it. None of that logic made sense, but nothing in Boulder seemed to make sense without my grandma in it, and so I trusted her instincts over mine.

The tattoo shop was small and dark and smelled of cleaning chemicals, which I suppose is what you want when dealing with many people bleeding in the same place at the same time. Part of the reason Katie and I chickened out in Bangkok in 1996 was because the AIDS epidemic was rampant, and people were terrified and confused around the spread of blood-borne pathogens. By now, in 2003, we are clear on how HIV is and isn't contracted. We have come for a consultation with the big-tipping artist who, I find out, is named Phill Bartell. He is easy on the eyes with a soft, low voice and a gentle demeanor. There was an instant connection between us, less like a spark than a familiarity, less like a lightning bolt and more like a cozy hug.

In my wallet, I saved a small, torn scrap of paper from Colombia bearing the logo of La Ruta Pacífica, the brave and outspoken collective of feminist peace activists; Colombianas who use their collective voice to denounce the war and keep each other safe from direct targeting...organizing colorful, loud, media-heavy caravans for peace using art and puppetry and imagination. Something about their energy stuck to me and, now, with the loss of my mother's mother, I wanted to design a custom tattoo similar to their logo, which was multiple women's bodies contorted into a circle, representing the unbreakable force of women coming together, continually saving each other, continually sacrificing for womankind, continually imagining a better world for the next generation.

I envisioned three naked forms, contorted in a teardrop shape, their features indistinguishable but their individual silhouettes reminiscent of the three stages of womanhood: the maiden, the mother, and the crone. In the center, the Tibetan symbol for indestructibility or "that which cannot be broken," called a "double Dorje." Phill listened to my tattoo ideas intently and we talked briefly about Grandma Martha and the matriarch that she was. Katie was raised up by a strong single mother and molded by a fierce grandmother who had raised five children as one of Boulder's pioneer families. We agreed to get matching teardrop designs with the slight variation that she replaces the double Dorje with the astronomical sign for "Leo," as only a Leo would do. We booked appointments for one week later.

"I can tell you're really nervous," Phill says, close enough to my ear that I can feel his breath and only I can hear his concern. I'm not sure if it's my white knuckles gripping the tattoo table or the giant sweat stains encircling my arms that gave me away, but I nod, embarrassed. He puts his extra-large hand in the center of my back, right over my heart chakra where the tattoo is about to be engraved into my body forever, adding, "Let's just take three deep breaths together, and we will begin when you are ready." His voice is intoxicating and as we breathe in unison, I, again, have the overwhelming urge to hug him, or, more specifically, crawl into his lap like a cat and fall asleep...which is saying something, 'cause I'm still barely sleeping more than six hours at a time. He makes me want to rest, or at least pause.

The tattoo is excruciating, and I cry most of the way through, some for the pain and some for the loss of life it memorializes. Phill doesn't skip a beat with my tears, and it occurs to me that he must see people at their worst all the time. He has the bedside manner of a hospice nurse, helping people through their pain, even as he is the one causing it. The tone of his voice seems custom-tuned for calming people down. When it's over, I feel triumphant, adrenalized, better than I have in the weeks since I returned from the DRC. I feel bonded for life with Katie and with Phill, and, before we part, he gives me the deepest, longest, most magnetic hug I have ever received, leaving everyone else standing around us awkwardly. At the last minute, we tell him we are going out for a whiskey at a local dive bar and he perks up with, "Okay, see you there...."

▪ ▪ ▪

"Fortune Favors the Brave," I say aloud, reading from a book of 1920s New York sailor tattoos. I am lying in Phill's bed, the tattoo on my back now several-weeks-old. Once he walked into the bar later that first night, I knew we had a future together, but I assumed it would be short-lived. I was moving to Nairobi in a few months and I had no idea when I'd be back. I was attracted to Phill initially because we had nothing in common and I thought it would be easy and uncomplicated. He knew nothing about the work I did or where I'd been, and he had barely even left the country. I set up his first email address and registered him to vote, which were dating prerequisites to my twenty-six-year-old psyche.

Phill filled his days with making art and reading books about art. His room was crammed with piles of reference books, from popular artists to the obscure, and stacks of minidiscs filled with punk-rock music (I listened to hip-hop and pop). He had dropped out of art school to go on tour with his punk band, "One Nature," in the late '90s (that same year, I was sneaking across war-torn Cambodia). He claimed he "didn't really like to read," which was practically blasphemous in my world (I read the *New York Times* every morning and a novel before bed). He had never had a use for email and couldn't manage to keep his phone charged nor have it on him (I checked my email and phone every few minutes). He was an enigma that fascinated me, and he was also the perfect spring fling to get me out of my funk: easy, non-confrontational, and fleeting.

"Fortune favors the brave," I repeat.

"What?" Phill finally replies.

"Well, it's just that it's quite similar to a Buddhist teaching from my childhood. We might say, 'Good fortune comes from fearlessness,' with 'good fortune' meaning good karma, and 'fearlessness' meaning the courage to overcome fear and defeat conflict." He looks at me cockeyed. Phill was raised in an Episcopalian church and had attended private Catholic school, so, in that respect as well, we seemed to come from two entirely different planets.

"Yeah, I guess when sailors adopted that slogan, sea travel was still a daring adventure to places unknown...often with actual fortune to be found."

"Exactly!" I say, "We must go to the unknown, physically and mentally, if we are to gain the knowledge we need to evolve. Humans are still evolving, now mentally faster than physically, but we still haven't figured out how to stop killing and exploiting one another, nor how to peacefully coexist amongst our differences."

"Maybe I'll get that tattooed on me someday. I really love it," I say, surprising myself, shocked to be talking about getting another tattoo so soon.

"Maybe," Phill says with a smile and a knowing wink.

Six weeks later, civil unrest breaks out in Kenya over tribal land disputes, delaying my work visa approval and suspending my plans to end things with Phill. With all of our differences, I am astonished that we are still hanging out and enjoying each other's company, and how easy it is to be my whole self around him. I live in a collective of makeshift apartments that fit inside a turn-of-the-century mansion in Boulder, ninety percent of which are rented to nomadic activists. We call it The Bat Cave and its proprietor, our landlord, contributes to the causes of its inhabitants by offering cheap, lease-free rent to those of us who traipse around the world fighting for peace and justice. Phill has made friends with my many radical housemates (cavemates?) and blended into our counterculture naturally, introducing the house to the lesser-known sport of stair diving. He gets me in a way that no other person ever has.

I will be going off about the U.S.-led invasion of Iraq, our housemate Shannon broadcasting live from Baghdad, and Phill will listen quietly and simply offer to cook dinner again. I shaved my head in protest of the Iraq War and he thought I looked stunning. He is patient, generous, and kind, even if the music he listens to gives me a headache. And my dad likes him! Which feels like a miracle after his obvious disdain for most of my previous partners. Phill may not know the capital of Mozambique or even how to locate it on a map, but he knows how to bring me down to earth and absorb everything I emote…which is often a lot. Like me, he has an acutely-developed gift for listening.

▪ ▪ ▪

A few months after meeting Phill, UAF receives word from The Bear that the border between southern Sri Lanka (under the control of the recognized Sri Lankan government), and northern Sri Lanka (under the control of the L.T.T.E., one of the most notorious rebel factions in the world) has opened for the first time in twelve years. There is an opportunity to not only spread the word about UAF funding to an entirely new network of women activists working on the other side of the conflict, but a chance to hear directly from women in the north about what they've experienced and where our network can be helpful. We decide that I should go to Jaffna, the capital of the north, with my colleague, The Mongoose, who is still working for Oxfam in Colombo, and a Tamil translator. I am thrilled at the opportunity to spread our work and anxiously recalling my last trip to Sri Lanka and all the mistakes that I made.

After Sri Lanka, I plan to meet The Sparrow, who will be my replacement at UAF headquarters when I move to Nairobi. Much of what I do in the field can't be taught in an office in Boulder, Colorado, and, thus, we need to do some outreach together to see what situations arise and to train on how to respond in real time. We plan to meet in Kuala Lumpur and, from there, travel towards Aceh, Indonesia, where a separatist movement has made its violent claim for independence, women and children caught in the crosshairs. Indonesian women have been organizing and distributing resources, building an underground network. It's time for UAF to be there.

I will be gone at least a month, and it's my first dangerous trip away since meeting Phill. This is the time in most of my previous relationships where my leaving becomes an issue and the other shoe falls right in my lap. But, when I tell Phill of my plans—leaving many of the details out—no issue arises. Instead of saying anything negative or fearful or controlling, he got to work on a mixtape to "properly introduce me to the roots of punk rock" along the many long flights ahead. He didn't try to change me one hair, as if he knew full well who he'd fallen for, eyes wide open.

As the miles between Sri Lanka and me decreased, my heart rate and nervousness increased. I can't say I was ever excited to see The Bear, but I was anticipatory and curious to be with her, especially given our last disappointing conversation. She was placing a lot of trust in me, and I didn't want to let her down again. The Mountain Goat had hired a professional writer to compile the mountains of information we have from our first five years of funding women's actions on the frontlines. UAF was planning to publish its first book and use it to advocate for changes within the major funding structures. In addition to outreach, The Mongoose and I would be conducting interviews for that book and much was riding on my shoulders. It felt like a lot of pressure and a far cry from what other twenty-six-year-olds were worrying about. At the same time, I felt I had something to prove, and I was ready for the chance to do so.

The flight from Colombo to Jaffna was aboard a military plane with an armed female soldier pacing up and down the center aisle, the way a stewardess would. There were no drinks offered and no in-flight entertainment, unless you count the movie unfolding before us, the thrilling anticipation of seeing something for the first time. The Mongoose, myself, and the Tamil translator she'd hired all stayed strapped to our seats for the short flight, eyes alert. My reunion with The Mongoose had been sweet, and she and I spent a few days together in Colombo preparing for the trip and meeting with several Colombo-based NGOs, gaining trust and contacts for the trip ahead. The Bear sent a clandestine note to my hotel that she was unable to meet with me in person this time around. I had learned enough to know that sometimes my white American profile was an asset and sometimes it was a liability. I didn't take it personally but was glad for the company of another brave young activist in The Mongoose.

We landed on a grass and dirt runway, no airport to speak of. Another soldier reviewed our paperwork and asked us questions through our translator. Everyone looked at me sideways, but no one spoke to me directly. I was immediately aware of how many women soldiers there were, semiautomatic weapons strapped to their backs. A cargo truck pulled up and started throwing our bags onto the ground. The Mongoose arranged transportation and, before long, we were speeding along in the back of an ATV, taking in sights very few people had seen in more than a decade.

We stopped at a roadside tea-seller, not much more than a compilation of wooden boards for shelves, a small gas burner keeping the tea warm. Sri Lanka, once called Ceylon, is the tea capital of the world. The Mongoose and The Translator ordered in Tamil. I picked up a package of cookies and noted that they had expired years earlier. Inspecting all the other packaged foods for sale, I saw that they were all well past their expiration date. I'd always thought of expiration dates on highly-processed and packaged foods to be arbitrary suggestions, but I'd never thought about how war makes such regulations obsolete; and never been in a situation where those dates were put to the test. I bought the cookies and ate them, deciding that they were probably just as bad on the day they were made.

We got to our reserved hotel and were given a hard time straight away. The manager of the hotel was not comfortable with three women traveling alone, coming and going as they pleased, and his first serious question to us was, "Where are your husbands?" Hotels can be tricky in war zones, especially if they take your passport information, monitor your comings and goings, and have access to your stuff. This particular hotel manager and his obvious distrust of us immediately raised my hackles. We were going to have to be incognito and deceptive about our whereabouts.

The following day, we met with the few women's rights groups that managed to stay active and involved during the war. Their resilience was phenomenal, and all they had managed to accomplish with few resources or outside support was impressive. Their work wasn't sophisticated, like their Sinhala counterparts in the south, but it was effective; the nitty-gritty, hand-dirtying work of saving lives. They housed and fed orphaned children, offered income-generating skills to war widows and injured soldiers, documenting the horrors and the disappeared, counting the dead that accrue after decades of armed conflict. They were surprised and happy that we'd come and that we had resources to offer; at the same time, they felt forgotten and abandoned by the world. I could offer very little other than to say that I would take their words with me and amplify them to others, thinking of the advocacy work UAF was just starting.

Arriving back at the hotel, we find an L.T.T.E. soldier waiting for us, Sneaky Manager by his side offering tea. *So much for staying incognito.* The Translator explains that he is there to extend an invitation. The L.T.T.E. leadership in the area have learned of our presence and our involvement with the women's groups. They would like to "invite us to come to their headquarters and meet with their women as well." The Mongoose and I eye each other widely and both start nodding our heads, agreeing to go. While it didn't necessarily fit into the outreach nor the research aspects of our trip, it was an incredibly unique opportunity to see inside an L.T.T.E. camp and neither of us wanted to upset our hosts by refusing.

The security to get inside the camp was intense and thorough. Female soldiers did a body search that included grabbing my breasts to feel if I had anything hard concealed in my bra (the place no other soldier or security guard had dared to go). Our phones, recording equipment, and pens were confiscated, offering me a pen of their own choosing and allowing me to take notes by hand in a small notebook. The L.T.T.E. is notorious for the deftness of its suicide bombings and was the first armed faction to use young women as human bombs. Their security measures reflected a level of expertise I had not yet encountered.

We are escorted into a small room with a few high-up officials, all male, making small talk via The Translator and sipping tea awkwardly. Eventually, four uniformed female soldiers enter and fill the four empty chairs waiting. They are all exceptionally clean and well-pressed, various pins to denote rank, disciplined in their every move. I begin by asking them the same question I've asked all the women activists we've met with, "What are the priorities of your work right now? How can we help?" All four women, to varying degrees, talk about the need for more supplies and support for their cause. Of course, UAF doesn't fund armed movements but, other than that, their concerns mirrored that of the other Tamil women on the outside of their walls: they needed more food and more resources.

Amazingly, each woman then opened up about joining the L.T.T.E. straight out of the refugee camps, saying that they had slain family members to avenge and that their options lay in either staying powerless refugees or picking up arms and joining the fight. In a way that sounded well-rehearsed, they outlined all of the "modern freedoms" they enjoyed as L.T.T.E. soldiers, or "Tigers" for short.

They were incredibly proud to be Tigers and recited all of the "codes of conduct" that they adopted, which abolished the dowry system, allowed for "love marriages," and gave women roles in the fighting that included driving heavy machines, supervising other soldiers, and operating complex artillery. One woman says that they are "still women who want to get married and have children," but their first duty is to the cause of liberation and to their fellow soldiers.

I imagine that many of these Tigresses, like me, were not naturally drawn to motherhood, that they had leadership skills and agility that had them excelling as soldiers instead. In America, these women may have become professional athletes or CEOs. I instantly recognize their innate qualities and wonder, in that moment more than ever in my life, if I had been born a Tamil girl in Jaffna, if life had offered me the same choices it had offered them, who would I have become? Would I have taken up arms to protect my family or community? Was there always a third option to conflict, as I'd been taught, or is it sometimes black-and-white, "us" versus "them," "me" versus "you"? I had not expected to have so much in common with the Tiger women and I was surprised to learn that their chief concerns—food, shelter, water, medicine, freedom—were the same as the Sinhala women on the other side of this conflict…they were all fighting, and killing, and dying for essentially the same thing.

Sometime during those interviews, I started to get suspicious that our translator wasn't fully translating. The Mongoose confirmed those concerns later, pulling me aside and saying, "Dude, I don't think our translator is translating correctly." For me, it was something about the intonations that didn't match up, but The Mongoose understood enough Tamil to know that something was off. Those trusty old bells started chiming their warning, softly but surely.

Arriving back at the hotel, we again find Sneaky Manager questioning our plans and motives for being in Jaffna. I explain that we are planning to leave the next morning, by car, pointing to our hired driver who is going to take us south and across the eastern coast of Sri Lanka to Trincomalee. "Oh?" Sneaky Manager questions, his eyebrows shooting upward, head tilting sideways waiting for more explanation from The Translator. A conversation ensues that I cannot understand, save for the intensity of it, between our driver and this man who just can't seem to leave us alone. "Your driver is not comfortable taking you along that road," he states, and then adds "but he says he will do it for double the money."

I can't tell if we are being scammed for money or if there is a real problem. Studying the driver's face, his eyes shifting uncomfortably, hairline beaded, hands fidgeting, I ask "Why doesn't he want to go?" as directly as one can through a third person, eyes directed at Sneaky Manager.

"Landmines," is all he needed to say, as if the word itself contains some of its explosive power.

It's a crazy proposition, to say the least. If the driver isn't willing to risk his life to drive across a minefield for a certain number of rupees but is willing to go for double that amount, then he's just put an exact value on his life and, in a very nonchalant way, he's named a price for my life, The Mongoose's life, and The Translator's. My legs go wobbly and my head spins, making me instantly nauseated. I head to my room to "think about it," and not only do I vomit the minute I enter, my entire body starts to shake. I can't decipher if I'm terrified or ill, having premonitory visions or a bout of food poisoning (wondering if expiration dates aren't so arbitrary, after all).

I don't know what to do. I'm terrified of making a mistake, which could be deadly. I should call The Bear, as my main local contact, but I can't take anymore criticism in my fragile state. I need a pep talk, not a reprimanding. I call The Mountain Goat instead. Of all my mentors, she is the most like a mother to me, though she chose to birth organizations instead of humans in this lifetime. Calling my real mother is out of the question, lest I fall apart completely. The

Mountain Goat helps me think through the pros and cons of pushing forward, through an active minefield with a terrified driver and a suspect translator…of which there are many cons. The only major upside would be to spread the word and legitimacy of UAF funding, which less conspicuous others can do now that we've delivered outreach materials in Tamil. When I think about going on and check in with my body, I feel sick and the bells are clanging; when I think about turning around, I feel stronger and my head quiets.

We work through the details of aborting the mission, while I work out the bacteria that has invaded my body. In the morning, I tell The Mongoose, who is disappointed about the change of plans. By the next afternoon, we are on a small commuter plane back to Colombo, the Sneaky Manager's winning smirk engraved in my mind. I will never know if I made the right decision to turn that mission around, if I was influenced by my past trauma and giving in to fear or if I prevented a disaster. I learned that day how to listen to my body over my head and decided that is what they mean by "trusting your gut."

▪ ▪ ▪

From Colombo, I fly to Kuala Lumpur, Malaysia, where The Sparrow is already connecting with our network of women's groups. From there, we are aiming to fly to Medan, Sumatra, the gateway to Aceh. Working on human rights in Indonesia can be tricky, and foreigners have spent years in jail for working without government permission. The Sparrow and I met with one such activist who had been imprisoned for working without a specific visa, and she gave us tips on how to stay under their radar and blend in. I hadn't spoken Indonesian in years and, according to her, all the better. We should look and act like tourists, not too knowledgeable about Indonesian politics, and use visibility as our cover. We should never meet with local activists in public and instead invite them to a private room in an upscale tourist hotel. The Sparrow and I were only planning to be in Medan for two days…

get in, make our connections, get out without being recognized. That was the plan....

The hotel in Medan had marble floors and wide columns in the spacious reception area. The Sparrow and I were dressed like tourists, she always a bit more glamorous than me, and we approached the check-in desk with an attitude that only American white girls can conjure. In this case, it was maybe too much attitude. The smiling man behind the reception desk seemed to light up at the sight of us, exclaiming, "I know you!" At first, I thought maybe he actually did know me from my teenage trips to Bali, but then he said, "And you!" pointing to The Sparrow (who had never been to Indonesia before). "From MTV!" he says so loudly that others in the lobby look over, making us the least-inconspicuous guests in that giant room. So much for getting out without being recognized. I had a choice to make and only a couple of seconds to make it. I only had a fleeting hope that The Sparrow would follow my lead, but if anything was going to show her how to think on your feet in a war zone, this was it.

"Yes! That's correct!" I beamed, flashing my teeth and winking. The Sparrow nodded and started acting aloof.

"I knew it!" the receptionist exclaimed while stepping away into the back office. He returned carrying a large poster board, covered in signatures of actual famous people, a smiling colleague behind him with camera in hand. "All famous people who stay here sign this," he proclaimed, his pride palpable. The Sparrow looked at me for a brief moment, as if to say, "Have we gone too far?" but I smiled and nodded and took the offered pen to sign something illegible. She did the same, and we snapped a photo with the man who "recognized" us. He also gave us an upgrade to their best suite and, by the time we got up there, a complimentary gift basket had been delivered.

It seemed to me to be the perfect cover, as far from grassroots activists as we could possibly appear, and we were both feeling confident in our new roles as American music stars, laughing at all the possible musicians they could have been mistaking us for. Then the phone rang, and it was the head manager of the hotel, inviting us as his special guests to their in-house karaoke bar. He also wanted to know the names of some of our most famous songs to pre-program in. Neither of us could even carry a tune and we still had no idea who they thought we were. I accepted their offer cautiously and hung up without answering the second question, unsure of our next move.

"What are we gonna do?" the Sparrow worried, "We signed their special board and everything! We're totally gonna get busted and blow our cover."

"Oh, no, we're not," I assured her, "We've just got to think of a good way out of this," wracking my brain for the next best move. In many ways, this was the perfect training ground for The Sparrow, in terms of what's required to do this delicate work: a little bit of improv theatre, a dash of Western entitlement, a huge dose of confidence and courage, all combined with a lot of bald-faced lying for the greater good. I personally rely on lessons that began in my childhood acting classes, taught by a fabulous ex-Broadway actress in our Buddhist Sangha, much of which was improvisational and outrageous. My father acted in an adult production company and taught high-school acting classes, much of which trickled down to me. I continued acting through college, staring in a dear friend's senior thesis production as the martyred Russian poet Anna Akhmatova, and, at one point, thought of acting as a possible career path. The fact that I could employ all of those learned skills with reckless abandon, holding firmly in my mind to the mission at hand, was the best part of my job.

After thinking it through, debating and considering many options, we agreed that the best card to play—kind of our only card to play—was the Diva Card. We would channel Mata Hari's wiles, here on her actual stomping ground in Indonesia, and regain control of the situation on our terms. I called the manager back and expressed our gratitude at their warm welcome but regretted to decline their evening offer, as we were both performing in Jakarta the following evening and were resting our vocal cords (we were, in fact, flying to Jakarta the following evening, after a full day of meetings with some of the bravest activists on the planet). "Furthermore," I continued to push it, "while we appreciate your staff's attention, we are having discreet music industry meetings for the rest of the day today and tomorrow and require less of a scene and absolutely no more photo requests." I continued to heap it on, explaining that we'd chosen to stay at their fine establishment because of their reputation for professionalism and we were hoping he and his staff could help us welcome a few guests in and out of the hotel quietly.

"Of course, madam," was his willing reply. I thought of The Pelican in Bogotá, teaching me how to use my privileged voice and skin tone for good, how to leverage my presumed innocence and hide my intentions in plain sight.

For the next day and a half, a hilarious scene unfolded in that grand hotel reception room. Like something out of a *Pink Panther* movie, we would receive word from the front desk that we had visitors and one of us would head down to the lobby to receive them, each time a different group of women, most wearing traditional head scarves, none of them looking like music promoters. I would find a moment to wink at the receptionist, when none of our visitors were looking, and he would attempt to clandestinely take my photo, more than once spooking our guests. Two distinct storylines, converging in one awkward, nerve-busting moment after the next, The Sparrow and I trying to juggle and explain and dismiss their concerns. It was a good thing we only stayed two nights and miraculously never got busted. The Sparrow had gotten the perfect lesson in creating a spontaneous cover, and sticking to it, while we both got away with a good story about "that one time we were treated like rock stars for a day or two."

▪ ▪ ▪

By the time I actually move to Nairobi, plans have been severely delayed, and Phill and I have been dating for over a year. I know his family and he knows mine. His strange ways have grown on me like a fungus. I'm even starting to like punk rock music. When I told him my work visa had finally come through, he said two things: "How long will you be gone?" and "I just want to know because I'm planning to make a new painting for every month you are away." Not once did he say "What about me?" or "Don't go," or "I need you." He saw me for exactly who I was, and he had no intention of trying to control me, own me, or make my life about him. It was refreshing and freeing and, because of that, I agreed to maintain a long-distance love for as long as it felt authentic. And then, without much thinking, I gave him the dare of his life.

Standing in front of the security gates at Denver International Airport, locked in one of our epic hugs, both of our faces wet. I can already feel the lack of him in my daily life, as if the absence of him has its own weight and volume. This was the stuff my mentors were talking about in that speakeasy in London. This feeling was what made all the sacrifice and risk worth it. If we don't know what we are fighting for, then we are just blindly battling without a sense of purpose.

The Raven's prophetic words ring out in my head, "What makes you historic?" And I finally realize just what she was getting at. That this—this soft, kind, generous, love feeling—was equally worth fighting for. That maybe this punk rockin' artist could be my worth-fighting-for. And, with that realization, I pull Phill close and whisper in his ear, "If you are serious about this love, if you are brave enough to seek that unknown fortune, then save your money, come to Africa, and ask me to marry you." And, with that, and his wide-eyed reaction hanging, I walk away through security and towards my unknown.

▪ ▪ ▪

The work in Nairobi was both challenging and fun. Kenyans did most things differently than Americans and, without the guidance of The Eagle and our resourceful office manager Maki, I would have been completely lost. To set up a working grantmaking program, banking out of Kenya, was not only groundbreaking in the philanthropic world; it was also painfully slow and full of obstacles, requiring that I set my American-ness aside and learn to think more like a Kenyan.

In my mind, we would just make a trip to the office supply store, get some files, a cabinet, and a printer and we'd be in business (the way The Mountain Goat and I had done in Boulder four years earlier). In reality, it took Maki and me weeks to track down the supplies we needed and to get a working telephone with dial-up internet. It took even longer to get our materials translated into Kiswahili and other local languages, and longer still to get a working NGO license and an operating bank account. The Eagle, whose legal work took her flying all over the world, would check in on us regularly and offer support, but, mainly, it was Maki and me, using matatus (local transportation), banging our heads against walls trying to accomplish what would take hours in the United States.

All of my entitlement and unmet expectations were laughable to my Kenyan friends and colleagues, who seemed to regard me as more of a strange alien than a regular person. I was an anomaly for sure: a twenty-seven-year-old woman, unmarried and without kids, living alone in Nairobi without any family or linguistic training, and all I wanted to talk about was work and war. "Thousands of innocent Iraqis are dying in the name of 'American freedom!'" I would rant, "American soldiers are dying to somehow avenge a terrorist attack that had nothing to do with Iraq. Bombs are dropping on Baghdad, destroying centuries of cultural tradition and wisdom, because Americans want more cheap oil, a nonrenewable resource that is choking our planet to death!" The United States was the international bully, not the hero. It was the first official war during my lifetime—having grown up on stories of my grandfather fighting in WWII and my uncle fighting in Vietnam—and, for the first time in my life, it made me ashamed to call myself an American.

Kenyans, however, had lived through wars and suffered for decades under a dictator who would not allow free and fair elections to replace him. The tribal warfare in the south had calmed down, but it could flare up again at any time. Unlike me, none of my Kenyan friends had any delusion about their government being "the good guys," and, unlike me, they didn't equate a government's actions with the broad public support of its people. In other words, they didn't see me and think "There's an American girl who supports the insane and illegal actions of her overbearing government"; they looked at me and saw an individual, most likely powerless to stop her government from making any major decisions and, therefore, blameless in the matter. But I did blame myself, and all of my fellow Americans, for letting our leaders dupe us into believing their lies about "weapons of mass destruction," their falsified connections between the Taliban (who took credit for the attacks on Sept. 11th, 2001) and Iraqi leadership.

Two thousand and four hundred Americans died in the 2001 attacks, which were horrific, but tens of thousands of innocent Iraqi men, women, and children paid for it. *How was that justice?* While I knew that the U.S. had been funding foreign wars and arming revolutions worldwide for decades, up until "Operation Iraqi Freedom," I still held to the illusion that we were operating that way on behalf of increased freedoms, that our fundamental intentions in the world were for the good of humanity. Maybe that was naïve or blind, but invading Iraq unprovoked was the moment I released all remaining allegiance to the United States and began to envision living outside of it. I would not be associated with the bully on the international playground. I would stand up for the underdog. It may sound trite, but it was a profound moment in my mind and heart, a complete personal emancipation from any remaining patriotism I was holding on to. The "American dream" was just a fantasy, and it was time to wake up.

Maki and I worked night and day to get a Rapid Response Grantmaking program up and running for UAF-Africa. We also spent time adjusting and questioning the way we did things out of the U.S. office and how to apply that to a Pan-African context. In the U.S., we were able to respond to urgent requests almost twenty-four hours per day, seven days a week, and we could move money around the world in about a week. In Kenya, the internet and phone were unreliable, staff often didn't have service when they were not in the office, and no one was willing to work on Sundays, which was "God's day." I had never been around so many devout Christians and, on a daily basis, I was asked—often by complete strangers—if I "had accepted Jesus Christ as my Lord and Savior." And, try as I did to explain, no one understood how it was that I was a "Tibetan Buddhist," who didn't believe in their god and was convinced that Jesus was an enlightened brown man…not the blonde-haired, blue-eyed version of a savior that they had been sold by European colonizers. But the roots of their faith were inextricable from the chains of colonization and all my young, brash, blasphemous opinions came across more judgmental and offensive than convincing.

We hired our first full-time "program officer" to help run the grantmaking program, and I was excited to have a new colleague. Within a week of working, however, she posted an announcement in the center of the office, written by the Pope and the Vatican, outlining the unraveling of society that occurs when women begin to work outside of the home. I was shocked. I was all up for healthy debate around what we should or should not be supporting within the context of women's movements, but this was debating our worth outside of family life altogether! *How could someone work (outside of the home, albeit young and unmarried) and still argue the benefits of women in the workforce? Hadn't we all read the 1995 Beijing Platform for Action?*

Didn't we all identify as feminists? But I would soon learn that we hadn't, and we didn't.

Next there was an anonymous complaint to The Eagle that I continually used the words "lesbian" and "gay" in open discussion about our work, and it was making others uncomfortable. Homosexuality was still illegal in Kenya, and most of East Africa, and I was being insensitive and uncouth. *How could we purport to champion the rights of women to live free of sexual violence and not think, above all, that that would mean extending protection and support to people targeted for their sexual preference?* It was soon clear that my understanding of feminism was drastically different from my Kenyan colleagues'.

We'd recently had a heated debate amongst UAF's Colorado-based staff, which spread to a board meeting discussion about whether or not to extend protections and security for targeted transgender rights activists. The younger generation of employees and interns, of which UAF now had a handful, didn't see any problem in extending our grantmaking to protect and advance trans rights, while UAF's founders didn't quite see how it fit into protecting women's rights, as the two movements had always been separate. There was a brief discussion about UAF supporting male-to-female trans activists, targeted specifically for their expression of womanhood, but not supporting female to male trans activists who often passed for men and enjoyed male privilege in a patriarchal world. But then, we argued, who would protect threatened trans men when their gender identity was questioned or their trans identity outed? And the trans rights movement, on a global scale, was young and unsophisticated compared to the more powerful women's human rights movement. If we didn't extend a hand, who would? The younger employees, myself included, could see the power in intersecting our goals and we pushed the founders to expand our grantmaking language and criteria to include protection for all activists being targeted for violence because of their gender identity. But, here in Kenya, I needed to be more careful about how I talked about our work, especially our support for the underground and often persecuted LBGT community.

Shortly after my clashes with the new staff member, the tension in the office palpable, The Eagle took me out to a fancy lunch and gave me my first lesson in "African feminist diplomacy." She explained that we needed to be wary with our words, to avoid being reported to the national NGO Office, which could pull our license to operate. We had to stay subtle and vigilant and hold our cards close, which went against all of my loudmouthed, call-them-out American ways. The Eagle had traveled the world, opening her eyes and her mind, and shared with me that her sister was gay, living in New York City, and working for a well-known lesbian rights organization. In Kenya, there was a different way of doing things, and my bravado was making things worse and endangering our work overall. I recall The Eagle saying something wise like, "In America, you like to hit issues over the head and let your constitution protect your right to do so. In Kenya, we approach issues softly, swaying public opinion slowly, and then create new laws to support our positions down the line."

I spent months watching The Eagle work, awed by her skillful diplomacy and intellectual capacity to outsmart her foes and sidestep obstacles. Compared to The Mountain Goat or me, it was the difference between pushing an agenda, bullheaded, into becoming reality, and watching a careful dance, a ballet of sorts, that surprises you with how much it accomplishes in the end. I took careful note of the way The Eagle used her grace and her kindness to sway people's opinions and began to emulate the subtle ways in which she moved seemingly unmovable forces. Although I was always adept at acting and deceiving others for the greater good, The Eagle showed me how to create radical change while remaining invisible, never getting caught. She was the force behind so much advancement of women's rights in the region, and yet her strength lay in her anonymity; her power rested in never taking much credit.

While I had learned from The Tortoise, The Elephant, and The Bear about how to be subtler and less-assumptive, more strategic in my approach to work, The Eagle directly encouraged me to drop the last shred of self-centeredness and any "white savior complex" that I was holding on to, wanting to take some credit for the strides of African women. I learned from The Eagle that real success means fomenting power in others to create change without anyone ever knowing you were there. The Tortoise had also begun challenging all of our definitions and assumptions as an organization, cautioning us away from feminist fundamentalisms, which left blind spots in our growth and centered Western women's concerns.

That month, a colleague from South Africa, who had been instrumental in the anti-apartheid movement, challenged me further.

"I don't mean to sound like an ungrateful ass but what are you doing here?" she asked. "Your government is currently deceiving the entire world and burning Iraqi cities to the ground for access to more oil. Why aren't you, and every other American with a conscience, marching by the millions to challenge your leaders? If you want to end war so badly, why not start with your home, the world's biggest war machine?"

It was harsh and honest, and I honestly couldn't answer. Finally, I replied, "I suppose I'm here to learn from you, The Eagle, and other African activists. You who have toppled corrupt and oppressive governments, survived colonization and taken your power back from dictators. You have been resisting and organizing and winning for longer than I've been alive."

"Well, okay," she replied, "Learn what you can from us and take it back to teach your sisters at home. But don't stay for too long. They need you more than we do." And she was right. The African women's movements didn't need me, nor my way of trying to create change with my in-your-face feminism. I needed them; the whole world would eventually need them, to help prepare us for what lay ahead and to show us how to survive it.

I was out of my league, out of my comfort zone, and unsure of everything that had once felt certain. Fortunately, Phill was there on the other end of short, scratchy phone calls; sending me cute daily emails and handcrafted care packages, which arrived weekly. One of the rituals we had developed during our year in Boulder together was him reading aloud to me. His lack of interest in reading had not only stemmed from a life focused on making art and music, he was also dyslexic and had never been taught tools to work with that gift. I had a friend in college with severe dyslexia who went on to become our class valedictorian, so I knew that one could be dyslexic and also well-read and highly-educated. Early on in our romance, I encouraged Phill to read aloud. At first, it was slow-going, and he would get frustrated and want to stop. But, with patience and practice, he got faster and more confident. We spent hours together before bed, him reading to me from his favorite fantasy series, *The Wheel of Time* by Robert Jordan, and me finally relaxing and putting my mind on something other than violence against women and war. When I left for Nairobi, he bought a small tape recorder and continued the ritual without me. His care packages arrived full of treats and smells from home, and a new bundle of cassette tapes covering our brave heroes' latest quest, his voice keeping me company from 10,000 miles away.

I found an old tape recorder in the Nairobi street market and began recording over his tapes with books of my own, sending the tapes back to him in between. For months, this is how we loved each other; not in real time, but in well-thought-out packages of affection. And this type of love worked for me. It was slow, considerate, and un-controlling. Phill was opening up his heart to me in patient, meticulous prose and curated bundles, and, weeks later, he would receive my reciprocal affection and our love would grow. Meanwhile, I could focus on my work and he could focus on his. I wished all of my relationships had had such spaciousness and care. My being thousands of miles away had only brought us closer.

Other than The Eagle and Maki as my main confidants and support system, I also had John. John was my driver on paper, but he was my friend and a father figure in reality. He was roughly the age of my actual father and he looked after me like one of his own kids. John first started calling me by the Swahili name Njeri, which translates as "traveler" in English, and, by his grace and kindness, I never felt too alone in Nairobi. Any time, day or night, I could call John and he would be there in minutes, ready to take me wherever I needed to go or solve whatever problem had arisen. When Phill finally arrived in Nairobi—rising to the challenge of my airport dare—it was John who accepted him and all of his tattoos with the open, nonjudgmental arms of a father.

▪ ▪ ▪

Even though I'd told him to do just that, I was caught off guard by Phill's marriage proposal…most likely because he asked me on his second day in Kenya. By then, I knew he was coming to Nairobi and I took all of my remaining vacation time from UAF to explore East Africa with him, showing him much of what The Eagle had originally shown me. And I knew Phill had been by my parent's house to pick up gifts from them, and maybe the wedding ring I'd inherited from Grandma Martha? I assumed that, if he were going to ask me, it would be at the end of a successful month of traveling together.

He assumed that, the sooner he got the proposal out of the way, the more time we'd have as an engaged couple before separating again. Another example of how we were always viewing the world from opposite perspectives. I suppose, when it comes down to it, someone who sees what you don't is an ideal partner to have, as annoying as it sometimes is. At this stage of our relationship, I was fascinated with the way he did things and endlessly entertained by his approach to life.

We began our exploration of my favorite places in East Africa with a private safari from northern Kenya down through Tanzania, leaving Nairobi the morning of Phill's second day in town. On our first drive through the Samburu National Reserve that evening, we were treated to a magnificent show. Elephants, lions, giraffes, and monkeys all came out to play and delight in one of the most spectacular sunsets I'd ever witnessed. Florescent pinks and oranges filled the sky, from one horizon to the next, bathing the wildlife in a neon glow. We rode on top of our Land Rover, taking pictures and holding hands, soaking up the full magic of the moment.

Phill will say that he knew then that he was going to ask me to spend my life with him, that the sunset was the sign he was waiting for. It had already been one of the more remarkable days of his life, and he wanted to remember it forever. By the time we reached camp, we had just a few moments to freshen up before dinner. Our tent was on the edge of an embankment, overlooking the Ewaso Ng'iro River, and the views were stunning. I was taking it all in when Phill stepped inside to "check the time." When he returned, before I knew to notice, he was down on one knee. My initial reaction was that he'd tripped or was hurt, but then I saw the ring in his hand. Our eyes met, and his lips moved like he wanted to speak, but no sounds came out. We sat there like that, in silence. He, trying to find his words; me, taking in all the details and the enormity of the moment, frozen.

At last, he managed to squeak out the words, "Will you marry me?" in an octave above his normal speaking voice. I nodded, and we embraced, my torso catching his enormous exhale, his weight falling onto mine.

Phill would later admit that he had had a long speech planned, which he'd practiced a dozen times, but that the power of the actual moment, looking into my eyes, had stolen his words away. We told our waiter at dinner and our driver the next day, but it would be another week until we were able to call our families, remote as we were. I was so excited to share my life with this wonderful, enigmatic being. There was just one problem…I didn't believe in the institution of marriage.

▪ ▪ ▪

We traveled on together for another magical month, from the rolling grasslands of the Serengeti, to the pristine white beaches of Zanzibar, to the ancient wonders of Egypt. With each new adventure, our love grew bigger and more trusting. My mom always told me that the best way to know someone, and decide if you want to commit your life to theirs, is to travel together. "You see someone's true colors once they're out of their comfort zone," she'd insisted, and I thought of all the terrible trips I'd taken with ex-lovers, bickering over little nothings, a clear but unseen premonition of where the relationship was heading. If Mom's advice was true, then Phill was proving to be my perfect partner and, after a month of African exploration, we returned to Nairobi even more in love than when we'd left.

Phill spent a last week in Nairobi while I went back to work, where he connected with two tattooers, brothers named Abraham and Newton, who had built their own tattoo machines from scratch with no formal training. Phill passed the days tattooing with them and revealing coveted tricks of the trade. Before he flew home to Boulder, he left the brothers a professionally-built machine, high-quality inks, and answers to hundreds of questions about the craft. He was the first professional tattoo artist either of them had worked with, and they were the first self-taught Kenyan tattooers he'd heard of. The experience of working with the brothers left an indelible mark on him, revealing just how much access and convenience he had at his fingertips when it came to the work he loved. He was waking up to his privileges in the world and beginning to question how to better utilize them. He stayed in contact with Abraham and Newton after he left and started sending them packages of otherwise unattainable tattoo supplies.

Phill with Kenyan tattoo artists and brothers, Abraham and Newton, 2004.

When The Eagle informed me that fighting in northern DRC had subdued and the United Nations had successfully established a peacekeeping force (MONUC), headquartered in the northeastern city of Bunia, we agreed there was an opportunity to go and that I was the right person for the task. "Fortune favors the brave," I said to Phill upon telling him I was going back into the DRC, feeling both courageous and like I had more to lose than before. I finally had my reason for being historic, but it meant the risk felt greater too.

I had made the recent decision to return home to Colorado once this contract was over, in just a few months, and planned to build a life with my new fiancée. One last mission into the Congo, and then I could think about a future with Phill and the remote possibility of creating some personal happiness.

Chapter Ten

MEETING MARY

Just when I think that I've seen the worst of humanity, that there is nothing left that could shock me, I find myself face-to-face with a level of misery that proves me wrong. I am back in the Democratic Republic of the Congo (DRC), the place where everything changed; back in Goma, the lava-covered border town where I learned to mourn the Congolese way two years ago.

This time, we're on a mission to support the work being done by Congolese activists to document the rampant sexual violence that has become the weapon of choice throughout this complex and bloody war: women's bodies, small girl bodies, the literal stomping grounds of soldiers, fleshy fields upon which rebel armies compete, leaving unmistakable scars. Earlier this year, the Congolese government authorized the International Criminal Court (ICC) to investigate and prosecute war crimes allegedly committed anywhere in the territory of the DRC. The ICC opened its first formal investigation into the recent battle for the Ituri region—where we are heading—formally issuing arrest warrants for some of the men responsible for masterminding that bloody conflict which left 60,000 dead in the span of a few short years.

The Gazelle, a sharp-minded Algerian activist from Canada, is traveling on behalf of an international coalition of feminist lawyers who are pushing for charges of rape to be included in those ICC prosecutions. We are travelling together to Bunia, in northern Ituri, where a large United Nations peacekeeping force of 4,500 soldiers has established a "safe zone," now home to the region's largest refugee camp, Camp Aero, holding roughly 20,000 residents. I am hoping to expand Urgent Action Fund Africa's network in Ituri and find out firsthand what can be done to support women activists on the ground.

I'm holding my breath a lot. I catch myself gasping for air at the last moment, on the brink of passing out. Perhaps, unconsciously, I'm only surface-level breathing to keep everything around me superficial too, less-penetrating; as if even one deep breath could let in too much pain, pierce my fragile nervous system, and throw me off my adrenaline game. I don't want another "Sri Lanka" on my psyche. So I stay nimble, airy, and I hardly breathe. Or maybe, now that I'm deeply in love with Phill, finally have something concrete to live for, I am hoping to slip in and out of this madness unscathed. *Holding my breath while I tiptoe through the Congo.*

The Gazelle and I flew into Kigali, Rwanda, a few days ago and arrived uneventfully at the Congolese border via four hours in a taxi. I'd made the long trip across Rwanda before, marveling at its stunning beauty, but this time the hours slipped by unnoticed, my thoughts anticipating all the details ahead; all the possible exit strategies. The security measures involved in entering a heavily-militarized—practically forgotten—war zone are always shifting, and I've long learned strategies for shifting with them. *Practically forgotten?* In prepping for this trip, I tried to get a weather report for Goma, only to discover that there simply isn't one. It turns out, no one reports the weather over the Congo. There is no Lonely Planet guide, no tourist information website, no hotel reviews. We are entering a place that much of the Western political world has decided, quite intentionally, to disregard.... *Is there anywhere else on Earth where five million people die, hundreds of thousands of women and children are raped, in a war that involves troops from nine separate African countries and a massive United Nations intervention, and it doesn't even make the evening ticker tape back home?* Practically forgotten in Western supremacy's shadow.

The border has changed significantly since I was here last, due to a tenuous peace accord holding over the region, disorienting my earlier confidence, all my preparations now futile. I'm going to have to be on my toes. There are still plenty of meandering boy soldiers, machine guns slung at awkward angles across too-small chests, bloodshot eyes staring from underneath too-big berets, but now the place feels more legitimate. Crisp new uniforms declare allegiance to the recently elected "transitional government," while eager hands stamp my actual passport with an embossed seal that is also, apparently, brand-new and entirely novel to the embosser, who smiles achievingly every time it works. Last time, I got a passport-sized piece of paper slipped between the official pages and was told not to let it slip out, though it bore no legitimate authority. Now the army controlling Goma feels more like its own corrupt branch of an elected government and a regular bureaucracy has emerged—or rather, reemerged—weary but desperate to awaken after several years of civil war dormancy.

Crossing into the DRC is a far cry from the handshake and nod we got last time, the makeshift tree trunk replaced by an actual security arm, the handshakes and conversations replaced with formal paperwork and procedures. As I fill out my paperwork, I notice that my hands are steady, my writing fluid. I'm poised, as my high school basketball coach used to say, alert but at ease. By now, I've grown used to the attention that two blondes will provoke in a sea of darker, curlier hair, so I rely on my training for confrontational and bizarre scenarios. Just as I had been trained to do on the mock battlefields of my youth, I will surrender first; show submissiveness to soften my opponent's resolve, dissolve the tension to move the situation forward.

It's a well-rehearsed strategy: first, make myself as unthreatening as possible (smile, laugh, speak only English, hunch, bow head slightly); second, flirt and flatter all the egos in the room (usually male); third, paint my intentions as harmless or, better yet, useless ("just here to help the women and children learn how to sew"). When in doubt, mention babies. If things get tense, let out a little fart, or an amusing burp, to bring things to a human level. No one can resist the laughter a well-placed fart can inspire. Or, as Trungpa taught us, "Never be afraid to play the fool."

My approach works smoothly. With the subtle flick of a commanding officer's hand, a bevy of young soldiers—sitting on the shiny, new metal barrier-arm that hugs the border with surety, now sunken into the earth by fresh concrete, strong enough to hold the weight of their collective fears and the recently-added burden of hope—lower their guns and let us in. The Rhino is waiting on the other side. Last time, she picked me up in Kigali. This time, she cannot cross the border without a lot of difficulty and drawing unwanted attention. We smile and hug, a familiarity born from sharing my most profound moment of loss. Grief bonds people like nothing else.

We spend the next two days in Goma, meeting some of the better-known women's groups, learning about their work and current needs. Life here has improved for everyone, concerning infrastructure and regular access to goods, but the overall situation is still sketchy, and strangers rarely make eye contact. Checking into the "Foreigner Hotel," still the only licensed hotel in town, is smoother than last year. The room I was sleeping in when the death call came looms ominously at the end of the hallway. I make sure to request a different room on the other side of the grounds. If I keep feeling loss everywhere I look, I'll never have the strength to get through the challenging days ahead. I put Grandma to rest in the back of my mind.

We visit a rehabilitation center for raped women and girls, many of them struggling from severe mutilation, each rebel faction with their preferred way to maim and mark their territory. In this war, rebel armies send messages to each other, notes about their power grabs carved with bone-quills on skin-canvases, machetes against lips. Government soldiers answer back in smoke signals from burned villages, reusing the same human canvases like scratch paper. Yet, somehow, these small, breathing messengers continue to live, battle scars and all. They've dragged their used bodies, carrying their broken baby girls, thousands of miles to find safe refuge. Thousands of miles to sit on a cot, in a tent near the lake, drink Coca-Cola, and talk to me.

I record their stories, touch their wounds, and witness their pain. I have been training for this work since my childhood days with the trees. Listening medicine. I become a tree and, sentence by sentence, swallow their grief. I can offer no other solace and, with no clear way to make good on it, I promise to hold their pain, to carry their stories with me when I go and to share them with the world. If I were in their place, that promise might make me feel better, might even help me to let go of the burden of survival. "I'll carry it now," I whisper, leaving out the fact that nobody in the West wants to listen to me either. I am twenty-seven, and my soapbox is tiny, the weight of their stories enormous.

Last night, I lay awake in the dark, the overhead fan offering a slight breeze as company. Listening to far-off gunshots and footsteps running in formation. As if waiting for thunder after a lightning strike, I started counting after each explosion, convincing myself that there was a correlation between the perceived lapse of time and my physical safety. I waited for something to happen, each outside noise confirming my fears. But the only thing that happened, eventually, was the dawn. Orange and gold, just like it is at home, just like it is everywhere. Even here, in the middle of the world's most horrific war, there are such sparks of luminosity.

In our Sangha, we had Sunday school, just like the Christian churches, which we called Bodhi School. We read stories and enacted plays about the great Buddhist saints: Milarepa, the Murderer; Marpa, the Translator; Naropa, the Enlightened. With each yarn spun, significance was placed on their eventually learning compassion and generosity, on outfoxing the deceptions of materialism, on building merit for future lives. When someone in our community died, we all went to the Sukhāvatī. Friends and family meditated with the body for three days until the soul was ready to pass into the Bardo. We would collectively watch the decomposition of the corpse into rigor mortis, amidst incense, mantras, and rituals, and then burn the body on an open fire pit. My earliest memories are thus steeped in witnessing suffering and interacting with death. Over breakfast, my mother would read the obituaries out loud.

"Oh, look, Chani. So-and-so died yesterday," she'd chime into my sleepy reveries, not that we ever knew the person. "Hit by a bus when they were least expecting...taken by cancer...bested by AIDS. You know, we could both die today too. So what are you gonna do with your precious day today, just in case it's your last?" It would be years before I understood this to be a unique household conversation.

This morning, however, over a breakfast of French fries, eggs, and too-strong instant Nescafé, The Gazelle and I share an uncomfortable chuckle about our non-deaths from last night's firefight, confirming with the hotel staff that there had been an attempted ambush at a nearby army outpost, confirming that it wasn't my imagination; confirming that neither of us slept. We're heading north today, through rebel-held territory, far from the "comforts" of Goma. If "anxious" were a perfume, we'd both be wearing it.

Driving across Goma to the airstrip, the road under our tires is made entirely of lava rock from the massive volcanic eruption two years earlier. It makes squeaky, almost concerning sounds against the car's rubber tires, like every rotation is breaking something. Molten lava charred a mile-wide path straight through town, taking out half the airport and covering everything in soot and jagged rocks. Last year, as my heart was drowning in sorrow, these streets were still smoldering, parts of the city off-limits for the glowing, active lava flows. Today, they've all hardened, beaten into submission by thousands of newly-displaced feet. Some buildings that were burned beyond salvation lay still untouched, black monuments to nature's awesome ability to render us to ash. Most streets though manage to function in an emaciated way, serving as access paths and conduits to improvised housing and markets. Commerce, like lava, cannot be stopped.

The town's main square is packed with widows and orphans, sleeping in rows, waiting for a share of food passed out daily by the humanitarian missions and the local churches. Little kids are wandering around in rags, barefoot, unattended, though most of them are working in some way or another. They scavenge lava piles for food and salable goods. They carry wood and water on their heads. They bang on the windows of our car, hands outstretched, eyes vacant, hoping for some kindness, some relief from their hunger and loss and confusion. My spirit shatters at the sight of all those childhoods destroyed, and I bite my lip to conquer immediate tears. I don't want The Gazelle to see me cry. I don't want our driver to think I'm weak or, even worse, too overtly female. The Gazelle was in Rwanda during the genocide ten years ago and lost some dear friends, butchered in her own house, escaping with her life by sheer happenstance. When she told me about it, how her colleagues were murdered in their homes, she barely flinched, eyes dry as bone. It's not that she's numb, or even hardened; just that she's learned to control her emotions to carry on with her critical work, and I must do the same.

I focus my thoughts instead on the journey we are just beginning. Keeping my eyes on the horizon, I will the tears back inside my body, catch my held breath. We share the ride out of town in silence; tiny finger smudges on the window the only evidence of the plight disappearing behind us; no way of knowing that the refugee crisis laying ahead will dwarf what we've just witnessed. I tell myself to remain open-hearted, not to shut down or be consumed by such profound pain. So much of this insanity is out of my control. I begin to practice *Tonglen,* a meditation technique taught to me by my mom. I inhale the insatiable sorrow of the Congolese people, and exhale compassion and love. While it helps to slow my heartbeat, it feels about as effective as dropping blades of grass off a tall building hoping to create shade. I do it anyway because at least it's reminding me to breathe. The driver says the rest of the road to the airport is "clear," as if reporting on traffic rather than the movement of troops. We are about to board a small plane to Bunia, high in the northeast corner of the country. A horrific massacre took place near there last year, and the United Nations peacekeeping mission (MONUC) has established a security operation with an operating airport. It's the deepest I have ever gone into an active war zone, and we've both been reminded, repeatedly, that our safety cannot be guaranteed. The Eagle told me before the trip that she has contacts within MONUC and will do her best to get us evacuated if the fighting intensifies. *What are the odds that will happen in the next three days?*

In my right pocket, I obsessively finger several folded twenty-dollar bills, set aside to pay the driver, separated from the large wad of cash, thousands of dollars, that I've hidden deep in my luggage. Activists in Bunia are counting on that money and, if we are robbed in transit, I don't want anything of real value on my person. Though, realistically, if we're held up out here, I will most likely not recover any of my luggage after I'm dead. As we approach the airport, the tummy-butterflies begin their ritual dance, preparing for the unknown, the chance to meet contacts in Bunia face-to-face. I have heard about the flight north and how spectacular this country's rainforests appear from the sky, something few people get to see. The Gazelle is also planning a reunion in Bunia with an old friend working within MONUC and seems eager for the journey to begin. Neither of us has ever been north of Goma, so neither of us has any idea what's in store.

▪ ▪ ▪

He can't be more than eighteen years old, but the semiautomatic weapon in his hands and the wild look in his eyes make him seem older. I hear him yelling far behind us and know something is wrong, even as the words he shouts are unfamiliar. Like a toddler caught in the act, I slip the tiny digital camera back into my front pocket, turning to profess my ignorance, arms raised high. "Donne Moi l'appareil photo!" *Give me the camera!* he demands, spitting.

"Quelle photo?" I reply in bad French, just as I notice The Gazelle is still holding a camcorder in her hand. He shoots me the glance my grandma reserved for when she *knew* I was lying. I can feel the drops of sweat rolling down his face and smell his unwashed uniform as he draws even closer, eyes raging, raising his machine gun directly in line with my nose. He motions with the nozzle, as if the weapon is an extension of his arm, and, in a rapid dialect, orders us to move. We walk hesitantly, The Gazelle apologizing profusely in her native French tongue, toward a dilapidated wooden building entirely out of sight from the ancient, twin-engine plane that contains all of our belongings, our passports, and all that hidden cash. When our aircraft stopped earlier in Butembo, we had gotten off to a crowd of smiling children and a sense of calm. But now we are in Beni, in the Ituri province, and no one is calm. We are in the middle of the Congo, in a town recently taken over by a rebel faction, and have just committed a major faux pas by taking photographs of their operations. The Gazelle and I glance at each other only once during the long walk away from the landing strip to the shack, gun to our backs, and it's clear from that look that we both know we're fucked.

Just inside the wooden building, two desks, supporting several soldiers, stop us in our tracks. "C'est très grave ce que tu as fait." *What you have done is very serious*, a solemn-faced man chides, upon hearing a quick report of our transgressions. He speaks slowly, as if he's not bothered to negotiate, and appears to be the one in charge.

"Nous sommes tellement désolés." *We are so sorry,* The Gazelle offers, continuing to excuse our mistake in her perfect French. I keep my eyes down, unchallenging, energetically prostrating. The conversation quickly becomes a raucous argument, as more soldiers jump in to offer their opinions on possible consequences, The Gazelle doing her best to fend off questions with submissive tones and innocent tenors.

I only understand about half of what is said. My mind floating away from the words to take in the room, count the number of guns, the number of possible exits—seven guns, five men, and two women, both of whom are writing frantically in large ledgers. The only real exit is the way we came in, behind us. There's a room in the back, but my instincts tell me that's not a place I want to get trapped. Outside, a rooster crows and the fear in its cry mixes with my chalky saliva. Perhaps today is his day to die as well. My throat tightens as I imagine the many different, equally-horrible outcomes of this preventable scenario. The stories of the women we met yesterday come to life, but, this time, I am the protagonist. I grasp both my arms, often the first limb to be chopped off, in a way that feels desperate and defensive. Looking down at my shoes, attempting to be as non-threatening as possible, I notice that The Gazelle's cotton pants are trembling. She's also terrified, and that freaks me out even more. I have to think of something, employ my tested strategies, and diffuse this situation. With the argument still raging, I brainstorm ways to appease our captors, calm them down, get them on our side. I'm acutely aware of the fact that our plane, with all of our essential possessions, has probably taken off by now. If not, then our lifeline to the outside world is quickly slipping away, and we need to move.

Surprising even me, my paralysis thaws and I spring to life, responding to their demands that I hand over my camera with a friendly lesson on digital cameras, which are evidently still new around here. "You see, this is a special type of camera. Ç'est Nouveau! Il n'y a pas de film!" I explain in slow French, laughing at my own mistakes. Using humor to diffuse their anger, innocence to appease their confusion, wondering if I should try for a little fart at this point, not sure if I can relax enough, afraid I might actually shit my pants. "I can erase those photos by pushing this trashcan button, la petite poubelle içi. Et voila! Au revoir! Bye bye!" My smile falls on deadpan faces. *Have I lost my mind?* I am clearly not amusing anyone, least of all The Gazelle. She shoots me a confused look, and I can't tell if it's for butchering her language or for the stunt that I'm not pulling off. She has already relinquished her camcorder and tapes, equipment we desperately need for our work in Bunia, and I don't fully understand why I'm so determined to hold onto my cheap handheld camera. Perhaps I am trying to hold onto proof that this nightmare war is real, to find out a way, someday, to make people care. And then I feel it. Inside my pants pocket, the corner of the last remaining twenty-dollar bill, poking me gently in the thigh.

Hoping that this one piece of printed paper is our key out of this fear-box, I plop the money down in front of the women with ledgers, like a desperate gambler betting his last. The Gazelle lets out an exasperated sigh, giving me a pained look, head slightly shaking as if to say, "What took you so fucking long?" An unmistakable shift in the commanding officer's tone sends the saliva rushing back into my mouth....

The plane is still there. I meet the glares from the pilots with my best look of gratitude for not abandoning us and feel their annoyance over the intercom as they apologize for the long delay. Not one person from the plane spoke up or came to see where we had been hauled off to, not one bystander, though most of them are foreign workers just like us; a painful reminder that it's everyone for themselves in war. We sit quietly at first, listening to the whirl of the plane's propellers, taking in the stunning views below, thick, lush forests as far as the eye can see, each lost in her own terrifying version of what could have been. I catch my held breath again, just as little stars enter my vision telling me that I am close to blacking out. *Just keep breathing,* I command myself.

Astonishing that it only took twenty bucks to secure our freedom, when back home in Colorado that would barely cover the cost of a decent meal. The Gazelle and I agree that it's best if we don't recount this part of the trip to anyone…ever…especially not our bosses (mine being The Mountain Goat and The Eagle, hers being The Tortoise). She admits that she got in trouble before, traveling with The Tortoise in Afghanistan, after accidentally taking a photo of a soldier. I admit that I almost got thrown out of Cambodia for taking pictures at the border with Vietnam. We both knew better. The mistake was ours, and it almost cost us everything. I squish my face up against the window like a gnat, the cold plastic providing some form to my inner free fall. Surveying the jungles below, I wonder what else I will have to learn to forget about the Congo.

▪ ▪ ▪

"Shit!" The Gazelle says loudly in the dimly-lit bar. "We're already past curfew." It's our second night in Bunia and, through The Gazelle's friend in MONUC, we've gotten incredible access to the inner workings of a wide-scale UN operation, including how they let off steam to have fun. "Join us and enjoy some music and beer," her friend encouraged, "Just don't stay out past curfew." He'd arranged beds for us at a local nunnery, run by an Italian nun who had lived in Bunia for decades. While her tiny frame looked entirely out of place, her home was considered the safest place for foreigners to stay, her reputation garnering respect from the locals. There are no hotels in Bunia. Tomorrow, we will be visiting Camp Aero, and, even after four years of working on human rights in armed conflict, it will be my first time inside a refugee camp. The vision of myself that I first saw in Cambodia at age eighteen, finally being realized. But, first, we were gonna have to get back to the nunnery from this closing-down bar without losing our heads.

All the other patrons seem to have had a safe place to retreat to nearby, leaving just The Gazelle and me standing out in front of the bar, eyeing the long walk back through the center of town. The road, suddenly abandoned and only partially lit, looms ominously. But what choice do we have? There are no taxis in Bunia. In Boulder, I would feel nothing but a sense of calm and peace to be walking quiet midnight streets, but, here, every shadow and dog bark feels like a warning. It is probably only a ten-minute walk to the nunnery, but it's daunting as hell.

Eventually, we come to an empty crossroads, save for a sandbag bunker that has a small slit about head-level. As we draw closer, I can see the end of a machine gun pointing through the slit directly at us. "Hello?" I try in English, hoping it will make us seem less threatening and more out of place. A tall, olive-skinned soldier emerges from the bunker, face serious, and asks us a question. Only nothing he says makes sense to me. He is not speaking French. The Gazelle, miraculously, responds. I have no idea what she says, but she explains to me that they are speaking Arabic because he is Moroccan, which she speaks from her native Algeria. His expression lightens at her reply, and he smiles as he continues to talk, The Gazelle meekly explaining that we got stuck out after curfew without a safe path home.

Just then, another soldier emerges from the bunker. A short, brown-skinned man approaches, speaking a little English. His accent is familiar though and, without much thought, I ask him, "Tapai Nepali hunuhuncha?" *Are you Nepalese?*

"Ho!" he replies, shocked, his head wagging a familiar greeting. None of us can believe that I speak his language as well and, for a brief moment of mutual, unspoken awe, we look around at each other thinking: *What are the odds?*

Both soldiers agree to escort us back to the nunnery, which we can practically see from here. Along the way, the Nepalese soldier asks us to translate some of his needs to the local boys who are hanging around. He wants them to go and buy him cigarettes and beer, as he can't leave his post. Neither of the stationed soldiers speak French. *What the fuck are a Nepalese and a Moroccan doing keeping the peace in Bunia?* I wonder, just as I am sure they are wondering: *What the fuck are these Western women doing on this road in the middle of the night?* The Gazelle and I later marvel about how they were the perfect guardian angels, tailored just to us, making sure we got home safely. It's a complete 180 from our last run-in with soldiers after breaking the rules, and it restores my sense of confidence and calm.

UN "Blue helmet" peacekeeper emerging from his bunker in Bunia, DRC, 2004.

UN Tank patrols a major crossroad in Bunia, DRC, 2004.

The next morning, I am up with the sun, nervous for some reason, a lifelong goal about to be fulfilled. At one point, I thought I'd become a doctor and work for the Red Cross or Doctors Without Borders, but my unique talents lent themselves more to writing and listening than to suturing and injecting. I was never sure how I was going to write or listen my way into a job that works in refugee camps. Nevertheless, here I am, and it's downright exciting. As I understand it, there are several impromptu women's groups that have emerged in the camp to address the specific needs of women and girls. They are expecting us, and I am ready. Before I leave my room, I take a minute to sit in meditation, to feel the enormity of this moment and to prepare myself for the large-scale suffering that we will undoubtedly encounter. "Death comes without warning. This body shall be a corpse. At that time, the Dharma is my only help. I shall practice it with exertion." The words echo in my mind with my mother's voice.

I am back at the breakfast table, and she is asking me what I am going to do with my one, precious day. "I'm going to alleviate some suffering," I promise to her spirit, knowing she is proud of my resolve, even 8,000 miles away. I take a moment before I leave my room to mentally put on an invisible Kasung uniform, as I was trained to do in my youth, to ready myself for what I am about to witness and, with a "strong back and a soft heart," to hold fast to the improbable vision of "victory over war." I feel as if I've been training for this moment since I was eight.

Camp Aero is enormous. Twenty thousand people living side by side—all needing water and shelter, food and toilets—is a sight to behold. People are milling about everywhere, carrying water and firewood, selling food and goods, talking and washing. We are led through the crowds, all eyes taking in our white skin, our light hair, our well-constructed clothes. We are aliens from another world, one we will eventually return to, one they have no access to. I feel the distance between us distinctly, wondering how we are going to bridge such a vast divide. What can I possibly say, or offer, to make things better for them? Suddenly, I'm struck by a profound sense of imposter syndrome. *What am I doing here?* I interrogate myself. *What did you think you were going to be able to do? How did you envision piercing though this much suffering?* It's overwhelming and nearly paralyzing. At least The Gazelle is a lawyer and can work towards creating concrete change for these folks. I have little to offer but my attention and care, a bit like putting a cheap Band-Aid on a gunshot wound. I continue walking but my confidence is waning.

We are led into a crowded tent, equipped with dozens of chairs, arranged in a square. Most of the seats are taken and, behind them, women have packed into rows of standing room. There are three empty chairs at the front, or at least the entire audience is staring in that direction. The Gazelle and I both sit down, with our host taking the last open seat. She introduces The Gazelle first and then me, essentially saying that we are women who work with other women to solve problems. They are all pleased we've come and mainly want to share their stories with us so that we will better understand the unique suffering that Congolese women face. While we are both acutely aware of the atrocities they have suffered, I know there is power in telling one's story and power in witnessing that strength. Several women have been chosen to share their personal tales of woe with us, and I steel myself for the inevitable sadness and anger it will provoke. One by one, they begin to share....

After nearly an hour of testimony—my taking notes rapidly, for no real reason except to seem more official, to let them know that someone is recording the wrongs they've endured—Mary enters the room. I should say that her smile enters the room first, reminding me of The Dreamer, big as the moon and just as infectious. Both of her arms have been cut off at the elbows, and her face has deep keloid scars, signs of her violent run-ins with more than one rebel faction. Despite that, she is laughing when she comes in, as if to an inside joke. We lock eyes immediately and, just as happened many times before, with Maria and Wayan, Seema and Pratima, we instantly recognize one another's spirit. As she shares her incredibly tragic story, one in which she is orphaned by watching her family murdered, after which she was raped and brutalized so many times her uterus falls out of her body. There is an inexplicable lightness to her, a joy that cannot be diminished no matter how dark her tale gets. I am fascinated and deeply impressed by her.

After Mary's testimony is done, we wander around the tent seeing evidence of their skill-training workshops, providing girls with income-generating work. They are learning to weave and cook and sew. *But what about the girls like Mary?* I think. *What happens to the ones with no hands and no family to care for them*? Just then, Mary comes over, surrounded by a gaggle of giggling girls, curious to know anything about me. They ask me a dozen questions and, when I say that I am from the United States, Mary's face brightens. "Oh! Do you know my friend, Angelina?" She asks innocently. I am sure that I do not, as there are hundreds of millions of people in my home country, and I don't know a single one named Angelina. "Oh, that's too bad," she says, shrugging. "I was hoping you could give her something from me," she admits.

"Well, I could try," I respond, thinking maybe I could mail a letter or make a phone call for her. I have been desperately searching for some way to support these brave girls, and maybe I can help by contacting her friend; it's the least I can do. "Tell me her full name," I offer. "And pass me whatever you want to give her and I will do my best to deliver it."

"Really?" She perks up, her smile enough encouragement to do what I can. "Her name is Angelina Jolie, she says, and I'd like you to give her this." With that, she throws her half-arms around me, squeezing tight with her elbows and burying her head in my neck. It's one of the best hugs I've ever received, busting open my heart. It might be all that she has to offer but it is more than enough.

"Okay," I laugh, embracing her back, "I will try," knowing full well that the chances of my hugging Angelina Jolie are slim to none. The Gazelle later confirms that the actor and U.N. ambassador was recently here, visiting with these girls. I don't own a T.V. and rarely watch movies, except on long flights, but anyone who's made it to Bunia is legit in my book.

Leaving Camp Aero shortly after, I promise to return the next day to visit Mary and her friends and make some crafts with them. If I have nothing else to offer, I can at least provide my time and my attention, get to know more about their lives. The Gazelle and I return to the nunnery exhausted and overfull of emotions. She heads off to dinner with friends, while I turn in for an early night, clicking off the lights before 9:00 p.m.

The sound of a cell phone ringing wakes me in the dark but, at first, I am not sure whose phone it is. The Gazelle's sleeping form is in the bed across from me. I finally gain enough clarity of mind to root around for the ringing object. "Hello?" I say groggily.

"Oh, thank God." The Eagle's voice is crisp and concerned. "Are you awake? I've been calling and calling," she says quickly. "It's not safe anymore. You and The Gazelle are leaving Bunia now. There's a plane at the airport waiting. Get your stuff and get moving. I'll call ahead and say you're on your way." I can't quite grasp what is happening and try to probe for more information, but she's already hung up.

"Wake up!" I say loudly, rising to shake The Gazelle's sleeping form. "Get up. We've gotta go."

"What?" she says, confused.

"I don't know why, but we've gotta hustle."

"Shit!" she says. "Okay. Let me find out what's going on. She rises quickly and leaves the room, phone to her ear. Before I can even finish packing, she's back, and she's moving double-time. "The rebels breached an important security point outside Bunia. The U.N. has ordered all non-essential employees to evacuate."

"What about Mary?" I ask innocently, knowing the answer.

"What? Who?" She snaps. "Come on, move!"

I put Mary out of my mind, finish shoving items into my bag, double-check the room, and head into the nunnery courtyard. It's a chaotic scene, with other aid workers running around, most on the phone, packing their things, making exit plans. Some have been stationed here for months and have practically moved in. The Gazelle and I are in a car within minutes, speeding to the airstrip. Along the way, we pass Camp Aero and I begin to cry, no longer caring what anyone thinks. I want to take them all with me, all the women working hard on sowing seeds of peace and healing, all the innocent children who have already lost so much, now at risk of losing everything again. I feel torn into pieces. I have no choice but to get on that plane yet am nauseated at the privilege that allows me to do so.

Two children stand outside of Camp Aero, which held 20,000 displaced people in 2004.

Within minutes, we are sitting in an old Russian twin-engine plane, preparing for takeoff. I lean against the plastic window again and stare out at the scene behind us. I will not fulfill my promise to return, nor ever see Mary again, but her exceptional hug will always stay with me. In a sense, she is me; brave and undeterred, even in the most painful of life circumstances. I draw on her infectious courage, infuse myself with her unbreakable attitude, and turn to face my future, just as she and the others must bravely turn to face the outcome of yet another impending battle.

I realize that it's not what I will have to learn to forget about the Congo, but what I will have to vow to remember that matters.

Chapter Eleven

MARRIED TO TIBET

Not long after my trip to northern DRC, I found myself saying goodbye to Nairobi and my dear friends, The Eagle, Maki, and John. A Kenyan woman named Susan had also looked after me for the nine months I'd been in East Africa, cooking and cleaning to support my non-stop work schedule. She held me to her bosom and we both cried like family when saying goodbye. In my final conversation with The Eagle, she confirmed that the staff member we'd hired to run our new grantmaking program had tendered her resignation while I was in the DRC. Somehow, using her raptor-ish cunning and grace, she'd convinced the new employee that UAF-Africa was not the right place for her to shine and, in a non-confrontational way, had solved the conflict that I could not see around; had found that third option and dissolved the problem. Even with all of my years of training and studying conflict transformation, I had much left to learn from The Eagle. I was beginning to regret my decision to leave.

The Eagle, who had a lasting marriage and three beautiful children, could see that I was torn. Half of my heart wanted to be selfish and nurture my new love with Phill, while the other half wanted to stay. "Go!" The Eagle proclaimed directly, almost screeching it at me, sensing my conundrum. "Get married, have babies, find joy, and know love." She added, "When you are ready, come back to us. This work will always be here; our battles are long from over." And with her permission, and invitation to return, I dared my fragile heart to take a chance on personal happiness, no matter how ugly or painful that may end up. I left Nairobi the next day—Njeri the traveler—vowing to be back, knowing it would not be anytime soon, and forever indebted for all the invaluable lessons it had provided me.

When I arrived home to Boulder, Phill and I moved into a larger apartment in The Bat Cave, which, for me, meant moving across the hallway from my usual spot. The house was full of anti-war activists decrying the policies of a newly-reelected George W. Bush, the outcome of that election being decided by a torn Supreme Court, sowing distrust in the American voting process. Shannon had also just returned to live in The Bat Cave. She had barely survived a car bombing in Baghdad, which destroyed a hotel next to hers and killed some of her close colleagues. We leaned on each other, and the entire activist community, to help process all that we'd seen and experienced in the realities of war…and how to reconcile that with a daily life in Boulder, Colorado, one of the wealthiest towns in one of the wealthiest countries in the world.

I did some consulting work for UAF's headquarters, stepping in to help The Mountain Goat and The Sparrow manage the enormous amount of funding requests out of Sri Lanka and Indonesia, as well as Malaysia and Thailand, in the wake of the 2004 tsunami, which claimed 230,000 lives across fifteen countries. The tsunami wiped out the entire northern peninsula of Sumatra, leaving much of Aceh and its separatist war (and most of the network The Sparrow and I had connected with) simply gone. The giant wave then devastated war-weary Sri Lanka, adding more death, poverty and disease to an already-festering conflict. The aftermath of the tsunami was tragic, amplified by the confusion of war, and UAF's existing contacts proved invaluable to getting resources into the hands of women quickly. We worked around the clock to distribute as much support as we could, our budget dwarfed by the immense need the tsunami left behind.

After helping respond to that crisis, I didn't technically have a job, nor did I want one. I was twenty-seven and burnt out after five intense years with UAF. I needed time and space to digest and decompress from all that I'd seen and done. I needed to be un-contactable and I needed a good night's sleep. But I found it impossible to rest in Boulder. Phill wanted time with his fiancée after nearly a year apart, and all I wanted to do was leave again.

The Mountain Goat and The Sparrow, along with a packed office of new employees and interns, were working away, just down the street, glued to their laptops, staying one step ahead of the news. Leaving The Mountain Goat had been the hardest decision of all, as if I were abandoning her to carry on with all the dreams we had envisioned together. Of all my mentors, she had become the most like family and I missed working with her. It soon became clear that if I was going to break my workaholic cycle—and figure out how to sleep again—I was going to have to go far, far away. *But where? And how?*

The answer to that conundrum came quicker than I anticipated. As soon as I asked those questions out loud, two things happened that gave me answers to both. First, Phill and I rented the movie *Tibet: Cry of the Snow Lion*, about the Chinese government's horrific occupation of Tibet, and the undying and unlikely hope that Tibetans still maintained for their basic freedoms. Even though I had been raised in a Tibetan Buddhist sect in the West, led by a Tibetan refugee, and had adopted a Tibetan brother who had barely escaped Tibet with his life, it was surprising to learn how little I knew about the Chinese occupation of Tibet before watching that film. Phill was also shocked and weeping by the end. That led us to talk about my Tibetan "brother from another mother," who I will call Romeo, and what I knew about his journey across the world to Boulder and into our family when he was just eighteen and I was an awkward thirteen-year-old. Romeo was married to another Tibetan refugee, who I shall call Juliet, who he had actually met once during his harrowing escape across the Himalayas and a second time, coincidentally, years later, at a dinner party in Colorado. They had a small wedding ceremony the week after re-meeting, my father acting as both the marriage officiate and the stand-in parental figure. It just so happened that Romeo and Juliet were having a Tibetan New Year celebration the following weekend, and neither of them had met my new fiancée nor seen my face in over a year. That gathering was the second thing that oriented our paths towards Tibet. Once all the momos had been devoured and all the tsampa thrown into the air, Romeo and Juliet announced that they were going back to Tibet, after fifteen years in exile, this time as full American citizens. They were leaving in three months and were taking a small group of others with them, including a documentary film team. Romeo announced that there were a few spaces left on the trip and, before the party ended, Phill and I signed up to go.

A couple of short months later, we were packing new hiking boots into new Gor-Tex backpacks, prepping for a month of hard travel, mainly camping, around the Tibetan Plateau, with Romeo and Juliet as our trusty guides.

In the end, there were ten of us, in addition to Romeo and Juliet, who boarded flights bound for Chengdu, China, with the hopes of making it into the highly-guarded Tibet Autonomous Region (TAR), where the ancient city of Lhasa is located. Even though they had earned American citizenship, Romeo and Juliet were cautious and alert when it came to Chinese authority figures and extra careful not to break any laws. It was their first time since leaving Tibet to have the chance to see their families and we did not want it to be their last. There is no greater pain than being forcibly separated from one's people and I was looking forward to witnessing Romeo hug his mom and his siblings again, who he hadn't touched since he was seventeen years old.

Part of me thought of Urgent Action Fund and how little access they'd had in Tibet, wishing I could bring translated outreach materials with me. But I wasn't there to be political, and wouldn't dare involve Romeo, Juliet, nor their families in any such drama. I would remain as touristy as possible, follow all the rules, and just observe Tibet as she revealed her magnificence to us.

Going through the extensive paperwork for permits to enter the TAR, I was a bit concerned that my name might pop up on some no-fly list. But, for as much as I'd moved in and out of war zones, I had never given up my anonymity. We each got our permits approved easily after a few smog-filled days in Chengdu, and then we were on a small plane bound for Lhasa. The views from 30,000 feet, as the Himalayas begin to ascend, reaching upward towards you, eventually giving way to the Tibetan Plateau, were breathtaking, unlike any landscape I had seen before.

The reunion with Romeo's family was much more emotional than any of us anticipated. The raw and heart-wrenching moment when a mother, who, for years, believed her son to be dead, clutches him in her arms again turned me inside out. Romeo sobbed and sobbed, unfiltered, as he hugged his grandmother and grandfather, both in their eighties, and embraced his younger brother and sister, who were infants when he'd fled. Their family reunion pierced all of our hearts and laid the foundation for what would be one of the most magical and memorable months of my life.

During our week acclimatizing and exploring in Lhasa, we stayed in an upscale hotel near the Jokhang Temple, the center of spiritual life in Lhasa. One could walk out the front doors of our hotel and right into the stream of people doing Kora (circumambulation), and once around three times, walk straight back into the hotel, placing us smack dab in the center of Tibetan cultural life, known as the Barkhor.

When you are in the Barkhor, you have the feeling of being in old Tibet, and Tibetan faces outnumber the Han Chinese ones, but that section of the city was small and obviously shrinking. As we drove the considerable distance from the airport to downtown Lhasa, we passed evidence of modern-day China everywhere, clearly clashing with the architecture of ancient Tibet. Such clashes were apparent on every street in Lhasa, as the old and ornate were co-opted, remodeled, and overpowered by the shiny and new.

Visiting the holy sites around Lhasa meant security checks, cameras, and eyes monitoring your every move. The Dalai Lama's iconic winter palace, the Potala, had been transformed into a tourist trap, one that failed to include a single photo or mention of the exiled leader, whose home we were treating like a museum to an extinct culture, despite evidence of that culture holding onto its shrinking existence just outside the Potala's doors. We passed Tibetan women and children begging on the streets, their clothes in rags, their cries overwhelmingly ignored by their occupiers; their lives valued less than the cost of a photo in front of what was once a marvel of the Tibetan world. It was like being in actual Tibet and visiting the theme-park version of Tibet at the same time. Thousands of tourists per year being gaslighted into not believing, or even discussing, the cultural genocide they could see with their own eyes.

As we walked around Lhasa—and we did a lot of walking that first week, visiting monasteries, hospitals, and supply stores for our journey north—people were fascinated with Phill's tattoos. Not only staring at him, captivated, but grabbing his arms to get a better look, with one older woman using her own spit to try and wipe them off. Phill's gentle demeanor took it all in stride, both of us knowing that, if this is how the big-city folk responded to his tattoos, the remote villages were going to see him as a true stranger in a strange land. And that's how it felt, driving out of Lhasa, passing smaller and smaller townships and villages, modern Chinese buildings giving way to low stone and earth homes, like we were entering a world that had existed long before the arrival of Western civilizations and witnessing a people whose way of life, while under threat, needed nothing from us save for recognition and equal treatment. That is to say, they clearly needed the outside world to speak up for their dwindling rights and basic freedoms, but they certainly didn't need anyone to try and save them from their way of living.

We hadn't even been in Lhasa two days when Phill and I shared a wild idea with the group. Since Romeo and Juliet, married in the U.S. now for seven years, had never had a traditional Tibetan wedding and, since neither Phill nor I were interested in a traditional American wedding…why not throw a joint wedding in Lhasa, at the month's end, inviting everyone we meet and like along our travels, as well as Romeo and Juliet's family and friends? The group was all for it, and not just because they would experience a Tibetan wedding ceremony, but because it meant we had a big party to look forward to; and we were quickly learning that no one parties harder than Tibetans.

Once Romeo and Juliet were on board with the plan—Romeo's mom was smitten with her new daughter-in-law and the chance to welcome her properly into the family—and before we left Lhasa, we booked a venue, sent out word to both families far and wide, and were measured for custom-made wedding attire. Romeo would wear the customary dress of Juliet's region of Tibet, since her father had passed away, while Phill and I would wear whatever the family dressed us in and try not to look ridiculous, nor too appropriative. With wedding wheels in motion, and our own travel supplies prepared, we left Lhasa heading north through the province of Ü-Tsang, where Romeo grew up.

The weeks we spent traveling around Ü-Tsang, camping, hiking, visiting villages, and interacting with nomadic communities, were both enlightening and heartbreaking. The people we met were fiercely proud of their Tibetan culture and their exiled leadership, even if that meant presenting one face to their Chinese occupiers by day and another to their children by night. It was forbidden to teach the Tibetan language or to possess any imagery of the fourteenth Dalai Lama. Undeterred, household after household showed us how they used brushes dipped in water to teach their children Tibetan script, which then disappeared by morning; and they showed us their secret places of worship, their underground shrines to their exiled spiritual leader. Nothing the Chinese had done, in over fifty years of occupation—an estimated death of over a million Tibetan dissidents and innocents, hundreds of religious institutions and thousands of texts destroyed, the forced sterilization and reeducation/relocation camps of the nomads—had succeeded in killing the devotion and spirit of the Tibetans we encountered. I was simultaneously inspired and appalled by all they had survived—and were still enduring—often smiling and singing their way through collectively.

Our local guides, as well as the many nomads we picked up and traveled with, sang constantly. They sang as our bus drove along the one available road, and often off-road; they sang as they pitched our camp for the night, as they made a fire from scratch, and then cooked a delicious meal over it. Then they sang while they cleaned up and prepped for bed and sang around the evening campfire as they passed homemade chang (Tibetan barley beer). It seemed our traveling companions knew hundreds of different songs, those for work and those for play, for expressing joy and for emoting sorrow. They sang out loud and proud, voices filling canyons with long musical notes, yak herders calling to each other in song from one mountaintop to the other. As if song alone was a cord that tied them to their diminishing culture, the voice always with us and accessible, un-imprisonable. There is a well-known group of nuns who were imprisoned in Lhasa as teenagers and kept each other's spirits alive during years of torturous abuse in the infamous Drapchi Prison, through the nonviolent act of singing. The "singing nuns," as they became known, bravely recorded their protest songs on cassette tapes that were smuggled out of the prison and then played a million times over by Tibetans in exile, as proof of the undiminishable spirit of resistance inside Tibet. You can break a people's history, steal their land, brainwash their children, but here was a subtle, vibrating defiance; song by song, note by note, Tibetans were kindling their heritage, holding on to something deeper than their captors could hear or understand.

As part of my training in Buddhist summer camp, I was taught to use my voice to move other campers across a parade field in military-style drill, as part of the practice of Kasungship. With call-and-response songs, we would fill the valley of the Rocky Mountains in northern Colorado with chants for ending war and waking up the world. We would yell all day until our throats went dry and then, at night, we would gather around a fire and sing. Those starry nights in Tibet, gathered around a fire, sharing song after song, felt familiar to my child-heart; the deep connections with our hosts forged in flames and smoke, song, and endless laughter.

In addition to song, it was the color resistance that struck me the most. I had grown up with Tibetan prayer flags hanging in houses or the backyards of Boulder, but I had never considered their power before. Here, amidst the oppressive black uniforms and mandatory white, tiled buildings of the communist government, were bold signs of Tibet's colorful and improbable spirit. From mountaintop to mountaintop, massive gardens of flapping colors bloomed, reminding everyone that this was Tibet, with its bright yellows and reds and blues that could not be subdued. It reminded me of The Butterfly's subtle activism in Zimbabwe and her parting words to me. "Never lose your color, not for anyone or anything." Phill and I hung as many sets of flags as we could, as did Romero and Juliet, who had both lost so much since fleeing into exile, and we shouted slogans of freedom and victory over war, leaving drops of radical color all along our route.

Halfway through our month, we reached a monastery in the far north, surrounded by a fragrant and ancient pine forest. We hadn't seen many trees in Lhasa, which sits at 11,995 feet above sea level, but here was a magical forest, special trees that had been looked after and cared for, over centuries, by others who could hear and speak with trees. They were the happiest trees I'd ever come across. Phill and I spent hours walking through the forest, following a well-worn circumambulation path around the monastery. At one point, we ran into an old couple, greyed and bent, helping each other along the crooked trail, reciting mantras on worn prayer beads, offering gifts to the gnarled evergreen roots. I thought, "That is what I want to do if I ever grow old. Walk slowly, every day, amongst trees like these." I honestly couldn't see myself living past thirty, a premonition I hadn't shared with Phill, though I'd told my friends and family since I was a child. If my vision was correct, I only had a few more years in this particular lifetime and I planned to make them count. Maybe next time around I'll have more time for walking amongst trees.

We came to a clearing, one of five such sites in Tibet, where people bury their dead in the sky. Most of Tibet liberates their dead by fire, as we did in our Sangha in Boulder, but, in a few places, and often with specially-recognized people, Tibetans release them by vulture. A specifically-trained monk performs the funeral rites, which are held in utter privacy for the family, no photos or video allowed. The corpse is prayed over, cleaned, and then dissected and deconstructed carefully. Slowly, body parts are added to tsampa (barley flour) and ceremoniously fed to the waiting vultures who, after centuries, have become an integral part of this unique ritual. The deceased is fed back into the belly of nature to be digested and discarded, fertilizing this sacred ground. While it was slightly grotesque to most of our American minds, to the Tibetans we spoke with, the Western practice of embalming corpses and locking them in sealed boxes under the earth, where it can take hundreds of years to decompose, sounded like utter madness, bordering on soul abuse. One of our guides told us that the thought of his body flying high in the belly of such a mighty bird was the definition of the freedom that death allows.

Juliet asked if anyone would like to be guided through a "death meditation," her nonchalance reminiscent of the way my childhood community viewed and talked about death. Phill came out of a culture that rarely talked about death and often did everything imaginable to avoid the subject, even if someone close was actually dying. Given the fact that I most likely only had a few years left to live this life, I was thrilled to join in, not knowing what lay in store. Phill joined too, apprehensively, more like accepting a dare than making an informed choice.

Juliet asked us to consider our entire lives thus far, from our earliest childhood memories, through our adolescence, and into adulthood. To think about all of the people we'd met and the lessons we'd learned along the way, starting with learning to walk and then to talk. Then she asked us to imagine all of that energy and incorporate it into our bodies, to feel all of the people, alive or dead, who contributed to the miracle of our existence. Then she guided us to fully contemplate that this moment, right now, was the moment of our death, the second that our unique story ends; nothing left to say or do, nothing left to achieve or process. It's over. What was once a living body is now a corpse laying on the ground. She instructed us to let go, to collapse into the earth, releasing all muscle tension. "Now imagine your corpse devolving back into parts, limbs separating, skin shredding and disintegrating, muscle and bone ripped and smashed, devoured, returning to cellular form, returning to the ecosystem, food for the planet, the completion of the cycle, returning to the speck of life from which you grew."

When we collectively came out of the meditation, something changed, at least within me. I can't say that I'd ever been afraid of death, but I was deeply attached to this particular life, to my specific storyline. The truth is, I was going to die; maybe soon, maybe a long way off yet. When that day came, I wanted to be ready for it, not surprised. I wanted to witness my own death, be aware for it, no matter how painful. I wanted to jump confidently into the next realm, not creep into it angry and confused that my story was over. Juliet gave me the tools to do just that. I hoped that, whenever my end came, I would remember this teaching and embrace death like a magical flight across an unending sky.

While our travel around Tibet provided us with so many blessings, it was the teachings on death, not life, that affected me the most, freeing me from any remaining fear of death I was harboring. I began to sleep again. Deep, dream-filled nights that included bizarre and optimistic visions rather than the dark nightmares that had been haunting me. My love for Phill expanded alongside my love for the Tibetan land and culture. While I was fully American in most respects, my childhood within a Tibetan Buddhist Sangha resonated more with this place and its people than the country on my passport. I recalled the pain of entering into mainstream America, all the fear and confusion that arose from not being able to trust my surroundings nor people's intentions. I began to think deeply about family, examining my fears around having children and sacrificing my personal pursuits in deference to another's. I was about to commit my love to just one person, a person who loves to cook, and clean, and sew, and I could no longer see why that life couldn't expand to include children. I began to see the love between Phill and I as worth passing on and, even though I worried constantly about the state of the world and the future of humanity, I began to see how raising more nonviolent warriors to combat the rampant forces of ignorance and hatred was part of what the world needed. If Tibetans were brave enough to have children while living under a brutal occupation, if they could hold on to the hope that those children represented despite all the fear and uncertainty surrounding them, perhaps I could be brave enough too.

I couldn't speak Tibetan, though I was learning as we travelled along, and my Tibetan middle name "Norbu" became the source of endless laughter, as it's usually given to boys. I imagined a foreigner visiting the U.S. for the first time and telling me she was raised in a small community of American refugees who had given her the traditional American name "Bob." It was hilarious. My name thus never failed to fill in awkward moments and by the time we returned to Lhasa, we were as close as family, a handful of Americans and a handful of Tibetans, brought together by the courage of Romeo and Juliet to overcome unimaginable odds. We had slayed all of the conceived differences between us and, through laughter and song, became more similar than different. Now there was only one thing left to do, to celebrate like a family as we bonded the life paths of Romeo and Juliet, as well as Phill's and mine.

▪ ▪ ▪

The wedding attire was perfect. The food, the performers, and the local Rinpoche had all been arranged. Along with about seventy guests from Romeo and Juliet's families, we were converging in an ornate gathering hall called the "Crazy Yak," which seemed the perfect moniker for doing something as crazy as getting married. The idea of marriage terrified me. I was more comfortable walking into the DRC unarmed than I was with the concept of marriage. It wasn't the monogamy, nor the monotony, that worried me. It was the very idea of owning another human being, of being held to a relationship by an outside authority, of being legally-tied to another person's happiness. I didn't want to be responsible for anyone's future. I had no pets, no houseplants, and no children. I was a completely whole human being who wasn't "missing a piece," and didn't feel that I needed anyone "to complete me." Caring for another was not the issue, controlling another was. To me, the institution of marriage felt more like a sacrifice than a blessing; an age-old method for owning and subjugating women, a betrayal of the basic democratic tenets of separating church and state. In addition to its problematic roots, the institution of marriage, as defined by the U.S. government, denied rights to people who loved and shared their lives with other people of the same sex, and that felt fundamentally wrong. I wanted no part of participating in a legally-binding contract based on unequal, sexist, and archaic belief systems. By this point, Phill understood where I stood on that matter. But I could also see the benefit of making vows of commitment to one another, inviting our community to witness those vows, and using ceremony to mark those vows as sacred. Because Tibet is not an officially-recognized country and we felt held and surrounded by people who loved us and wanted the best for our future together, and because I had fallen deeply and madly in love with Phill by this time, I agreed to marry him…as long as laws and taxes had nothing to do with it.

Dressed in all of our brocaded finery, turquoise and coral beads braided into my hair, Romeo and Juliet dressed in her native Khampa style, we walked Kora first, around the Jokhang Temple, drawing a crowd of well-wishers and curious strangers. People's faces lit up at the sight of Tibetan culture being paraded around publicly, even as dozens of police officers bristled at the crowd we drew. We walked like that, an entourage of hundreds of supporters around us, across the Barkhor district and up to the entrance of the Crazy Yak. Nearly a hundred guests were inside waiting, most of whom I'd never met before. The smell of incense was thick and wafting through the open door, the sound of murmured mantras filling the air with a low buzz. I stepped past the hanging brocade tapestry blocking the doorway and took a brave step towards a destiny shared with another.

Juliet's family, those who had survived the occupation and managed to travel to Lhasa, along with Romeo's immediate family, were seated at a long table, slightly-raised, which had four empty seats in the middle. Guests filled the rows of seats that faced the long table, filling the spacious hall. All of our traveling companions were there, along with several people we had met and become close with over our time in Tibet. Everyone was dressed to impress, and the energy in the hall was electric. We took our seats at the ornately-carved table and were told that the Rinpoche and his attending monks had been there for several hours already, preparing the space and laying the groundwork for our sacred marriage ceremony. At that point, it occurred to me that we never talked much about what a Tibetan wedding ceremony entails. Phill and I, along with a dozen foreigners, would watch our wedding unfold, ignorant and curious about how it would proceed. I couldn't imagine a better wedding for me, especially the part about being surprised by the ceremony itself.

The Rinpoche, whose earlobes seemed to be making a run for his shoulders, eventually nodded in our direction, and we were instructed to kneel in front of him. He looked us each intensely in the eyes, said something that neither of us understood, then splashed water in our faces and hit us over the head with a book of sacred text. Romeo and Juliet then did the same, while their families smiled and wept. Phill and I stood and exchanged written vows (of which only a handful of attendees understood) and shared a gift with the other instead of traditional rings. We then leaned forward, touched foreheads, and it was done. No doilies, no bridesmaids, no stressed-out mothers-in-law, no long speeches…just a splash in the face, a bonk on the head, and a welcomed forehead-hug. We were married; by the power vested in no one but ourselves.

The chang was flowing, the singing and dancing outrageous, and the joy was prolific; spilling out of the Crazy Yak and into the night streets of Lhasa. For that one day, or maybe even just a few hours of it, it didn't feel like we were in an occupied country, as the Tibetans who hosted us celebrated and rejoiced in our love in a uniquely Tibetan way. In that, our wedding itself felt like an act of resistance, defiant of all that the CCP had been trying—and failing—to extinguish.

Me and Phill in traditional Tibetan dress after our marriage ceremony inside "the Crazy Yak," Lhasa, 2005.

Hungover and exhausted, with hearts full to the brim, we said goodbye to Lhasa the next day, parting from our many friends and newly-adopted family members, leaving for a honeymoon to Mount Everest Base Camp. As we drove out of the city and across the increasingly-barren landscape, I felt a deep sadness at going, a feeling of homesickness for a home I'd only just gotten to know. It was devastating. I didn't know if I would ever be back, given how remote and expensive Tibet is to reach, and the loss was measurable in my spirit. Driving away from what felt like sanity and comfort, back into the world of moral poverty and spiritual materialism. My vows to Phill extended to this land that held us and taught us, my allegiance to Tibet merging with my commitment to advancing human rights and equality. Though I didn't know it at the time, the roots of my bravest and riskiest mission were already being planted; the very road we were traveling along a foreshadowing of my future path.

The road to Everest took us two and a half days to complete. Three others from our original group joined Phill and me in hiring a driver to take us across the plateau and up to the highest peak on the planet. Past the hillside fortress of Gyantse, over several passes of more than 20,000 feet, along the only single road, which often curved so many times it felt like something out of a Road Runner cartoon. Through the large city of Shigatse, where the infamous Nyari Prison is located, where hundreds of Tibetan freedom fighters have been tortured and murdered. I had read their stories, and the word "Shigatse" sounded like a warning in my brain as we drove past high walls with barbed-wire fencing. It stood as a stark reminder that we were, in fact, in a conflict zone; a conflict in which one side held no weapons, fighting instead with unsilenceable songs and unbreakable spirits.

"Road Runner" like pass on the road to Mount Everest.

The night before we arrive at Base Camp, Phill got dangerously ill with altitude sickness. We didn't bring any medicine with us and, when it hit him, it hit fast with tunnel vision, vertigo, and a screaming headache. His body was pulling the emergency brake, shutting down his peripheral capacities in order to funnel all its available oxygen to the brain. We were crossing a very high pass and had stopped at a roadside seller to buy seashell fossils, from a time when the Himalayan Mountains were at the bottom of the ocean. Phill just walked away from me, as I was mid-sentence, stumbling downhill in the middle of the road. Something in his brain or his instincts told him to move downward, and, after a few hundred feet, his vision finally began to return to normal. So then he started jogging down the side of the steep mountain road until his head stopped screeching. I had no idea what was going on and thought he was trying to make some sort of strange, post-marital run for it.

We picked him up from the road several minutes later and, though he was feeling better, we weren't sure how to proceed. Our driver told us we had one last night to acclimatize in Tingri, the final town before the road splits—one way heading up to Everest, the other down off the Tibetan Plateau to Nepal. Everest Base Camp sits just below 18,000 feet, and none of us knew if Phill could make it back up to that altitude, nor if we could find any medicine at this point. The next day, after a horrible night's sleep for all of us, Phill felt a bit better and we decided to risk the ascent to Base Camp, promising to return to Tingri immediately if his symptoms returned.

Arriving to Everest from the Tibetan side requires one to pass through several security checkpoints and permit reviews before the road eventually ends at the Rongbuk Monastery, which has stood at the base of "Mount Chomolongma" (the Tibetan name for Everest) for centuries. From there, visitors can either walk for about forty-five minutes or hire a horse-drawn carriage to take them to "Advanced Base Camp" (ABC), from where the views of the mountain are unobstructed and spectacular. ABC is also where the expedition teams camp, preparing to ascend Everest's challenging "North Face." By the time we reach the monastery, Phill is again nauseated and dizzy, his vision blurry.

We plan to head back to Tingri, which will take several hours, after we have a hot lunch in the monastery's attached restaurant. Phill lays out flat on a carpeted bench after we order soup, falling asleep and making me wonder if we shouldn't just start driving down immediately. At that moment, the restaurant doors swing open and, along with a cold mountain breeze, two larger-sized men with deeply-brown skin and booming voices blow in, speaking loudly in Spanish. "Hola!" I call out, eager to know where they are from and to speak a language other than English. In the most miraculous turn of events, it turns out the newly-arrived visitors are Mexican and, because they were coming from sea level, have lugged a whole backpack full of extra oxygen canisters with them. I had never been so happy to see a well-prepared Mexican in my entire life. "Gracias a la Virgen, la Madre de Milagros," we agree, hooking Phill up to a canister of O2 and watching the color return to his face.

We buy extra canisters off of our new friends and decide to stay the night. Tourists can either rent a room at the Monastery or make their way up to ABC, where they can rent a bed in a traditional nomad tent and watch the sunrise over Everest. The choice feels clear to all of us and, while the others walk up, Phill and I hire a horse-drawn carriage and enjoy the ride. I would never have predicted that I would spend my honeymoon on the slopes of Mount Everest, as I'm more of a "hot chocolate in the warming house" type of mountain girl, despite my Colorado roots and the amount of camping I've done. I love the mountains; I just prefer to sit still and listen to them rather than try to summit their highest points.

We choose a tent with a wooden sign that reads "Hotel California," which seems custom-painted for us. Inside, we find beds lining the outside edges of the tent and a warm stove burning in the middle. Three Tibetan women, their cheeks rosy from the altitude, set in on taking care of our every need. They offer packaged soups and rice dishes for purchase and warm tea to sip on. The Tibetans have evolved with this land, adapted to living with less oxygen, learned how to survive and thrive here. For the first time since entering the TAR, I notice that there aren't *any* Han Chinese around. This is Tibet's mountain, their natural habitat and, if anyone wants to visit, they will need a Tibetan to guide them. Their Chinese occupiers, like Phill and me, are ill-equipped anatomically to stay up here for very long. As such, try as they may to claim all of this land, the Chinese can't fully occupy the Himalayan mountains; they simply don't have the physical capacity to do so. Way up here, this land feels like it still belongs to Tibetans, even if by sheer stamina alone.

Sometime around 2:00 a.m., Phill wakes me up from a deep sleep, under a mountain of blankets. He'd just gone outside to pee and saw that the cloud cover, which had been thick for weeks, had suddenly cleared, unveiling the entire Milky Way winking back at him, stars almost close enough to touch. "Kiri, you've gotta see this!" he says, as delighted as a kid on his birthday. "Come on! It's AMAZING!! I know it's cold, but you'll survive," he nudges me and insists that I get out of bed. Since I was about ten years old, I haven't been able to see much beyond twelve inches from my face, and I use maximum strength contact lenses during the day to make up for my extreme near-sightedness. At night, I wear glasses, which is what I reach for now, stepping out of my blanket cocoon and hopping barefooted and long-Johned to the tent door. By the time I reach the outside, which is significantly colder than the inside of the tent, I have about two seconds of stars before my glasses fog over from my body heat, and then freeze over completely. I take them off, now blind as a mole, and lick the icy lenses, melting the frost. I then expose my bare belly to the elements trying to wipe the lenses dry and quickly put them back on.

I get another second or two of stars before they fog, freeze, and even crack a little. Phill stands, head straight up, mouth agape, staring at the wonders of the universe, while my myopia prevents me from seeing much and leaves me bone-cold in a matter of minutes. I bound back to bed, annoyed at the interruption of a good sleep, which was totally not worth it to my blind eyes.

At dawn, the sky is still clear, and when the sun crests the ridge around Everest, it lights up the canyon like a spotlight. The locals say that it is the first time the mountain has appeared in weeks and how lucky we are to catch it. Everest stands naked and sparkling-white, like a glistening sword piercing upward another ten thousand feet above our heads. I could not, for the life of me, imagine wanting to climb it, but I can understand wanting to be in its presence forever, where the squabbles and suffering of mankind mean very little.

We stayed all day, hiking around and taking pictures of her beauty. We spied some Himalayan blue sheep, which also like to prance and prostrate at Everest's feet. The one downside to the entire experience were the toilets, both the foul and overflowing pits at the otherwise picturesque Monastery, and the equally vile and overused latrines at ABC. I emerged from one of them and declared to Phill that I never, ever, under any circumstances, wanted to return to that cesspool of un-biodegrading shit. The way the Chinese were treating this holy mountain, covering it in crap and garbage, was disgraceful. By the second nightfall, we were all ready to head back down to Tingri, none of us feeling very well from the lack of oxygen to our systems.

We left Tibet the next day. Winding down the craziest and most dangerous road I'd ever traversed, descending more than 10,000 feet in elevation, no guardrails, mud and vegetation competing with strips of loose asphalt, busses and construction trucks joining the caravan creaking slowly down off the Tibetan Plateau and into a valley that runs into Kathmandu. I was looking forward to seeing my adopted Nepalese family again and introducing them to my new husband. The hajuraama, or grandmother, of the family was still alive, now roughly a hundred years old, and my younger sister Pratima had recently gotten married as well. She had chosen to marry for love, the first in her family to do so, and it was causing some drama with the older generation. I wanted to be there to support her and yet I was already missing the feeling that Tibet had gifted me. I felt I was abandoning our new friends to their fate, not unlike leaving Mary in the Congo, wondering if I'd ever have the chance to return, and why some of us have the privilege to move around this globe as we like, while others are chained to invisible borders that people are killing and dying to defend. I tried to be like Everest, to channel the strength and big vision of the mountain, but my heart felt bruised and guilty as we watched Tibet shrink in the rearview.

Chapter Twelve

DYING IN TIBET

Phill and I were offline, drunk, and dancing the night away at Eve's wedding in central Mexico, which is why I didn't see the missed calls or listen to the voicemails Shannon left over the week we were away. The same Shannon who had been in Baghdad when the bombs were flying, resident of The Bat Cave, part of my activist family. When I finally call her back, her voice is urgent and serious. Phill and I are on our way to Dot's Diner for brunch, back in Boulder, and Shannon is on her houseboat in Sausalito.

"*Amiga*, I need your help." Shannon is half-Mexican, and we sometimes speak in Spanish. She continued by asking me to consult on a confidential action. She and some colleagues (of whom I only knew Jeff…soft-spoken, mountaineer Jeff, who had inhabited The Bat Cave longer than any of us), were attempting to do something that no one—not even I—thought possible. They knew it was a long shot, full of dozens of unknowns and dangerous obstacles, but they were going to try, and the timing was right. When she said that the protest they were planning was going to be inside Tibet, at Everest Base Camp, I knew why she was calling me, but I still didn't grasp the entire picture of my involvement. I began to rattle off what I knew about the complex permitting process to get into the TAR and then out of Lhasa towards Everest. Shannon was quiet, I assumed taking notes or something, and then said, "Would you be willing to join us?"

"I know that being public isn't your thing, but we could really use you on this one," her tone was welcoming and flattering as she added, "No one I know is better at crossing borders undetected." I told her I needed to think about it, and she said, "I can give you twenty minutes. We leave in a week."

I hung up and looked at Phill, who had been listening to every word. He nodded and winked, adding, "Looks like someone's going back to Tibet." By the time we were parking at Dot's, I was calling Shannon back and mentally preparing to head back to "The Land of Snows" in just a few days' time.

■ ■ ■

Arriving at the houseboat community in Sausalito, famous for its artsy and activisty residents over the years, I find a busy action-training center set up in Shannon's living room. Her couches and chairs are covered in technology hardware and donated mountaineering gear. I feel out of my element. Although I am confident that my knowledge of traveling to Tibet will be helpful to the team, the others are hard-core, the type of activists who scale buildings and shut down cities. I am used to working alone, remaining anonymous, and I have never been arrested.

Laurel, on the other hand, who Shannon introduces as her teammate, has been arrested several times, mostly for physically blocking access roads to old-growth forests and taking on the logging, mining, and coal industries. He is blonde and beautiful, extremely outspoken and bold. He reminds me of a real-life Lorax, laying his life on the line to "speak for the trees." I admire him instantly. Laurel, Shannon, and Jeff will make up one team, traveling to Everest completely separate from the team I will make up with someone named Tendor. I learn that

Tendor works for the organization Students for a Free Tibet (SFT), who has invited Shannon to lead this action and recruit her team. I have never heard of SFT before, but they have been planning this protest for a while and have successfully executed two other Tibetan freedom protests in Beijing over the past few years, giving them an idea of how the authorities may respond to our protest. Only in that moment do I understand that getting arrested is a major part of the strategy. I also learn that, with Shannon running the video camera and Jeff running the satellite equipment, it leaves Laurel, Tendor, and me to conduct the protest. I wasn't prepared for the possibility of being seen on camera, most likely in handcuffs, and, with that, my anxiety doubles and the stakes rise, not that they could get much higher.

I decide to go into the protest with my face covered, hoping to stay unrecognizable publicly. Even with years of activism under my belt, I have never had to put my name, reputation, and future on the line like this. Something about this mission feels ominously different than anything I've risked or tried before, and I have the sneaking suspicion that it could change everything for me…at the same time, the chances of us actually making it to Everest with a Tibetan American amongst our group are so slim that I figure I will cross each bridge as it arrives, rather than worry about practically impossible scenarios at this point. I doubt that Tendor will even be allowed to enter China from the Beijing airport.

I receive a grainy photo of Tendor, whose alias is Jim Jordan, from which I'm meant to identify him at the airport in Chengdu, China. He left a few days before me, just in case he didn't get in, as I've predicted. But he did get in and he then made his way to Chengdu and I've received word that he will be at baggage claim holding a bunch of flowers. I sent a message back saying I'd be wearing a bright orange scarf. Our backstory is that we are boyfriend and girlfriend, who met in college at Brown University (where Tendor actually went) and are traveling around China together post-graduation. Tendor is meant to tell anyone who asks that he was born in Sikkim, where he was given a very Tibetan-sounding name, but that he was adamantly, definitely not Tibetan. He was instructed to wear expensive Western clothes, keep his distinctly Tibetan-shaped eyes covered with sunglasses, and to speak English in public. I was to play the bubbly, oversharing American, batting my lashes and befriending everyone too loudly, which was a role I was used to performing. My alias was Donna Snowbunny, chosen to add to my ditzy façade.

Before leaving Sausalito, I spoke briefly with a woman named Lhadon, who is the Executive Director of SFT. She talked passionately and eloquently about their work for Tibetan freedom and their long-laid plans for this action. She helped me understand how the CCP is using their newly-won Olympic platform to present a modern face of China to the world, one where there are no chained Tibetans and monks are not setting themselves on fire to protest their restricted freedom to worship. Lhadon promised me that, if we made it to Everest and if we were arrested or disappeared, she would dedicate her life to seeing us freed. I believed her, recognizing the tone of her conviction. I wanted to tell her about my lifelong connection to her people and my marriage commitment to the Tibetan land itself, but, instead, I simply promised to use every trick in my toolbox to help Tendor get home and raise his voice high. I felt a lot better after speaking with her and being empowered to support their work in speaking up for Tibet, knowing this was a Tibetan-led strategy and that SFT had our backs all the way. With my parents offline in Mexico (they knew I was going back to Tibet, but they didn't know why), I left Phill's name and number as my primary media contact, hoping they never had to use it and knowing that none of my family members, not even my husband, knew how much risk I was about to take.

I said goodbye to Shannon and Laurel in Hong Kong, and headed to Chengdu alone. If all went according to plan, I wouldn't see them again until the night before the protest, somewhere near 18,000 feet.

I wasn't exactly sure how Tendor was getting to Chengdu, but he had better be there at baggage claim with flowers and he better give me a huge hug, as instructed. The moment you touch down in China, it is best to assume that you are being watched and never break character. Even the smallest mistake could ruin everything.

Over the few days I had in Boulder prepping for this action, I found time to take a walk with Romeo. Before his escape from Tibet, he had been a student organizer and was eventually arrested and tortured for his calls for freedom. During a well-documented prison break, he managed to escape but was shot in the wrist. The CCP spent months looking for him, hunting him, while he lived in caves and tended to his festering gunshot wound. Eventually, he made his way on foot over the Himalayas to Nepal. He knew a lot more than I did about the Chinese police and what might go down on the other end of our protest.

"Never let them get you alone," Romeo warned as we strolled the maple-lined streets of Boulder's historic Mapleton Hill district, where I grew up, Tibet feeling a world away. "And don't eat anything they offer you," he admonished, not a hint of sarcasm. "Friends of mine were poisoned in prison. Some never even showed up to the prison after our arrest, disappearing in the distance between, never accounted for."

"The CCP acts with total impunity," he reminded. "Remember, they gunned down their own children, thousands of young people protesting for democratic rights in Tiananmen Square were murdered in plain sight. Your American passport will only get you so far with them." Romeo was genuinely worried. We discussed hiding almonds in my pant cuffs and bra and keeping a close eye on my colleague's whereabouts. He didn't want me to go and didn't think losing anyone else to the Chinese was worth it. But he was also proud of me for having the courage to try, for still believing in the difference that one person can make. I knew that, even if we were caught before we reached Everest, the chances of my ever going to Tibet again, of ever seeing his mom or sister again, were nearly nonexistent, and that was a hard pill to swallow. But, if I had to sacrifice my access to Tibet in order to speak up for the freedom of all Tibetans, it was worth it. I left for Tibet with Romeo's blessing and with the full weight of all of my loved ones' worries and fears on my shoulders.

When Phill dropped me at the airport in Denver two days ago, I flashed back to the last time we'd parted there and the silly dare I'd given him. Married for two years now, those two lovebirds seemed like babies, our commitment now spanning three continents. I was confident in my choice to sacrifice my freedom for Tibetans, but the thought of losing the freedom to be with him hurt like hell. It's a fate that most of the world's refugees have to face, losing access to family. Though I suppose it's one thing to flee from oppression when it comes to your door, and quite another to sneak into the oppressor's home and let their highly-guarded secrets out of the closet...which is precisely what we were attempting to do.

Touching down in Chengdu airport, my senses are on full alert, taking in details of the people around me, memorizing faces to see if they appear again later. It's not unusual for the Chinese government to assign "minders" to tourists, guides to both show visitors around and to report on their every move. We wanted to avoid attracting any minders at this point, and that meant looking like I knew where I was going, without looking like a journalist or an aid worker in any way. So much of my work over the years had come down to appearances, and I had become adept at changing mine drastically to meet my goals. I donned my bright orange scarf and large sunglasses and tried not to look around too much on my way to baggage claim. Jim Jordan was a Mandarin-speaking, Sikkimese-American student, and Donna Snowbunny would be his savvy, yet totally harmless and nonpolitical, counterpart.

The first person I see at baggage claim, coincidentally, is a Tibetan monk, dressed in robes, holding a large bouquet of flowers. I'm shocked at first, wondering when we changed the plan to have Tendor parading around as a monk? At which point, another woman walks up and bows, accepting the flowers graciously. I realize all of my prejudices and stereotyping have made me the ass. Just then, I notice a skinny man in a leather jacket and sunglasses, holding a sad bunch of recently-picked posies, wilted and dropping dirt from their exposed roots. He smiles, winks, and walks over to embrace me awkwardly. This is the first moment we've met yet we are meant to act like lovers. And, from that uncomfortable moment, it's on. I become Donna Snowbunny and leave all traces of Kiri behind, drawing on all of my theatre skills and deception training to project someone entirely new.

We find a semi-crowded restaurant and slip into a booth where we can get acquainted un-overheard. Still we speak in hushed tones and never mention anything specific about the mission ahead. I learn that Tendor was born in exile, a refugee from his first breath of life, raised in the Tibetan Children's Village, started by the Dalai Lama's sister to preserve Tibetan language and culture within its first foreign-born generation. He is incredibly smart, excelling in U.S. Ivy-League schools, and speaks several languages. But he is also green when it comes to direct-action work in the field, young at heart, and prone to absentmindedness...like the fact that he forgot to bring flowers to the airport and so he pulled some public ones from outside at the last minute, or that he is not supposed to be Tibetan, yet keeps ordering Tibetan butter tea, a taste that only Tibetans love. I begin to worry that we are not going to make it to Everest, thinking of the dozens of checkpoints and security reviews we will have to pass through to get there. Tendor seems genuinely stoked to have made it to Chengdu. He has been here for two days without any trouble or drawing any attention and is feeling confident. I am thinking of how far we have to go and feeling trepidatious. Tendor informs me that he found us a hotel and a tour office to work with the next day, as we attempt the challenging process of procuring permits into the TAR.

Walking into the tour office the next morning, I know that these first permits will be the hardest to attain and that, once we are approved in Chengdu, it will be easier to acquire the permits we need to leave Lhasa on the road to Everest. There is a young woman sitting behind the desk alone and, with a few moments of forethought, I decide that the best approach will be to make this woman my new "best friend." Through laughter and compliments and, thankfully, being from America, which still carries a certain level of coolness, we fill out the permit forms together, dropping—and making sure she sees—my purse full of U.S. dollars. Tendor and I are both wearing high-end, brand-name mountaineering clothes and expensive sunglasses and trying to put out the vibe that we're not just Americans; we are rich Americans and used to getting our way. We then purchase, with cash, a day tour to a nearby Giant Buddha statue, giving my "friend" another large commission for the day. She pauses slightly at Tendor's name in his passport (his full name Tenzin Dorjee being the most Tibetan-sounding name I know), and I insert the story about his being born in Sikkim, where he was given a similar name to Tibetans. I am not sure she is convinced and can feel her hesitation mixed with her desire to please me. I lean in with a good ol' American hug, catching her off guard and breeching the physical barrier between us to try and seal the deal.

When we return from our tour, several hours later, we find our tour agent distraught and confused. She explains that my permit was approved, but that Tendor's was denied. "Why?" I begin too loudly, obviously upset, fake tears welling up. "Simply because of his name?!" I question, incredulous.

"Yes," she admits, head bowed.

"Why is that?" I am almost yelling. "He is an American citizen, just like me. What if you came to visit my country and we wouldn't allow you to visit Disneyland because you had a Chinese-sounding name? Wouldn't that break your heart? To deny someone access to a part of your beautiful country just because of his name, when he has done nothing wrong, is shameful. This is not the modern China I thought I was visiting." I worked on her throughout the evening, while Tendor said nothing, resigning himself to the fact that we had tried and failed. But he didn't know me and had no idea how persistent and persuasive I could be; I was just getting started throwing my privilege around. Gently but steadily, I eventually convinced her to reapply for a permit for Tendor, using a slight variation of his name… namely, not Tenzin, which is also the Dalai Lama's given first name.

To my surprise, and Tendor's utter amazement, our new "friend" came through the next day with permits for both Tendor and me to travel to Lhasa. She made it clear that she was bending the rules slightly (not something a Chinese citizen does lightly) and that, no matter what, we could not break any laws in the TAR, nor try to leave Lhasa. We promised, both fully aware of our deception. I hoped she wouldn't get into trouble if we made it to Everest and actually executed our plans, knowing that she was just the first in a long line of people we would need to dupe along the climb to Base Camp.

The flight to Lhasa was on a small commercial plane, perhaps even the same one I'd flown on two years earlier. I offered Tendor the window seat, figuring I'd seen the incredible sight of ascending up onto the Tibetan Plateau before, not quite grasping the enormity of this moment for him, of his getting to see Tibet emerge before his own eyes. He studied the land below from the small oval window, gasping at the Himalayas, as they began to rise out of the earth and reach for the sky, as if he wanted to memorize every peak and take even the smallest detail to heart. When we landed, I saw pain and joy, fear and excitement flash across Tendor's face. At the age of twenty-seven, he was going to see his native home for the very first time.

As we drove the long road from the airport to Lhasa, Tendor felt lost in his own thoughts, as if he couldn't believe he had made it, or maybe thinking of all his community in exile, most of whom will never have the chance to see Tibet. When we passed the Potala Palace for the first time, sitting high and majestic above the city, Tendor started to cry. Soundless tears streamed down his face, sunglasses barely masking the deluge soaking into the collar of his t-shirt. I didn't know him well enough to comfort him but the enormity of what we were attempting had dawned on both of us. I was also thinking that I was glad that we had taken seats in the back of the airport shuttle and that it was not going to be easy to hide Tendor's Tibetan-ness now that he was finally amongst his own people, walking on his rightful land.

Luckily, our first few days in Lhasa were uneventful, acclimatizing and prepping for the protest, and, other than the constant scrutiny of the police officers posted on every corner, we drew little attention. I figured that Tendor could act a little Tibetan, have his butter tea, but I wanted him to seem more like a "Tibetophile" outsider than an insider to the culture. At no time, EVER, was he to speak in Tibetan. In fact, neither of us were to speak to anyone outside of a few words to order food and arrange transportation. There were cameras on every corner, and it was common for the CCP to go back and review footage, persecute anyone they thought we were associated with, which was no one. We visited all the major tourist sites (otherwise, why were we there?), giving money to the oppressors while Tendor bit his tongue and suppressed his rage. His people and their history were being presented to tourists as if they were "liberated" by China from their "primitive" and unsophisticated former way of life. It infuriated me, and I couldn't begin to imagine how Tendor was feeling. It fueled our resolve to make it to Everest and set the record straight, tell the world a Tibetan side of the story.

The Olympic spotlight on Everest was SFT's golden opportunity to be heard and, after two painful, propaganda-filled days in occupied Lhasa, we fully intended to steal it. China had contentiously lobbied to host the Olympic Games for decades and Tibetan activists had fought it for years, arguing that the spirit of the Olympics stood in stark contrast to China's brutal human rights record; that the games were developed 111 years earlier to spread harmony and sportsmanship around the globe, and China's track record disqualified it. Eventually, enough money and influence swayed the International Olympic Committee (IOC) to give China the honor of hosting the 2008 summer Games. The CCP was using this moment as their big "coming-out party," wanting to be seen as a major player on the global stage. They wanted the world to believe that the Tibet issue was over, and that China was a free and modern nation with only happy citizens. We were going to Everest to send the opposite message, to fill that global platform with a healthy dose of the truth about the brutality of the Tibetan occupation and the decimation of all those who dare to resist it.

The Chinese expedition team was heading to Everest, which is only summit-able for a short window in the spring every year, to attempt a trial run of their ambitious plan to carry the Olympic torch to the summit of Everest. In a few days' time, the IOC was gathering in Beijing to announce the "Torch Relay Route" to the world, marking the official countdown to the opening ceremonies, about fifteen months from now. We were planning to hijack that media attention one day before the IOC's announcement, to steal all of their thunder, and poop on their parade in the name of human rights, and on behalf of all the silenced, imprisoned, and murdered Tibetans.

Leaving Lhasa was almost as hard as getting in. I had to play all of my worst cards—the Diva, the Racist, the Totally-Entitled American—to get us permits and a private driver to take us to Everest. Tendor remained quiet and aloof, letting me do most of the talking and planning. The morning we were set to leave Lhasa, we met up at our tour office, which was a fancy Chinese outlet, only to find that our driver was Tibetan. We had specifically asked for a Chinese driver, not wanting to involve nor implicate any innocent Tibetans in our plans. Tendor talks to me outside for a moment and says, "You're going to have to go back inside, talk to your new 'best friend,' and tell her as much racist shit as you can to get us a Chinese driver."

But, no matter how many vile lies I spew about "my discomfort with a lazy, ignorant Tibetan being our guide" (to which she too readily agrees), she also admits that she could not find a Chinese driver willing to go.

The other team was also in Lhasa, and we had developed a complex system of passing paper notes in an emergency. We learned that they too were having trouble finding a Chinese guide/driver and that they had left Lhasa the day before with a person they believed to be Chinese, but, as none of their team spoke Mandarin or Tibetan, they simply weren't sure. In truth, while we knew that innocent Tibetans caught in our path could reap the worst consequences that our protest would create, even Chinese citizens we came in contact with may have to suffer the repercussions. It was too late to change course, and the crux of the problem, when it came down to it, as my "best friend" explained, was that there were no Han Chinese drivers willing to take the chance of crossing the Tibetan Plateau alone, much less with tourists in their charge. Most were afraid to leave Lhasa, and didn't do well physically at the altitudes we would reach. Tendor and I made the painful decision to press on with the plan, but neither of us were comfortable with the possibility of our driver carrying some blame down the line. Also, Tendor was going to have to be extra guarded about his Tibetan-ness if he was going to fool another Tibetan man into thinking he was from Sikkim for the entire three days it would take to reach Everest.

And then it was just the three of us, miraculously flying along the one road leading south out of Lhasa, towards Mount Chomolungma and our uncertain destiny. Tibet is massive and spacious, so the hours we drove found Tendor and I speaking English, talking about our lives this far and what led us both to this fateful point. Tendor pointed out—which I'd never fully considered—that it was quite incredible to think of Chögyam Trungpa Rinpoche, a revered Tibetan tulku and meditation master, fleeing the Chinese occupation by walking across the Himalayas (an entourage of devotees by his side), making his way to India, and then to the West, where he learned English, started a Buddhist Sangha, and raised American white girls like me in the path of nonviolent warriorship. He marveled at the fact that my early life training was the very reason I was here in Tibet with him, and the very reason he was able to get this far on our mission, because I didn't look like a Tibetan, even as my heart was wholly with the Tibetan people. To him, that was nothing short of a miracle. I began to see and feel how my being on this assignment with him was part of my karmic path, that I was exactly where I was supposed to be, playing a role I was uniquely prepared for.

Tendor and I stayed in the back of the ATV, quiet and sunglassed, through all of the many security checkpoints, letting our driver and our expensive paperwork do their jobs. Occasionally, I would roll down my window and bat my eyelashes, pay the guard a compliment. Tendor never said much, and we passed through easily, proceeding without issue through Gyantse and its mighty hillside fortress, over the winding "Road Runner" mountain passes, and past the Nyari Prison complex in Shigatse…which silenced both of us for a while, thinking of what our near future might entail. I was confident that, if we did get arrested as planned, we would be quickly expelled to Nepal, a short drive from Everest. Tendor wasn't so sure.

By day, we talked about the moral dilemmas around a nonviolent direct action like ours. Tendor had studied Gandhi's Satyagraha movement, Martin Luther King Jr.'s civil right's movement, and Gene Sharp's "198 methods of nonviolent action." In systems of oppression, resistance often makes conditions worse in the short term. It is usually the people who make waves that get blamed for oppressors' harsh retaliations. It can be hard not to think of our instigation as adding to the problem, even as we know that doing nothing, saying nothing, means the slow, calculated decimation of an entire ethnic group and its traditions. We are both worried about the effect that our choices and actions will have on Tibet and its people, but Tendor admits he's more worried about the consequences of inaction.

I mention that I am concerned about the response from the mountaineering world, from those who have trained hard and paid tens of thousands of dollars to summit Everest this week, whose plans we will most likely ruin. Tendor reminds me that Mount Chomolongma is in Tibet, a land that was brutally occupied over a span of ten years, causing the death of more than a million Tibetans; and that mountaineering groups pay the CCP to climb their holy mountain, contributing to China's oppressive rule in the region. As far as Tendor is concerned, the mountaineering community should be joining us, speaking up for Tibet, and boycotting the profiteering off their photo ops, which is used to further repress the Tibetan people's freedom, and grossly pollute the land that they consider sacred. His convictions bleed into mine, helping me prepare mentally for any fallout from our upcoming actions.

By night, Tendor and I stay busy in our hotel room, music blaring, discussing the details of the protest and making bright yellow protest shirts that read "Team Tibet" on the back and "IOC No Torch Through Tibet" on the front, ensuring that our allegiance and our demand is clearly displayed on our bodies. We construct our protest as a sort of Olympic opening ceremony for Team Tibet, with Tendor as our national champion, holding his own torch high and singing the banned Tibetan national anthem. I have been wearing the part of our banner that is written in Tibetan script inside the lining of my bra since Sausalito, about ten days ago. I explained to the team how a white woman's bra was the one place security guards rarely check and, thus, a place I considered my most secret lockbox. I will only remove it to attach to the larger banner on the morning of the protest.

And then, without much difficulty or suspicion, we are back in Tingri, at the same tourist hotel that Phill and I had stayed in when he was recovering from altitude sickness two years earlier. I explain to Tendor that it is a good thing that neither of us feel sick from the altitude and he explains how Tibetans have genetically evolved to live at high altitudes, underscoring their historical claims to this land. I have no idea why the altitude doesn't seem to affect me but am grateful for the reprieve, remembering how ill it made Phill just to be here.

The next day, our driver drops us off at the Rongbuk Monastery, saying he'll be back the following evening to get us. We both know that we'll never see him again and that, if things go well, we'll be leaving in police cars instead. We are both hoping like hell that he doesn't have to pay for any of our actions and will do everything we can to protect his identity. A new tented-camp has been constructed to house tourists in the two years since my last visit, now dividing the distance between the monastery and Advanced Base Camp (ABC), where the Chinese Olympic expedition team is camped. Tendor and I walk into that new tented village and spot Jeff, wandering around on a nearby hill, holding our satellite (which looks like a laptop) up to the heavens. We soon learned from Shannon and Laurel—once inside our cozy nomad tent where they've saved us two beds—that the trial run with the satellite that morning had failed, all of the equipment malfunctioning because of the freezing temperatures. All of our previous connections and tuned precision around the equipment are proving moot in the real environment of Everest. We don't know of anyone who has successfully sent a satellite signal from Everest before, and perhaps this was why. The team is dejected. Conducting the protest without live footage leaves us at risk of being arrested without witness and without getting our protest message out first. The satellite is the key to our security strategy.

Then Jeff (introverted Jeff, who brews his own kombucha and takes care of all the abandoned houseplants in The Bat Cave) has a brilliant idea. If the problem is the cold, we can use makeshift hot water bottles to cocoon the equipment inside sleeping bags, inside a warmed tent. The only trouble would be getting enough hot water by 4:00 a.m. to carry up to ABC to coax our lifeline equipment back to life. For that, we were going to need a fire and fuel. At this altitude, the only natural fuel available is yak dung. The team set in on boiling water and filling all available water bottles, a tedious process that would take hours. As Jeff tended the fire, he joked that, even with the most advanced satellite equipment in the world, nothing was going to work without the power of yak poop.

As we collectively prep for sleep that night, each internally preparing for the protest at dawn, Laurel shares a story from the day before. He had gone for a hike after arriving, taking photos and acting touristy, and found himself inside what seemed like an abandoned part of the Rongbuk Monastery, where he encountered an aged monk. Without much language between them, the monk had presented Laurel with a small handful of barley seeds, instructing him to carry it with him. While Tendor, Shannon, Jeff, and I each had a connection to Buddhism, Laurel seemed to have found his on the eve of our insanely-bold action for Tibet. And, in that—in ways big and small—we were all spiritually committed to our impending mission, each having made our own internal convictions around the sacrifices we were willing to make.

Me and the majestic Everest on the day before
our historic protest, Tibet, 2007.

▪ ▪ ▪

I hear the alarm beep on my watch, but I am already awake. Today is the day. In just about an hour, I am going to take the biggest stand of my life and my heart is already pounding. I stick a hand out from under the covers—so many heavy blankets that I have to punch outward to get through them—and feel the stinging chill of the air. It is still dark, only the dim light from the fire to see by, kept burning throughout the night by Jeff, who is already gone.

Moving in mechanical motions, I get dressed deliberately, just as Shannon has asked each of us to rehearse in our minds in the days leading up to this moment. She is our leader, and I place my trust in her completely. Warm socks, long underwear, Capilene layers, goose-down layers, heavy fleece-lined pants, strong hiking boots, double-knotted. Tucking energy bars and almonds into hidden pockets and pant cuffs, a few in my bra, just in case, I make sure I have my giant yellow protest t-shirt easily accessible. I know the t-shirt will fit over my down jacket, having practiced for this very moment in locked hotel rooms along our journey, and I laugh at recalling an image of myself in the mirror with all my gear on, looking like a giant yellow M&M. I also know that possession of the t-shirt alone can get us arrested and I have to make sure that doesn't happen until our message is successfully sent past the Great Firewall of China.

Tendor and Laurel are getting dressed as well, their silhouettes dancing on the tent walls in the firelight. None of us speak. At this altitude, wearing five layers of clothing, our movements are labored, my breath visible as quick, foggy bursts. Shannon and Jeff's beds are empty, and there is little sign that they've snuck out an hour earlier, very little sign they've been here at all. Last night, Shannon gave away practically everything she brought with her, clothing, sleeping bag, backpack, keeping only a few small items for friends and family back home, which she carried on her. I envied her ability to so easily give away all her belongings.

The three of us finished neatly packing up our bags, ready to grab them quickly if we ever had a chance to do so. I was still holding onto the hope that we would somehow be allowed to take our possessions with us after the arrest. Looking back, it seems silly that I was worried about losing my sleeping bag. Perhaps I was secretly hoping we wouldn't really be arrested at all, just given a good "talking to" by some local authorities and that we would be free to walk away a few hours after the action was complete.

I double-check my pockets to make sure I have nothing on me, no receipt or slip of paper with a phone number or name, nothing that can tie me to the hotels we've stayed in or where we've eaten. I am clean. I wear only two prized possessions against my chest: a Gao, which is a Tibetan locket, filled with protection cords and tokens from my immediate family and teachers, which I have been carrying with me since I turned eighteen, venturing across war-torn Cambodia; and a mala, Tibetan prayer beads, given to Phill the first time we were in Tibet, on the occasion of our wedding. These two items make me feel like I am not alone, like my actions are bolstered by my family and mentors, each walking with me into this historic moment.

The sight of three bundled tourists leaving their tent at dawn is not unusual at Base Camp, though I don't recall there being anyone around to witness it. What I do remember is that, as we came out into the growing light of day, the sight we all hoped to see was absent. Instead of seeing the black silhouette of Everest, we are surrounded by a thick cloud layer and can hardly make out the road that will take us up to ABC, much less the majestic and impenetrable shape of the tallest mountain on Earth. Our hearts collectively sink as we realize that, without sight of the mountain in the background, we will have no way of showing the world that we are indeed at Everest Base Camp, and therefore there is no point in doing the protest this morning.

But it has to be today! It is April 25th, 2007, and it is an auspicious day. The Panchen Lama, a key figure in Tibetan culture, a boy who has been held by the Chinese government in secret captivity since the age of six, is turning eighteen today. The three of us quietly debate our options and decide to make the long hike to Advanced Base Camp, regardless of the weather, where Shannon and Jeff are waiting. We will decide as a group how to proceed and then shift our plans accordingly.

As we walk, each of us lost in our own thoughts, I begin to recite a mantra from my childhood:

"Grant your blessings, so that my mind may be one with the Dharma."
"Grant your blessings, so that Dharma may progress along the path."
"Grant your blessings, so that the path may clarify confusion."
"Grant your blessings, so that confusion may dawn as wisdom."

I chant it in time with my footsteps: left, right, left, the way the teenage me had practiced military drills at summer camp. It occurs to me that I am marching up the very mountain range where Chögyam Trungpa Rinpoche led his entourage out of Chinese-occupied Tibet and that he had taught us this mantra. I thought in detail about the words I was saying, perhaps for the first time. I was asking for blessings to hold a clear mind in the moments to come, a mind that is in line with the Dharma of non-violence and compassion. I thought of how even such basic teachings were being held captive in Tibet, denied their right to be passed on, to flourish, to "progress along their path." I was asking for blessings to help carry the Buddhist Dharma along its path, out of Tibet, and into the hearts of everyone it touched. In doing so, I was praying that it may help to clarify the confusion and ignorance in this suffering world, so that wisdom can bloom in its place. In repeating the mantra over and over, time seemed to freeze and, as we got closer and closer to ABC, I felt less and less afraid.

Looking around, I notice Tendor is chanting to himself and building cairns with rocks along the road. Laurel is also reciting the short Tara Mantra, "Om Tare Tuttare Ture Svaha," taught to him by Tendor. We are all chanting, spontaneously, privately, and the air itself feels full, pulling us slowly up the mountainside, each step part of a collective prayer.

Arriving to ABC, we spot the yellow tent that had not been there the day before, during our scouting mission. Shannon is near the tent, which is pitched on top of a small hill overlooking camp, fidgeting with a camera. Jeff has made a nest inside the tent, surrounding the satellite equipment with sleeping bags and hot water bottles. Shannon is equally concerned about the cloud cover masking Everest, and we debate returning to our sleeping tent, when the skies magically begin to clear. Shannon says she's been texting with Lhadon about the weather and everyone with SFT—all around the globe—is praying for clearer skies along with us. Shannon suggests we wait a bit and get fully prepped for the action. Within thirty minutes of the team converging, it is as if an invisible giant has risen up above Everest and slowly blown all the cloud cover away; revealing, minute by minute, the magnificence of Mount Chomolongma, blazing silver in front of an increasingly turquoise sky.

Tendor, Laurel, and I are crouching behind some large rocks, each now wearing a bright yellow protest shirt. Tendor is holding the torch we have crafted from a traditional Tibetan butter lamp and a broom handle. Laurel is holding one side of the twenty-foot banner we have carried in pieces and assembled by night; I am holding the other end. At the exact moment Shannon announces the satellite connection is a go by yelling "Action!" we step out from behind the rocks as the sun emerges brilliantly over the valley ridge, lighting up the side of the hill like a stage.

Tendor lights our unique torch, while Laurel and I hold our banner high. We all remove our hats while he loudly and proudly sings the Tibetan national anthem. He then delivers a searing speech calling out the cowardice of the International Olympic Committee and China's false claim to Everest, which is on stolen Tibetan land. I am moved to tears by his courageous words, unable to speak. In removing my hat, I have shown my face to the camera, revealing my identity for the first time in all of my years of activism. Laurel speaks a few words as well, all while Shannon gives the thumbs up that we are still live recording to SFT headquarters in New York.

I look around, expecting authorities to move in, SWAT-like, and take us down to the ground. But, in reality, it seems no one has even noticed us, and we spend the next few moments regrouping and plotting our next move. We decide to march down the hill and into the heart of the Chinese expedition team's camp to "wake them up!" Shannon and Jeff plan to stay on the hill and film whatever happens from afar. We know we've gotten the protest footage we came for, and that it has gone beyond the Great Firewall for the whole world to witness. We march down into the Chinese camp at ABC where we begin to hoot and holler, sing, and make bird noises…we are having a birthday party after all!

▪ ▪ ▪

The moment we are arrested is anticlimactic. Prepared for batons and manhandling, the cold slap of handcuffs, or worse, I brace myself when the first soldier arrives into my peripheral view. He is shouting in Mandarin, to little effect on my untrained ear, and, though he forcefully rips the banner out of my gloved hands, there is no real violence. The machine gun remains strapped to his back as he struggles to get the other end of the banner free from Laurel, who has somehow tied his foot to it and fallen to the ground. The soldier actually seems more embarrassed than angry. *At having to arrest a bunch of kids? At wishing he could stand on our side of this ridiculous conflict? Or perhaps nervous that someone has read our banner calling for a free Tibet before he could rip it down?* What he can't possibly know is that, while he is bundling the canvas banner away from any peering eyes, we are secretly betting on thousands of eyes seeing its message in the next few hours alone.

Other uniformed men arrive quickly and surround us; a young man in a camouflage coat grabs my arm hard, shoving me in the direction of the concrete building he's just run out of. I walk in front of him obediently, no part of me objecting nor defying his orders. And that is how I am arrested for the first time in my life. No broken bones, no mace, no paddy wagon…nothing like what I'd been preparing for. It is so underwhelming, in fact, that I silently mock the men in uniform guarding us for most of the day. First off, they keep us all together, in one concrete room, while they scramble to follow remote protocols, none of them expecting to be stationed for a day like this, or that the "bad guys" would look anything like us. They seem unsure of what to do with us and have only captured four of us, causing a mountain-wide search operation to kick off. It could have been three arrests, but I stupidly looked over towards Shannon, still filming from a distant hillside, as we were being hauled in. The soldier behind me noticed my gaze and Shannon had just enough time to hand the videotapes to Jeff—who ran like a sprinter down the barren valley—and distract the soldiers until they nabbed her too.

So now there are four of us in a makeshift jail cell, huddling around an oddly-shaped coffee table, a strange hunk of dried meat hanging from the ceiling in the corner of the room, the majestic Everest still gleaming from behind the one small, barred window. And they haven't physically searched us, which means two of us still have hidden cell phones and begin texting madly with the teams in New York and Kathmandu.

"Jeff is on the run!"

"Do you capture the footage?"

"Yes! We still have phones, sitting in a concrete jailhouse, send contact info to media."

"Fuck yeah everyone! We did it! Free Tibet! [Insert photo of Everest behind bars]."

Once the initial shock wears off, we laugh collectively at the inanity of their response, so disproportionate to holding up a simple sign, the CCP's unwinnable war against free thought. A soldier comes in to check on us, machine gun safely on his back, offering cigarettes. What I really want is water, but it is the first small kindness shown towards us and most of us take his offer. He is ethnically Tibetan and young, which surprises me, even as I know the Chinese army has employed Tibetans to work against each other for decades. I refuse to smoke, at first. It was hellish quitting nicotine two years ago after twelve committed years. But, as the hours drag on and the cold sets in, so does the reality of what we've done. Eventually, I give in. When I'd finally stopped smoking, I'd told myself that I was absolutely done…unless, of course, I ever found myself in a cinematic "smoke 'em if you've got 'em" type of scenario. I suppose that being arrested at Mount Everest Base Camp, on the opposite side of the globe from home, while facing unknown consequences from a ruthless political regime, counts as one of those situations.

The tricky thing about cigarettes though, is that they're actually poisonous. It takes time for the body to adapt to, and eventually crave, that poison. Instead of feeling good upon finally taking a drag, my immediate reaction is nausea and a sore throat. When it's finally my turn to leave the concrete room and talk with the interrogating officer, I am wobbly on my feet and feeling feverish. Luckily, they've taken Tendor in first. As the only Tibetan amongst us, he was an easy target for their initial anger. When he returned from his interrogation roughly an hour later, he looked shaken up but strong. They took Shannon away next, leaving Tendor to tell Laurel and me everything they'd asked. We had carefully crafted backstories but, when you don't know the impending questions, it's hard to cram for an exam. The nicotine buzz, while turning my stomach, boosts my brain into overdrive, and I carefully memorize Tendor's replies and formulate corroborating responses. These initial hours of questioning—Tendor briefing me, then Shannon briefing Laurel—will prove invaluable when the real interrogation begins, though none of us know that this is just a dress rehearsal; not one of us suspects that this is the warm-up exercise, nor that the real marathon has yet to even begin.

A one point, I ask to use the restroom and am escorted outside by a young soldier, who leads me by gunpoint right back into the world's most disgusting toilet, where I had sworn to never return. The soldier posts on the outside while I go inside and have my first moments alone since the arrest. As I am squatting, the phone in my bra begins to vibrate. As if calling from down the block, the voice on the other line is clear, introducing himself as Peter So-and-So from the Associated Press, calling to get a statement from the Everest protesters. I am entirely unprepared, and my pants are around my ankles, but I do my best to send a clear message out to the world about why we have chosen to act on behalf of Tibetan freedom and why now. When we hang up, I feel utterly alone and scared. I want to call Phill or my mom, but I don't want to waste the little phone credit I have left. I stay inside for a few extra minutes, gathering myself. In an insane turn of the Karma Wheel, I not only find myself back in this foul pit toilet, but wanting to stay here forever rather than face what's waiting on the outside.

The first interrogator, Little Big Man, is the highest-ranking officer stationed at this remote outpost, if still a low-man on the overall military totem pole. When I was ordered to leave the others, the escorting soldier carried his machine gun slung across his back. But, as I sat down in the "hot seat," across from the interrogator, he lifted his firearm and pointed it to my chest. The effect was unnerving, and I struggled to find my words. Tendor and I had concocted an elaborate story about taking a public bus as far as Tingri, then hitchhiking up to Base Camp. We were attempting to protect the identity of our driver, who we didn't want associated with our actions. For now, it seemed that our bus story was holding water, so I continued to fill the bucket.

"We met in college. Fell in love instantly...." I weave a tale of love and intrigue, the dream of visiting Tibet at the top of our shared bucket list. I feign ignorance that holding up a sign to "help our new friends with their passion project" could be illegal. I act shocked that they have reacted so strongly and made such a big deal out of a little political statement. I ask to call my mom, fake some tears, then shed some real tears when he firmly says no. I tell him, "Where I come from, this wouldn't even make the evening news," and I offer unsolicited advice, "Maybe you could just let us go? Wouldn't it make everyone's day so much easier?" But Little Big Man is unmoved by my naiveté, and uninterested in my opinions on free speech, nor what I think he should do. I'm actually offering good advice. If only he'd listened and not made our big statement into a big deal, just sent us packing down into Nepal, our story would have died, and news stations would have turned their lenses elsewhere. If only he wasn't such a Little Big Man in the big picture, he'd have seen that the smart strategy was to bury our message, not amplify it. But that is not what happened. As I sat and lied, a pointed machine gun and two sets of deaf ears as my witnesses, our little "David vs. Goliath" story hit the international media stage and got bigger and bigger, my impromptu message from the toilet reiterated hundreds of times over, as our small cry for Tibetan freedom began to soar around the globe.

▪ ▪ ▪

The first time I saw The Worst was roughly fourteen hours after our arrest. Once it started to get dark, and we were sitting in the same cold, cement room at ABC, any hopes of being across the border by nightfall faded with the light. At this point, I was just hoping to be able to return to the nomad tent where we left all of our belongings, crawl into a warm sleeping bag, and face more interrogation the next day. But the soldiers and Little Big Man seem to be waiting for something else to happen.

As it grew darker, we did jumping jacks to stay warm and drank offered hot water with a couple of split Snicker's bars. I smoked a couple more cigarettes, which only made my nausea and sore throat worse. At 10:30 p.m., about an hour after the night's cold was setting in, a caravan of police SUVs arrived, lights flashing, sirens blaring. Their lights cast long, colored shadows across the valley, making sure everyone on the mountain was paying attention. Moments later, a group of crisp-looking officials walked in. They were dressed in full police uniform, wearing dark glasses, tall hats, and trench coats, and, from the moment they arrived, everything changed.

The Worst was the first officer I noticed, partly because she was the first uniformed woman we'd encountered this high up, but mostly because she looked so classically Tibetan, not unlike my dear friend Juliet, and it shocked me to see her. Shannon got the first dose of The Worst's psychotic techniques when she asked to use the toilet. They left the room together and The Worst began smiling, acting like they were close girlfriends going to the bathroom to gossip. When they returned, Shannon seemed visibly shaken and The Worst wore a steely glare.

This group of officers were what Little Big Man and his crew were waiting on, and the local authorities must have notified them of our arrest shortly after we were detained, for they seemed road-weary and seriously pissed off. We were each searched thoroughly, our phones finally confiscated, as they examined our seized equipment, seeming not to recognize the satellite. It was late and dark and, at first, they said we would be sleeping there, on the cold cement floor, which could have been a death sentence at that altitude. But then, suddenly, they demanded we get on our feet and march outside, down the hill, and into the row of awaiting vehicles. The Worst took my arm firmly but smiled sweetly, saying in English, "Everything is going to be okay. We are your friends." I was simultaneously terrified and comforted by her.

Five months earlier, sitting in the waiting room of my eye doctor in Colorado, about to have Lasik eye surgery to correct my severe myopia, I'd made a premonitory statement to Phill. "Once the surgery is done, if I ever make it back to Mount Everest, I will be able to see all those stars with my own eyes the way you could. Can you imagine?" Not knowing at the time that, in a short while, I would be back. The night before the protest, excited and hardly able to sleep, I peeked outside the tent expecting to be wowed. But the cloud layer was already thick and masking the skies, not a single star visible. I confided in Laurel how disappointed I was to have missed seeing a clear, starry night sky from Everest, thinking that it was my last night there and probably my last chance to fulfill that wish. Now, just as I am being hustled into one of the waiting police cars, I hear Laurel shout, "Donna, look up!" And there they are: billions of bright lights, the entire Milky Way sparkling and moving as if in a far-off night dance, one that I can finally witness for a moment or two. I laugh out loud at the irony of it and how this wasn't exactly what I'd had in mind.

Shannon sat next to me on the first leg down to the lower section of Base Camp where we had slept and left our bags. "You know what she is doing, right?" She whispered in my ear. "She is trying to get on your good side, get you to trust her." She recounted her trip to the toilet and how The Worst had snapped at her, screaming in her face, after Shannon told her that her little friendship ploy wasn't going to work. I vowed to keep my guard up, but I had no idea what I was dealing with. Eventually, it became clear that we were not going to stay at the lower camp either. After stopping to collect our bags, they loaded all of us and our gear into separate vehicles, each of us squeezed between two officers in a back seat. The Worst made a point of sitting next to me, smiling creepily and patting my thigh. Her comrade, The Lackey, the only other female officer, packed in on my other side.

Not long after we began to drive, The Worst began to whisper in my ear. Her English was quite good. She told me how much trouble we were in, how I was probably never going to see my family again, that we had broken her laws and that we were going to pay for it severely. She talked so softly and close that the others in the car didn't seem to notice her rant. Every so often, she would pat my knee or squeeze my arm and announce loudly that we were "becoming good friends." Then she would lean in and start again, painting a picture of the dim future that awaited us. She gave me the eeriest feeling and only added to my terror. That's when my crying fit began.

The realization that we were not heading south toward Nepal, but instead back north into Tibet, made my wailing even worse. Although The Worst would not tell me where we were going, it soon became clear that it was not south, toward the border. My sore throat, throbbing with every dry swallow, tightened further as it sank in that I would not be sleeping, not even in a cement jailhouse, for quite some time yet.

Earlier, when discussing our overall strategy, the group had decided that Shannon and Laurel would take credit for planning the action. They would draw a hard line during the interrogation, if need be, speaking to their beliefs about Tibetan freedom and, if it got ugly, stonewalling them while demanding to speak with a representative from the U.S. Embassy. I was to act like a terrified and confused tourist, who ended up in the wrong place at the wrong time. I was to give them misleading and confusing information, cry a lot, and try to get helpful information out of them by playing on their sympathies. If nothing else, we agreed to protect Tendor at all times, and had made a pact that none of us would leave him behind, no matter how bad it got. Tendor was planning to speak very little, act confused about the details, and stick to our story of being a couple on vacation who had mistakenly gotten involved at the last minute. At no time was he to speak Tibetan or respond to questions asked in Tibetan.

I worried that Tendor wouldn't be able to pull it off, his Tibetanness almost a part of the way he moved and spoke. And I wished for Shannon's role, which felt tougher and easier to me. My role, however, all this emoting and complaining, was way past the edge of my comfort zone. I was used to playing a ditzy role with security, perhaps even a flirty role, but acting this soft was actually turning me to jelly. I felt vulnerable and scared and, playing right into her hands, began to believe it when The Worst told me I was never going to see my family again. I started to panic about my unclear future. *What have I done? My poor Phill! My family! Shit, my mom is going to kill me. I don't think I can talk my way out of this one....*

I was spinning, unable to latch on to any reality, when I first farted on The Worst and it made me feel better. When I descend from altitude quickly, my belly fills with air and I begin to fart and burp relentlessly. It has always happened to me, as I grew up in the Rocky Mountains, ascending and descending thousands of feet regularly. So, as The Worst was leaning in to fill my brain with threats and fear-inducing images of what awaited us, I began leaning onto my far butt cheek and letting it rip in her direction. She gave me a shocked look, but it did not deter her much, though I was enjoying fighting back in some way. Eventually, after hours of verbal abuse, I reached my limit and turned to face her, saying firmly, "Stop!" She looked into my eyes and we stared at each other for several long seconds, scanning the other's face, and then she looked away and stayed quiet.

Even though I was able to end The Worst's whispered tirade, I was still terrified of her. At the same time, I was curious about her. Who was she? How on earth did this Tibetan woman end up being a high-ranking officer in the Chinese police? How was her English so good? I thought of all the stories I'd heard and read over the years, of all the sacrifices that are required to survive a war. Women in refugee camps turning to prostitution in exchange for food, mothers giving their babies away in a desperate act to save them, children forced to take up arms and kill their own families in order to save themselves. *What had happened to this woman? How had she become this terrible version of herself? How could she turn on her own people?* I loathed her.

▪ ▪ ▪

"Think of the ripples," Laurel says to me, the sound of urgency and importance barely masked in his naturally soft tones. We have stopped briefly at a sort of police station, and it is the first contact I've had with one of my colleagues since we began driving, hours ago. He is holding me tightly around my shaking shoulders and staring directly into my eyes, imploring me to calm down.

"The ripples?" I manage to squeak out, despite a never-ending flow of tears soaking my face, shirt, and hands. Once I'd started to cry in the car, it felt impossible to stop. I thought I must be in some sort of shock, having realized that we weren't leaving Tibet but instead heading, off-road, to an unknown destination, and I lost track of where I was on the map. I began losing my grip. But it was more than that. It was everything. All the sadness and violence in this world, all that I had seen, heard, kept stuffed down, all that I believed in and held dear about my individual life, all of it was pouring out of my eyes in huge drops, and I felt powerless to stop it.

"Ripples are going out right now across the whole world, golden ripples, as people are waking up and learning about our protest. We just threw a huge rock into the pool of global consciousness and right now, as we stand here, ripples of information are going out far and wide, and people will know the truth." Laurel is squeezing me harder, holding my face, trying to bring me back to the present moment. A seasoned activist, he can tell I am coming apart. As he implores me to focus instead on imaginary waves rippling across the planet, I am stewing in my own pity party.

It was the understanding that these could be my last free moments alive that started my fit. I suppose it had never fully occurred to me before the protest. I was simply doing what I usually did, jumping in with both feet and trusting my intuition. I had had some close calls, but my privileges and assumed innocence had always carried me to safety. Now I was red-handed and having to face the consequences of my actions, my face on camera. Images flashed into my head of the people who have mentored me, The Mountain Goat, The Tortoise, The Eagle…their faces clear and comforting. They are joined by others I've met along my path: survivors, advocates of equality, activists, professors, writers, rule-breakers, change-makers, rebels. I had hoped to tell their stories at some point. I had been sure there was still time. Now it was all going to disappear, lost amongst the rocks and glaciers of one of the most remote places on Earth. I had no idea where I was or what was going to happen to us, and I was losing my shit.

The others seemed to be holding up much better. Laurel and Shannon gathered around me once we stopped, and I felt embarrassed at my outpouring of emotions. *What was wrong with me? Hold it together, girl! You've been in scary situations plenty of times and always kept your cool.* But this wave of sadness possessed me beyond my control. The only benefit of my emotional collapse was that it was so disarming to the stoic, mechanical operations of the Chinese police officers that they seemed unsure how to respond. Shannon seized the moment and demanded that I be allowed to ride in the car with my "boyfriend," Tendor, and, miraculously, they agreed. Amazing that, with all of their military might and strict codes of conduct, a young woman sobbing uncontrollably had the power to make Chinese officials uncomfortable enough that they took direct orders from one of their prisoners. For the first time since we began driving inland, for just a moment, we had taken control of the situation, and I felt slightly stronger.

Perhaps it was due to this renewed sense of control or maybe it was Tendor sitting next to me, but The Worst finally left me alone. For the next few hours' drive, I focused on the ripples. I meditated on the ripples. I saw them majestic, white and gold, flowing endlessly through the air, stopping at one inbox, then another, multiplying, translated, printed, posted, photocopied, forwarded. I heard our message for Tibetan freedom repeated in dozens of languages, heard the echoes of Tendor singing the Tibetan national anthem bouncing around the globe. It helped enormously to calm my mind, and I finally stopped crying. Tendor had remained calm since our arrest, and I tried to draw on some of his strength. I began to see that, whatever our fate would be once this endless night-drive ended, we had taken a bold stand, spoken up clearly for those who are silenced, and our message would not go unheard…feeling sure that the ripples were multiplying and that the world was listening, my hands and heart steadied.

But the feeling wouldn't last. During the next stop, I was convinced the others were being harmed when I heard Shannon screaming, "Stop it! You're hurting me." Tendor and Laurel had long since been dragged into the police station, and disappeared from sight. Shannon was also forcibly taken from her vehicle and then reappeared briefly, flinging my car door open, blinding me with the internal car light, yelling "Don't talk! Don't talk! I have just been threatened with harm!

Embassy! Just say Embassy!" Before being ripped away by two officers. At that, I bolted from my car, and began running around the courtyard wildly, like a headless chicken, shrieking "Shannon! Laurel! Tendor! Are you okay?" over and over again, while pulling my best basketball spin moves on the gaggle of soldiers chasing me. Eventually, I was tackled by several of them and shoved back into an SUV, where the doors were firmly locked and guarded. After some time, Tendor and Laurel were led back out of the police station and forced into two different vehicles, leaving me alone again between The Worst and The Lackey. It was somewhere around 4:00 a.m., judging by the cold alone.

I have always been prone to car sickness, and I am infamous in my family for barfing on road trips before we even leave the city limits. Just as our caravan of SUVs was pulling out of that last terrifying police station stopover, shortly after my wild-goose-chase attempt to locate my hurt friends, I start to feel wobbly inside. The familiar sensation of saliva pouring into the back of my mouth confirms it. I am going to puke. I lean over and confess my situation to The Worst, covering my mouth. She stares at me, reading my face for signs of subterfuge, and then says something in Mandarin to the driver, motioning with her hands for him to pull over. It never occurred to me, being the final car in the caravan, that the other cars would not stop as well. *Surely, they will radio ahead and let them know we've stopped.* But, as we pull onto the gravel shoulder of the solitary road, I watch in desperation, counting one, two, three sets of red taillights as they turn a mountain corner ahead and then disappear completely.

And then I am alone with this psychotic policewoman and her goon. The Worst looks at me and smiles, a creepy smile that never touches her eyes. *This is the moment Romeo had warned me about. I am the one who doesn't make it from the arrest site to the prison.* The thought makes my stomach lurch and I dry heave over my lap. At that, The Worst and The Lackey usher me quickly out of the vehicle, each grabbing hold of one arm. I figure we will walk like that, the three of us, a few steps from the car, where I can discreetly throw up, as I've done many times on the sides of mountain highways throughout my childhood.

The Worst has different plans. Pulling me hard, each gripping an armpit, they drag me away from the car and onto the icy, windy hillside, urging me forward until we are hundreds of feet from the vehicle, looking over a cliff. One of them puts a hand on the back of my head, grabs a handful of hair, and bends me forward. I vomit on cue, bile whipping across the side of my face in the fierce gusts of wind and dirt, my diaphragm spasming over and over, emptying my belly into the blackness. My body collapses to the ground, face on rock, limp. And then I feel something hard and cold on the back of my neck. *Maybe a gun? Maybe a boot toe?* Enough to thrust me out of my physical form, abandon my body laying on the ground, and float above the scene.

I am back in the woods in northern Tibet, sitting next to Juliet, listening to her guide me through the death experience. I know that this is it for me. The final words to my story. Juliet's voice is calm and welcoming. I lean into it, let go of my life, take a final breath, and invite death in....

But I wasn't shot, and I didn't die.

The sound of The Worst's laughter is the next thing I hear, mixed with The Lackey's cackles, bringing me back into my body. I am a joke to them, hilariously covered in vomit and now piss, terrified. But I am alive and so, for me, the joke is on them. As quickly as they dragged me from the car, they are shoving me back inside, still chuckling at my expense; taking great joy in my suffering. And as we round the mountain corner, I see them. Four sets of red taillights, waiting for us. Like embers of a dying fire, they provide hope. Perhaps I will make it to the prison after all. Perhaps I still have some story left to write, some life left to live out. The joy of feeling my breathing body, of having even a few more moments with me, is so overwhelming that I too begin to chuckle, laughing at the beauty that blooms in the face of death, how even years of hard labor in a prison camp feels like a blessing now.

And I maintain this giddiness, this renewed sense of owning my life, for the rest of the drive. I feel kind of invincible. The Worst has done her worst, and I've survived. As the sun rises and we enter the outskirts of a town, I take a risk and ask The Worst directly, "Where are we? Can you please just tell me that?" Her answer turns my stomach and deflates all of my newfound confidence, even as it brings a small upturn to the corners of her mouth.

"Shigatse," she states, as if the place itself is our penance.

Chapter Thirteen

REBORN IN TIBET

It's dark now, and finally quiet. Once my body hit the bed, it fell asleep immediately, as if on its own and I was unable to stop it. In fact, I don't feel like I've had much control over my body since the arrest. That's the thing about detention that no one shares, just how alien it feels to have zero autonomy over your own body. You become an object to secure and move around, placing it here and then there, using it this way and then that, no longer an independent self making independent bodily decisions. I can no longer control when I sleep, when I eat, or when I shit. So, I am doubly shocked to discover, upon waking and peeing in front of yet another stranger in a police uniform, that my body has gone ahead and started its monthly cycle, bright red blood soaking the cheap toilet paper and staining my fingers. I laugh out loud at the oddity of getting my period now, in Chinese detention, and the adjoining relief to not be pregnant. Phill and I have been trying to start a family for two years, with one heart-breaking miscarriage already behind us. Two weeks ago, we'd had too much tequila at Eve's wedding in Mexico and spent the whole night doing the baby-dance. It's strange to imagine the sadness I would've felt today if I were home in Boulder, the blood another confirmation from the universe that I am not cut out to be a mother. *Has it only been two weeks since that optimistic wedding party? Phill and I batting around baby names as if we'd already conceived.* I'd completely forgotten to count days or watch for early pregnancy signs as I've been doing for months. To the watching-not-watching police officer, I must have appeared mad, sitting on the toilet, laughing at a wad of toilet paper, no clue about the non-baby it happily represents.

Using a trick from junior high school, I build a makeshift menstrual pad in my underwear, aware that it won't hold for very long. I slip quietly back into the bed I'd passed out in, crawling under the covers and curling into a fetal position, holding my now-aching uterus with both hands. I have a moment of panic realizing that I'm probably going to stain the sheets and may soon have blood running down my legs. Then it occurs to me, for the first time, what a powerful nonviolent weapon menstrual blood is. Just like my resistance-farts and my hysterical crying fit, another one of my body's natural functions could be used to my advantage. "Fuck it," I say out loud, determining that I'm actually okay with bleeding all over everything in this awful place, letting the blood stain my clothes, leaving a trail of red in my diminishing wake, freaking all of them out.

I must have fallen asleep again, cramps and all, fatigue beating the pain into the recesses of my brain, when the covers are thrown back and bright lights flash behind my closed eyelids. Opening on instinct, I see two young Tibetan girls, dressed in Western clothes, cell phones outstretched, snapping photos of me. Looking around, they are now the only two people in the room with me, which feels bizarre after having so many officers around since we'd arrived. "What's happening?" I ask in groggy English, hoping they might understand.

"You're very famous," one of the girls replies in a heavy accent. "We sell your picture for money," she adds, and they break into giggles, covering their mouths with their hands to hide their excitement. I'm wondering if this is a dream, and actually pinch my arm to see if I'm asleep. No luck; this is real.

"You're gonna sell those pictures of me?" I clarify gently, still confused.

"Yes. Yes. People buy photo of you, famous person!" I'm shaking my head, sure that not one person on the planet wants a picture of me right now, when the door opens and The Worst enters.

The fear that arises within me upon seeing her is simultaneously foreign and familiar. A paralyzing terror I've rarely ever experienced, coupled with a vivid memory of watching myself die at her hands, the back of my neck recalling the sensation of death. "I see you've met my little sisters," she says calmly, the way a teacher speaks to a student, or a predator to its prey. "They've been watching over you to make sure you didn't escape," she half-jokes. We both know there is no possible escape from this place with its walls within walls. She says something in soft tones to the girls, speaking her native Tibetan language in front of me for the first time. She seems to be praising them for doing a good job watching over a sleeping body. I wonder if I should mention the contraband on their phones, show The Worst that I'm a "good little prisoner," and get on her good side. But I also wonder if those will be the last photos ever taken of me alive. If I don't come out of this at all or emerge a shadow of the person I went in, those pictures may be the only living evidence that I was still me on April 27th, 2007. *What if those are the last photos that my husband and parents ever see of me?* Better that they stay secret for now. Plus, if I tell on the girls, they might send Angry Dark Man back in to watch over me and I could lose these potential allies to mine for information. I'm hoping The Worst will leave me alone with them again soon.

The Worst is circling the room quickly, though, The Lackey close behind her, following orders. They're both picking up loose papers and water cups, removing all signs that we'd been here. Her fast tones imply something important is happening and I get the feeling that we might be on the move. I take the opportunity to go to the bathroom one more time, this time closing the door to no objections. Suddenly, and momentarily, I am alone for the first time since the foul toilet at Base Camp. I hardly recognize the person staring back from the bathroom mirror, like looking at a strange photo of me in disguise. Once I had accepted that I would never leave Tibet, once I detached from my body completely, I stopped caring how it appeared. Now I'm looking at a puffy-eyed, bloodshot, wild-haired, bedraggled version of myself staring back and wondering: *Where am I? Who is doing the staring, and who is being stared at?* It's as if I've split into two versions of myself—my body and my mind—and I'm having trouble reintroducing them in the reflection. *What does it matter if I comb my hair or straighten my shirt?* I wonder. It's no longer my hair, nor my shirt. The Worst and her cronies have taken everything. She could order me to take off all my clothes, and I wouldn't put up a struggle. All anger and defiance are long gone. I have surrendered, bowed down on the battlefield, given up the fight. Once you call "uncle," the game is over, right? In this case, that game meant my personal freedom, and I have lost.

A loud knock has me jolting back from my desperate reverie, still staring at the strange woman in the mirror. "Coming!" I yell, and quickly fashion a new toilet-paper menstrual pad, stuffing handfuls of paper in my pocket for later. I open the door and walk out without combing my hair nor straightening my shirt. "We have to go." The Worst's tone is finite.

"Are you moving me somewhere?" I probe. "Are the others coming too? I'm not leaving here without them." I surprise everyone, even myself with those demanding words.

My small protest seems to amuse her because she grins as she replies, "No more questions now, Westin," the way a mother speaks firmly to an overly curious toddler. Just then, another officer comes in with paper and a pen, shouting in Mandarin. The Worst translates to me that I must write an apology letter. "Right now!" she barks to my unmoving form. *Am I going to get out of this with an apology after all?*

"To whom?" I ask innocently.

"To China!" she shouts.

"To China?" I ask confused, "Like, to the entire nation of China?"

"Yes!" she admonishes. "Do it. Now!"

So I pick up the pen and proceed to write:

> Dear China,
>
> I held up a sign that said Free Tibet. I'm terribly sorry for hurting your feelings.
>
> Love,
> Westin.
>
> Laramie, Wyoming.

It seems that this is good enough for their purposes, whatever those are, but I feel like I'm being *Punk'd*, wondering who in the world is going to read that letter and decide that everything is forgiven?

"What's this all about?" I ask, to no reply. The Lackey grabs my arm and leads me out of the room. A room I know I'm never coming back to. I glance around for a split second, feeling frightened to leave its relative comfort, this space that now holds so much of my sweat, and tears, and blood. I assume that we are being moved to more permanent cells, that I will soon see my new forever home. I prepare myself for much worse than a bare motel room.

Stepping out of the building, The Worst on one arm, The Lackey on the other, the scene in front of us is surreal and confusing. It's dawn, and the light is flat gray. There is a long line of police vehicles, with at least a dozen officers running around, and dozens of journalists with cameras and microphones. All of those cameras turn in our direction as I am led towards the motorcade. I feel the intensity of The Worst's grip as she shoves me into one of the cars and locks the door.

One by one, I see my colleagues emerge from the same door with the same disheveled look, broken but still alive and walking. At one point yesterday, Scary Fat Man implied that others were being hurt and the banging sounds from rooms nearby led me to believe him. It's a huge relief to see them physically whole.

Once all four of us are secured in separate vehicles, I assume we will begin moving to a new location. But we don't move. Instead, I see Laurel's thin body emerge from his vehicle's side window, thrusting five fingers into the air over and over again, shouting something inaudible. I roll down my window and, with no one to stop me, lean out to hear his voice. "Do we have all five of us? We're not leaving without all of us! We need five of us! Five!" *Five? Has Laurel lost his mind?* There were four of us arrested, four of us dragged here throughout the night, four of us that made the trip to Shigatse. But then I see the building doors open, and Jeff walk out, an officer holding each arm.

"Jeff!!" I scream. He looks over and smiles sheepishly. I had no idea that he had been arrested. All of those invisible, golden ripples that I had been imagining, the reverberating images and messages of our disappearance—would any of that have happened if the high-definition tapes didn't get out? SFT must have captured some grainy satellite images but when Jeff ran, he carried all of our hopes with him. Seeing him here, my heart drops. They caught him, and not only is he going to rot in prison with the rest of us; no one will ever see those stunning images of our iconic protest, or hear the crisp sound of Tendor singing the Tibetan anthem, or see us being led away at gunpoint. If there is no video, then there is no proof, and all of this—sacrificing my future, my marriage, my someday-children—is for naught. Sure, there will be stories and written accounts, maybe a newspaper article or two, some low-quality satellite images as proof, but no one will care without clear visual evidence.

And yet Jeff is smiling as he emerges. Maybe he's just happy to be alive and breathing fresh air, or maybe he knows something I don't. I leave room for the possibility, the fading hope, that he got the tapes out before being busted. I will take the promise of that smile with me into whatever the next chapter this nightmare holds. Wherever we are going, I'm going to need all the optimism and magical thinking I can muster. I have conjured up magic to help others all my life, and now I'm going to have to help myself. The motorcade full, each police car flips on its flashing lights and blares its sirens as we pull out of the prison complex, car by car, back onto the plateau. I picture a damp prison cell or maybe a stark labor camp on the other end of this drive, telling myself that I can survive either.

Where are we going though? This many vehicles, these many high-ranking officers, the media presence, what's it all staged for? I suddenly have to know more, not that I expect The Worst to tell me the truth after so many lies, but my imagination is working overtime and it is better to prepare for reality. Still, it takes me a long time to formulate the words, knowing her answer might mean the death of me. "Where are you taking us?" I finally utter, twenty minutes into the drive.

"Home," she replies flippantly, with an actual flip of her hand, as if it doesn't mean anything to give me back everything.

"Oh, really?" I snort-laugh, refusing to believe it, baiting her to prove it. And then she does, explaining that they can't hold us any longer under Chinese law unless they formally charge us with a crime. "I thought we had been charged," I challenge, and she just smiles back—another of her lies.

"Your American government secured your release from the Beijing authorities," she adds. I can feel the blood rushing back into my veins, my lungs drawing a first full breath, my nerve endings reconnecting with my brain, reclaiming control of my aching bones. I probably shouldn't believe her, nothing in our track record says I should trust her, and I know the disappointment will be enormous if she's fucking with me, but I've already bought in. Like a birthday present ripped open before the cake, I unwrap her gift and joyfully retake ownership of my future.

The more we drive, the more I believe that we are going to be free. There is only one highway leading south out of Tibet, towards Nepal, and our motorcade is flying along it. Fifteen police cars, a dozen high-level officers, and five "splitists," speeding across the Tibetan Plateau, lights flashing, sirens blaring, demanding everyone's attention. As it turns out, that was the plan. To let as many people as possible know that they had apprehended the American criminals who were trying to "split the motherland." China was safe again and, to hammer the message home, we stopped in several small villages and holy sites to put on a show.

First, they line us up shoulder to shoulder, and, with a strong and steady finger-wagging, announce to the villagers that we were apprehended for promoting Tibetan independence, which only harms the Tibetan people by separating them from their great liberators. We are outside agitators, most likely sent by the Dalai Lama and his clique (I wish I'd met the Dalai Lama or his clique!). Then, someone respected from the village would come forward and offer the officers white Khatas, a ceremonial scarf to denote gratitude and blessings for "keeping them safe." The entire tense charade is confusing and obviously vapid, yet we are forced to repeat it over again. I wonder how the average Tibetan feels about our protest and look for any signs of support, even as I know how dangerous it would be to show them.

I look to Tendor, to measure how he is feeling about this last dose of public punishment, but his expression is stone, just as it's been since the arrest. Unlike my crying, farting, snotting, whiny-brat reaction to having all my freedoms taken away, Tendor took on a calm resolve after the arrest, hardly emitting any emotion at all. It was as if he'd been training for this his whole life, and perhaps he had. At the very least, he'd been listening to stories of Tibetans being tortured and killed at the hands of the Chinese government his entire life, and he went into the protest with eyes wide open. I took the more privileged American white-girl route, kicking and screaming the whole way. But I'd also used that obnoxious archetype to our advantage, several times, during the interrogation, and it was precisely because of that American privilege that we were being released and not another statistic in this bloody occupation.

Somewhere around this time, I began to feel a little braver, even cheeky, and I started to "push my luck," as my mom would say, beginning with my one-woman bloody-toilet-paper protest. The thing you never see on the TV police shows is just how human everyone becomes during a prolonged crisis. You never see the make-believe police eating, drinking, or pooping, and you never see "the bad guys" having to go pee. But, in a real-life police drama, one including a cross-country road trip, a lot of human needs arise. Not long into the ten-hour drive to the border, we take our first bathroom break out in the open. Shannon and I migrate to the same small group of rocks to squat behind, sharing our first unobserved conversation in days. We were both worried sick about the other and hug for a long moment, feeling the miracle of our still-breathing bodies. As I squat, I realize I've soaked through another makeshift pad, and bloody toilet paper is falling all over the place. Shannon can't believe that, of all the times to start one's period, this was mine. I stop short of telling her that, compared to the alternative, which was being pregnant in a Chinese prison, this feels workable. And, just then, we spot a herd of rare and endangered Himalayan blue sheep, and they're breathtaking. There is no way I'm leaving this bloody trash on the untouched wilderness around us. In my newly-emboldened, slightly-mischievous state, I place my finger to my lips and motion for Shannon to follow me back to my police car. The Worst and The Lackey have gone to find their own open-air toilet. I wad the crimson paper into a ball and quickly shove it between the seat and the back support. Her smile says everything as she nods approval of my final, bloody act of resistance.

The pattern continues throughout the day's drive: stop for public shaming and village thank yous, then pee, wipe, shove, repeat. Eventually, we come to a place where the road begins to wind downward, off the Tibetan Plateau, toward Nepal. People say this is the most dangerous road in the world and, after making the trek twice now, I tend to agree. Our motorcade lurches and curves and creeps down thousands of feet in elevation, my imagination watching our vehicle drive off the cliff in several places. Eventually, we enter the overcrowded border town of Zhangmu.

A decade earlier, as a college student in Nepal, I snuck into Zhangmu by hiding in the back of a construction truck while crossing the fifteen-kilometer "buffer zone" that separates Nepal from Tibet. I was eventually discovered and kicked back into Nepal for not having a Chinese visa, but not before touching Tibetan land momentarily. A naïve twenty-year-old, I just wanted to feel a piece of the place that had birthed my Sangha's founder. I was reading Trungpa Rinpoche's memoir, *Born in Tibet*, at the time and trying to wrap my head around what it would be like to have your home country stolen from you and systematically destroyed. Now, entering Zhangmu from the opposite direction, I have barely tasted the foul flavor of such tyranny and, for a brief time, thought I'd lost everything that I hold dear. While my tiny sample is nothing compared to a million murders and the decimation of an entire people's culture and spiritual wealth, it was enough to feel the loss of personal freedom, which I'd always taken for granted. A part of me died on that windy cliffside "mocksecution," and that part will always stay in Tibet. But another part of me was awakened and would march back across that border with me, and that was the part that literally felt itself "reborn in Tibet."

Entering Zhangmu in our flashing motorcade feels a far cry from my fugitive college visit or the trip though here during my honeymoon. Soldiers, standing firmly at attention, salute as we pass, and all other traffic has been suspended. Arriving at the customs office, we are again lined up, pointed at, laughed at, and stared down by all the locals and travelers whose lives have been disrupted by our passing. The customs agent stamps each of our passports with a large sticker that reads "Expelled from China." And, just like that, we are ushered back into our vehicles and driven out of the country, through the buffer zone, towards Nepal.

I am with The Worst and The Lackey, plus a male driver, and we are no longer, technically, in China. This is my chance. Emboldened by my successful bloody-paper protest and fueled by the immensely warm sensation of owning my own body again, I take a risk, look The Worst directly in the eyes, smile, and bow my head slightly. I am surrendering on the battlefield, laying down my weapons, doing as I've been trained since age eight, transforming conflict with kindness. "What is your name?" I ask gently, as if we'd just met.

"Dolma" she replies, returning a smile that finally reaches her eyes.

"Well, then, Dolma," I continue, "I must ask you something before we part. As a Tibetan, how do you feel in your heart about what we did?"

The Worst/Dolma, stares back at me for a long time, eyes squinting as if she is fighting an internal battle, unsure how much The Lackey or The Driver will understand. Eventually, she begins to speak. "China is a great and powerful nation that saved Tibetans from the dark ages of serfdom, bringing security and technology to all of us. . . ." Her voice cracks just slightly as tears start down her face. She continues, "China has taken care of my sick parents and my sisters and, without them, we would have starved to death." Her words, long-memorized, don't match the anguish on her face, nor the tears bathing it. Without making a choice, my eyes well up too, my chin quivers with the dawning realization that she, too, is just like me. She is Maria in Costa Rica, and Wayan in Bali, Seema in Nepal, a Tigress in Sri Lanka, and Mary in the Congo. She is a fighter, a survivor, a daughter, a sibling, and a human.

Dolma's tears admit that she doesn't know if she is doing the right thing or standing on the right side of this fight, just that she is doing what she can to endure it. All the hatred I'd been holding for her melts away. We are two women warriors, forever bound to this painful moment in history. "I understand," I nod, trying to let her know that I forgive her for all the anguish she's caused me. She implores me to come back and visit her, even as she knows I've just been banned from China for life. I can picture a scenario, under different circumstances, where we could perhaps become friends. It's a wild sensation, and I finally understand what Palden Gyatso tried to teach humanity so many decades ago: that, even after thirty-three years of being horrifically tortured in a Chinese prison, what he feared most was losing his compassion for his torturers.

I know, in that miraculous moment, that it is my compassion for Dolma—not my hate or anger for The Worst—that will eventually heal me from this traumatic event.

My childhood teachings have, once again, proven true: all conflict is workable, and kindness is always available as a secret weapon for transforming hate. She and I met at that proverbial moment on the battlefield of life and mutually surrendered. She had harmed me, and, for a time, I thought she would be the one to end my life, but it was the unlikely love that I found for her—in that one profound, connected, human moment—that actually saved me.

It was my torturer, with her silent tears, who set me free in the end.

Epilogue

It is hard to put into words the global reaction to our protest on Mount Everest, because the responses ran the gamut. Once we'd safely crossed the Friendship Bridge into Nepal, I shocked the group by using Nepali to make the Nepalese border guards laugh and negotiate our impromptu arrival in their country without visas, nor the required passport-sized photos. I offered what little money we had to a random teenager talking on a cell phone outside the customs building. It was plenty for one short call. I had memorized Lhadon's burner number in Kathmandu and we both started crying when the phone line connected.

The international media had run hundreds of stories about our protest during the days we were detained, most of which included quotes from my toilet conversation (which was the last anyone heard from us for the following fifty-five hours). News of our action overshadowed the news about China's Olympic torch relay, reopening the question of its legitimacy as an Olympic host. The success of our message for Tibetan freedom going global was beyond what any of us could have foreseen. Not even the "golden ripples" of my imagination matched the impact that our simple, nonviolent action created.

The first days of freedom in Kathmandu were a blur of unending hugs, media interviews, and teary phone calls home. There were also buckets of gratitude expressed by thousands of Tibetan refugees, who invited us to a local school and showered us with white Khatas and praise. It was a far cry from the Khata ceremonies staged along our drive out of Tibet, which we soon learned sparked a sort of cross-country game of "telephone" that saw stories emerge in far eastern Tibet of Tendor summiting Mount Everest and planting the Tibetan flag at its peak! Throughout the Tibetan diaspora, we were lauded as heroes, especially Tendor, who had defied all odds, made it inside Tibet, and broadcasted his clear message of defiance, solidarity, and hope for the entire Tibetan world.

Outside of that world, however, not all the reactions were as congratulatory. Aside from the millions of Chinese citizens who considered us enemies of the state, there was a vein of Westerners who filled online comments with gripes like, "They broke the law in another country and they should have paid the price there, just like anyone else" or along the lines of "Spoiled Americans who had no clue what they were doing and just made things worse for Tibet; I just wish they had gotten longer punishment."

Nevermind that Hitler and his cronies were operating legally when they murdered six million Jewish people, nor that the Khmer Rouge gave themselves the legal power to murder two million people in Cambodia, at some point we have to hold the laws of basic human decency above the nationalisms and patriotisms that govern us. That is what the Universal Declaration Of Human Rights is meant to achieve, to protect our most vulnerable from the evil policies of a few, borders be damned. Tibet remains one of the world's last colonies and the six million Tibetans living under Chinese occupation are one of the most oppressed ethnic minorities on the planet. Despite these conditions, Tibetans have waged a nonviolent campaign for their basic human rights for more than sixty years. I am proud to have played a tiny role in our ongoing struggle for collective freedom and truly believe that one day, Tibet will be free.

In the two years that followed our protest on Everest, I worked intimately with Students for a Free Tibet, joining their board of directors, and helping to plan and execute a 2008 Olympic campaign that saw eight successful Tibetan freedom protests inside Beijing during the XXIX Olympic Games. That campaign recruited more than seventy activists from seven different countries who were arrested in Beijing for nonviolent actions on behalf of Tibet, each of which caught Chinese authorities by surprise. My husband Phill was one of the first protesters arrested in that campaign after scaling a 200-foot pole outside Beijing's iconic Bird's Nest Stadium and dropping a massive banner reading "Tibet Will Be Free" (in both Mandarin and English). Phill's passport joined mine in being permanently banned from China; he too willingly sacrificed his future access to Tibet and used his privileged voice to echo muzzled cries for the world to wake up to the atrocities taking place there. It was Phill's first time protesting publically and his convictions made our love, and our marriage, grow deeper and more respectful.

In 2009, I decided to take a break from human rights work and finally write that memoir I'd always talked about. I needed to write in order to heal. After three years of trying to get pregnant, having kids biologically didn't seem to be in the cards for us. I was open to adoption down the road and focused more on my creative passion for storytelling. There were many stories from my years working with UAF still bouncing around inside of me, desperate to be heard. They nagged at my psyche in the twilight hours, reminding me of promises I'd made in the field, lessons I'd taken in from The Bear, The Elephant, The Eagle, The Tortoise and The Mountain Goat.

Ed and Deb Shapiro (see acknowledgements) had just written a book entitled *The Unexpected Power of Mindfulness and Meditation,* in which they interviewed me about applying meditation techniques during my work in war zones. Phill and I flew to New York City the week of their book's launch with the hopes of supporting the Shapiros and getting away from Boulder for some fun. I was also planning to meet with literary agents and shop my first book around.

In the bathroom of a friend's apartment in Harlem, moments before leaving for the book launch at Barnes & Noble, all dressed up to meet potential agents, I pee on an old pregnancy test stick that I found in the bottom of my purse. When you've been trying, and testing, for years, those sticks infest every satchel and random back pocket. I was daydreaming about the first book I would write, how to accurately convey the lessons I'd learned and the people who'd handed them down, when, to my utter disbelief and groundless shock, I found myself staring at not one but two parallel pink lines: a message from the Bardo telling me that life as I knew it, and planned it, had forever changed.

Little did I know I was about to embark on my toughest mission yet…motherhood.

Acknowledgments

I wrote this book by hand, which surprises people younger than me and impresses people older than me. My whole life, I have pushed pencils across paper, writing being my main form of expression, the indent on my middle finger now a well-worn landing pad for a beveled No. 2. My back, shoulders, and wrist assume the writing position by memory, giving the familiar ache when I've pushed for too long. I have formed my body around my craft and, thus, become a physical part of my creations. For generations, writers have molded their bodies around quill pens, the printing press, and typewriters. Scribes who have sacrificed the way their bodies grew in order to smith words with which to shape the world. As part of the last generation to remember life before computers, to have been taught penmanship and calligraphy in school, I pay homage to the writers who came before me with their uniquely-twisted forms and offer this work into the ocean of our collective history.

So how did this book come to be in your hands? There is an outrageous New Yorker, a Jewish swami, both a dance champion and an accomplished hairdresser (who is so charismatic, I once heard him referred to as the P.T. Barnum of Buddhism) and, ten years ago, his path crashed into mine. Ed Shapiro and his brilliant wife, Deb, who have written a collection of books on spirituality and the physical body, insisted I write this book and then introduced me to all of the people who made it possible. That level of belief in someone is rare, and I will always treasure their love and support.

I took my first official writing class when my first child, Maya, was still an infant. I was thirty-three and drowning in post-partum responsibility and invisibility. It was just a weekend course, by author BK Loren, but I came away from those few days with confidence, assured in my unique writer's voice. Five difficult post-partum years later, when my second child was an infant, I took two semesters of "Memoir Writing 101," at Lighthouse, an adult literary community in Denver, Colorado. My teacher was columnist Kathryn Eastburn, who not only introduced me to some of the best memoirists of our time, but directly told me that I could, and should, write this book. Next, I took a semester of writing classes, entitled "Writes Of Passage," by novelist Sarah Elizabeth Schantz, who pushed me out of my rigid mental boxes to see how nonfiction and fiction could inspire each other to explore the limits of creativity in storytelling. And, lastly, as a surprise fortieth-birthday gift from my partner, Phill, I left our young kids behind and spent a delicious week in Tuscany learning from the memoirist Mark Matousek, who taught me how to actually build a book, like a sturdy house, and invite others in. That time in Italy, surrounded by other passionate writers and held by Mark's better half, David, filled my soul with community and encouragement, convincing me that I could take these wild stories and mold them into a book people would enjoy.

The Shapiros introduced me to my agent, Bill Gladstone, who's been in the book business since before I was born. Bill jumped into my boat to help navigate the murky waters of publishing and contracts, eventually captaining us to the shores of Post Hill Press and into the capable hands of Debra Englander. Debra, Heather, Seane, Casey, and the team of editors and designers at Post Hill Press took my rough manuscript and polished it into a gem. That work takes a special skillset and I am profoundly grateful for all the minds and hands that read over my words and molded them into the book you're holding.

Although, in many ways, I have been writing this book for decades, once the contracts were signed, I had six months to produce the first draft of the manuscript. Six months in the life of a working mother of two (whose partner travels for work) is like a blip on the lifeline. I was reading Stephen King's *On Writing* at the time and internally raging about the privileges and time afforded to white, male writers. King recommends that, in order to be a "good but not great" writer, one should spend at least five hours per day on their work. I could barely find five minutes per day to write! So I turned to the real heroes of our craft, women writers of color who have had to carry the world on their backs while also producing ground-breaking work. I looked to the greatest memoirist of all time, in my humble opinion, and took my cues instead from Maya Angelou. Ms. Angelou used to check in to a hotel, give herself a firm check-out date, and write like mad for the precious days she had carved out of life's constant burdens.

Phill and I looked at our schedules over the six months I was under contract and found five small windows during which I could get away and write this book. But we couldn't afford five long hotel stays over five months, so I begged and borrowed from friends and family, securing time in their empty vacation homes. I will forever be grateful for the Treehouse in Yelapa Bay (and the fierce community of creative and supportive women it came with), the luxury condo in Puerto Vallarta (belonging to the classiest and most generous men I know and love), and the spare bedroom in Sayulita where these words were crafted…and for the loyal community of friends who brought me food, listened to me gripe, read my early writing, offered suggestions, and cheered me on as my hands cramped and the memories melted my mind.

And speaking of friendships, I have been lucky to have had many lifelong bonds with other humans, but there are only a handful of people on this planet who I can categorically say would lay their lives down to protect mine. To the members of Team Everest—known and unknown—and to the staff and families of Students for a Free Tibet (SFT) who ensured our freedom from the Chinese Communist Party (CCP) in 2007, my family today exists only for your courage and conviction and I hold deep gratitude for that type of loyalty and camaraderie.

To my ever-supportive parents, who I have too often dragged through the wringer of worry, and whose travel stories infused my early life with adventure and intrigue, I am who I am only because of your love, guidance, and understanding. That gift can never be repaid, only paid forward, so I promise to do the same for your grandchildren. And, to my big brother Noah, who has always kept me grounded to family, no matter how far I strayed, I love you unconditionally. And lastly, at the end of each day, when the pencil dust and trauma were all laid bare, there was always Phill. My Punk Rockin' Artist, my biggest fan, the yin to my yang, father to our two greatest creations, Maya and Jupiter, and the delightful breeze that keeps me afloat. You helped me understand that writing my stories down would not only lighten my emotional load; it would introduce our children to sides of their mother they would never have known. For that—and for them—I am eternally grateful.

I wrote this book for all of the people listed above and more but, above all, I wrote it for the women whose stories are found within... to preserve what we were able to achieve together, to capture the crucial lessons my mentors imparted upon my journey, and to pass that wisdom along to you. May it be of some benefit in your life and in this world we are always creating together.[2]

2 Ten percent of my proceeds from the sale of this book will go to financially support the ongoing human rights work of Urgent Action Fund for Women's Human Rights (www.urgentactionfund.org), and the global efforts of Students for a Free Tibet to demand freedom for Tibetans living under Chinese occupation (www.studentsforafreetibet.org).

EGYPT
DEPARTURE
21 JUN
UGANDA
NOV 2004
MALABA
EXIT
REPUBLIC OF FIJI
PERMITTED TO ENTER AS A
FOR 4 MONTH
FROM 21 OCT 1995
NOT AUTHORISED TO
IN ANY BUSINESS
KENYA
JKIA-NAIROBI
20. 12. 2004
IMMIGRATION OFFICER
EXIT
KENYA
20. 12. 2004
IMMIGRATION
ARRIVED
21 NOV 1995
CAIRNS AIRPORT
IMMIGRATION DEPARTMENT
06 NOV 1995
JALISCO
10 ABR 08 E
MEXICO
15.08.07
REPUBLIQUE RWANDAISE
NATIONAL SECURITY SERVICES

POLICIA DE INVESTIGACIONES
CONTROL MIGRATORIO
0 7 JUN 02
CHILE
AEROPUERTO A. MERINO BENITEZ
SRI LANKA
20-8
LEAVE TO ENTER FOR SIX MONTHS:
EMPLOYMENT AND RECOURSE TO
PUBLIC FUNDS PROHIBITED
28 MR 2001
P.I.A./A.I.P.
497
774
IMMIGRATION OFFICER
-3 JUN 1999
CHANNEL TUNNEL
UGANDA
22 FEB 2002
ENTEBBE
AUG 15
REP. DEM. DU CONGO
IMMIGRATION
AERO - BUNIA
ENTREE - SORTIE
le 21.08.2004
Nguyễn Thị
入境后可停留030
DURATION OF EACH STAY
DAYS AF
T2007
R2007
签发地点
ISSUED AT
芝加哥
2007-04-27
ESTBY
VIETNAM IMMIGRATIO
210306
MOC BA
188
U.S. IMMIGRATION
MON
ADMITTED
AUG 21 20
CLASS
UNTIL
Děčín
ČR
15 08 7 0 8
D9
07.05
2005·0005